War and the
Soviet Union

WAR and the SOVIET UNION

NUCLEAR WEAPONS AND THE REVOLUTION IN SOVIET MILITARY AND POLITICAL THINKING

BY H. S. DINERSTEIN
The RAND Corporation

FREDERICK A. PRAEGER, *Publishers*

New York, N. Y.

BOOKS THAT MATTER

First published in the United States of America in 1959
by Frederick A. Praeger, Inc., Publishers
15 West 47th Street, New York 36, N. Y.

© 1959 in the United States of America
by The RAND Corporation

Library of Congress catalog card number 59-7696
Printed in the United States of America

This book is Number 79 in the series
of *Praeger Publications in Russian History and World Communism.*

For my father and mother

AUTHOR'S NOTE

The author owes more than the usual debt of gratitude to colleagues and friends. Military developments proceed so rapidly that even the few works of synthesis that have appeared have become rapidly outdated. The author, who brought some experience in work on Soviet problems to this task, could not have essayed or completed it without the instruction in military developments willingly furnished by some colleagues. Others with primary interest in the social sciences have in writing or conversation helped me think through many thorny problems. The following persons have all been of great assistance: James F. Digby, Raymond L. Garthoff, Alexander L. George, Jerzy Gliksman, Herbert Goldhamer, Leon Gouré, A. M. Halpern, L. J. Henderson, Jr., Victor M. Hunt, Anne M. Jonas, Herman Kahn, Paul Kecskemeti, Joseph E. Loftus, Andrew W. Marshall, Emmanuel G. Mesthene, Stefan Possony, Melville J. Ruggles, Myron Rush, Frederick M. Sallagar, Hans Speier, Allen S. Whiting, Eric Willenz, and Albert J. Wohlstetter. Probably none of these persons who have so generously helped me agrees with everything in the book; some would certainly dissent sharply on particular points. This variety of opinion, so common when large and contemporary subjects are treated, explains why individuals and not collectives write books on such subjects and why, as in this case, authors assume sole responsibility for the whole.

Ian C. C. Graham has brought to the editing of the manuscript a rare critical judgment that has contributed greatly to whatever merit this book may possess.

This study was prepared as part of the research undertaken for the U.S. Air Force by The RAND Corporation.

H. S. Dinerstein

Washington, D.C.
August 11, 1958

CONTENTS

War and the Soviet Union

THE CHANGING SOVIET OUTLOOK*

Since Stalin's death the world has watched the Soviet Union intently in the expectation of great changes. Some expected that Stalin's heirs would founder on the problem of succession. Others believed that the long-suppressed bitterness of social groups hitherto silent and impotent might find violent expression. But important as the changes have been, the Soviet leaders have thus far coped with them. The problem of succession has been settled for the present, and with much less bloodshed than in previous Soviet political crises. The new oligarchy has maintained political control, making concessions here and there but preserving the old system in its broad essentials. Nevertheless, there have been some gradual but important transformations in the system. The Western world has looked for more dramatic and obvious reversals so that its attention has been somewhat distracted from such changes as have actually taken place. The transformation of the Soviet appraisal of their own power position and of Soviet military thinking, for example, has not been properly appreciated.

The Soviet leaders now believe that the world military balance of power has changed decisively in their favor. They believe the new Soviet military strength makes a war not of

* This introductory chapter sets the stage for the rest of the book, and anticipates many of its arguments. The evidence for these arguments is set forth in later chapters.

Soviet choosing less likely. Yet the Soviet Union must be always ready to wage a full-scale nuclear war. Moreover, the Soviet Union's new military strength furnishes her with opportunities for expansion without the actual employment of military force.

A confident mood has replaced the feeling of constant peril which pervaded Soviet life from the Revolution until very recently. Instead of worrying about forces of destruction beyond their control, the Soviet leaders now see themselves as masters of their own fate. So radical a change has naturally entailed a re-evaluation of the prospects for the future. In the past the Bolsheviks feared for the safety of their regime in the short run and clung to the vision of a distant utopia. Today, however, their powerful military forces so greatly enhance the security of the Soviet state that many policies once seemingly dictated by the need to preserve it have come up for re-examination. Is it possible, for example, to relax the furious effort to industrialize the country and expand the armed forces? Are the ferocious security measures of the later Stalin era still necessary? Is it possible to yield somewhat to the pressures within the Soviet Union for more abundant consumer goods? Can the Soviet Union be more flexible in its foreign policy? Is the Soviet Union now secure enough to make small concessions abroad in the expectation of making large political gains? These and similar questions flow from the new confidence in Soviet power.

The mood of re-evaluation that now permeates much of Soviet thought will be examined in more detail at a later stage. It is first necessary to recall as vividly as we can the sense of insecurity that recently prevailed in the Soviet Union.

It is already becoming difficult for the student of Russia to recapture the feeling of extreme vulnerability that pervaded Soviet life for a third of a century after the October Revolution. The constant communist fear of the outside world was no product of a disordered imagination. The Western European powers failed to crush the Soviet regime in 1917-1920 only because their leaders to some extent, and peoples to a greater extent, were too weary of fighting to prolong their intervention in the Russian Civil War. By and large, however, the Western powers continued openly to detest the Soviet regime. In the years following the Civil War the Soviet leaders were not unreasonable in suspecting that the "capitalist" nations might well try at some favorable juncture to dislodge the Soviet regime even by violent means. Obviously the Soviet Union in its early years would have lost any major war in which it became engaged. Indeed this might have occurred had not its enemies been divided. Historical speculation is usually unsafe, but it is not unlikely that between the two world wars Germany alone could have beaten the Soviet Union. The Soviet Union could hardly have survived attack by a major power or powers without the aid of one or another of the capitalist countries. Such allies were hard to come by and unlikely to be reliable.

During the Second World War disaster often seemed imminent. The German campaign of 1941 fell only a little short of complete victory. The first stages of World War II reinforced the Bolshevik conviction that annihilation was a distinct possibility. After the defeat of Germany the Soviet Union faced an awesome spectacle. A large part of the country had been devastated and population losses had been fearful. Had the United States chosen to make war upon the Soviet Union in 1945, the latter would probably have been defeated. While such a course never occurred to any American in a responsible position, the Soviet leaders, suspicious as ever, could not be sure of United States intentions. From the Soviet point of view, security now depended on America's foregoing her opportunity. The Russian leaders must have been considerably reassured by the rapid American demobilization of 1945.

In 1947-1948 the United States announced her intention to rebuild her military establishment, but the Soviet Union realized that years must elapse before the American force level of 1945 could be restored. Meanwhile the Soviet Union had already built up new strength and was steadily improving her military posture. The exclusive American possession of nuclear weapons, however, added a new element to the situation. Many Americans contended that their country's initial monopoly of the atom bomb and subsequent preponderance in nuclear weapons and air power made it possible for the United States to destroy the Soviet Union at will. Since this position would be transitory, some prominent Americans even urged that an early attack be made on the Soviet Union. However slight the chance that such a reckless policy would be adopted, the plain fact is that for a number of years the United States *could* have devastated the Soviet Union with a minimal likelihood of retaliation. Hence the Soviet leaders, even after the great territorial gains of World War II, could not rid themselves of the fear of annihilation.

These apprehensions have sometimes been described as irrational, even psychopathic. Had this been the whole truth, no change in the power balance could have elicited the self-confidence now displayed by the Soviet leaders. Growing confidence has kept pace with expanding armaments, and this is one of several reasons for assuming the essential rationality of the Russian rulers.

The rise of the new spirit has coincided with the Soviet acquisition of nuclear weapons, so that one is tempted to ascribe the change *exclusively* to this phenomenon. It should not be forgotten, however, that the Soviet Union in recent years has made great advances in heavy industry and in the education of adequate numbers of recruits for a steadily expanding economy. The industrial strength of the Soviet Union is still far from matching that of the United States, but the gap is closing. Moreover, the Soviet Union is no longer the only communist country in the world. In recent years the Soviet leaders have boasted again and again of the accession of Eastern Europe and China to their camp. However doubtful the political and military value of the satellites at any given time, the expansion of international communism has raised official morale in the Soviet Union. The acquisition of nuclear weapons, then, has hastened the growth of Soviet power and self-confidence, but it is not the sole cause of that growth.

The change in the balance of power brought about by the Soviet development of atomic weapons differs in character from similar changes in the preatomic age. The increased destruc-

tiveness of weapons, coupled with their relatively even distribution between two hostile camps, seems to improve prospects for an extended peace. Their very destructiveness suggests
that they will not be employed on a large scale, since the risks
of retaliation are too high. In this thought there is an element
of reassurance for both the Soviet Union and the United States.

Finally, the Soviet leaders must derive some satisfaction
from the difficulties met by the West in present or former
colonial areas. When we add together all the above factors, the
new Soviet confidence is understandable. Some Soviet leaders,
as we shall see later, have felt that peace is assured, while others,
now dominant, have condemned this belief as reckless complacency. The official line now postulates that increasing Soviet
military and industrial strength improves the prospects for
peace but never guarantees it.

In the Soviet reappraisal of their situation, a careful examination of the implications of nuclear weapons has played
a large role. As we shall see, the Soviet leaders adopted a strategy
suited to the demands of the new situation. They did so, however, only after some waverings and backward glances.

Until the death of Stalin neither the Soviet specialist press
nor the propaganda media assessed, with any care, the implications of the existence of nuclear weapons. The Soviet press
usually confined itself to propagandistic charges that the presumptive enemy, the United States, falsely believed the atomic
bomb to be an absolute weapon that could win wars by itself,
and to charge that the United States tried to wring concessions
in the cold war by threats to use the atomic bomb. But such
verbiage did not meet the main issue at all. The fruitful question was not, Is the atom bomb an absolutely decisive weapon?
It was rather, How, if at all, do nuclear weapons modify warfare?

Of the many important questions that cried out for analysis,
none was discussed until after Stalin's death. In his last years
Stalin became ever more rigid and unwilling to entertain any
major proposals for change, unless he felt or was persuaded
to feel that he had initiated them. Perhaps the picture that
Khrushchev drew in his "secret" speech of a warped and

tyrannical old man was somewhat overdrawn, but basically it was probably true. Such a man would doubtless insist that his leadership in the last war, and the principles on which it was based, should not be re-examined. The disasters of the initial period of that war made it all the more likely that he would insist that everything had been perfectly planned. Soviet military literature reflected this hypothesis. It presented the war as a series of Soviet successes, and explained the withdrawals of the initial period as a planned policy of "active defense." But Stalin, though old and intolerant of new ideas, was not a lunatic. He did not commit the cardinal error of neglecting the development of nuclear weapons. Nevertheless, he failed to understand their true importance, clung to dogmatic, old-fashioned theories, and prevented the emergence of a military doctrine suited to the nuclear age. Stalin's personal conception of the nature of warfare governed Soviet military planning and was presented in the Soviet military press without debate, variation, or development.

In 1942, when it became apparent that the Germans had fallen short of victory in their first campaign, Stalin promulgated a dictum that became the last and only word on the subject for more than ten years. Stalin's position was that war was a massive social phenomenon in which two or more societies were pitted against one another. In this contest all the strength and weakness of the societies came into play. It was not a gladiatorial contest in which the superior skill of one man, or the accident of, say, a man stumbling over a stone, could determine the outcome. Since war was a social phenomenon, the laws of society were applicable to it. In the special social context of warfare, what were known as the "permanently operating factors" would determine the outcome. These factors were "the stability of the rear, the morale of the army, the quantity and quality of divisions, the armament of the army, the organizational ability of the army commanders."

This formulation is so truistic as to be almost devoid of meaning. Obviously the country with the stronger economy, the better morale, superior equipment, larger forces, and abler commanders will win the war. The only really substantive point in Stalin's formula was his conclusion from the above premises: that transitory factors such as surprise could not determine the outcome of war. He argued that the Germans, who had already lost the advantages derived from surprise, would lose the war because they were inferior in the permanently operating factors.

Stalin's view was relevant chiefly to the world wars. Whereas earlier wars had been fought, for the most part, with forces in being at the outset of the war, the Napoleonic wars inaugurated the systematic replacement of men and materiel lost in the fighting, often with an actual increase in their numbers. In the popular phrase, Detroit won the last world war for the United States. Popular morale was more important than in previous wars because of the need for all-out industrial production and for masses of draftees to replenish units at the front.

Stalin's view of the permanently operating factors could readily be applied to a war in which nuclear weapons figured. In a nuclear war it was certainly important to have a stable rear, high morale, divisions adequate in quantity and quality, good weapons, and skillful command. These things might well continue to be prerequisites of victory, but they did not necessarily guarantee it. Stalin's dogma merely provided a general framework for the discussion of war. The true criterion of its usefulness as a basis of discussion was its ability to solve the problems raised by the existence of nuclear weapons. This capacity was lacking in the doctrine of the permanently operating factors, which debarred any discussion of the real issues.

The obvious innovation introduced by nuclear weapons was their enormous destructive power. The development of the hydrogen bomb meant that a successful nuclear campaign could achieve more in a day than old-fashioned attrition and blockade could in years. The new power of destruction raised a whole range of theoretical questions: Do the new weapons mean that air power will determine the final outcome of a future war? What kinds of delivery vehicles, and how many of each, are required for various purposes? Can active defense measures frustrate a nuclear blow, or can they so blunt it as to render it indecisive? Can civil defense save enough people and resources to justify the investment in it? Will the initial disruption of industry be so great that a country that suffers nuclear attack must plan on fighting the war with weapons and materiel in hand at the outset of the war? Is the effectiveness of surprise attack so certain that a potential victim must strike a forestalling blow, when convinced that the opponent means to strike, and thus start a war that might have been avoided? Assuming that sufficient damage can be inflicted on the enemy to make him "surrender," what will be the cost in destruction to one's own country? How important will the role of navies and armies be in nuclear warfare? Naturally, no positive answers can be given to these broad questions, but decisions have been taken on the basis of such tentative answers as have been forthcoming.

Until late in 1953 the Soviet discussions of Stalin's doctrine evaded these important questions. The Soviet press mechanically reiterated Stalin's few paragraphs on permanently operating and transitory factors and touched on the new issues only in polemics against Western statements. If some American commentators and spokesmen stressed the greater importance of air power, the Soviet press would point to the fallacy of the belief that any single arm could win the war. If Americans discussed the possible decisiveness of a nuclear blow, the Soviet press answered with the charge that the Americans sought to revive the discredited strategy of blitzkrieg. If any American talked of preventive war, the Soviet press warned that the United States would be beaten. Many of the American statements singled out by the Russians for propaganda rebuttal were carelessly framed or superficial, but the Soviet treatment of them was even less impressive.

Stalin's framing of basic military doctrine was obligatory for Soviet theoreticians, which meant in practice that many subjects could not be discussed. Failure to discuss the decisiveness of the nuclear blow, however, did not prevent the decision to develop nuclear weapons. To make that decision it was necessary only to assume that nuclear weapons were important, not that they were decisive. That Soviet military doctrine failed to take into account the likelihood of an aerial blitzkrieg did not detract from the Soviet desire to possess all the latest weapons, including radar, interceptors, antiaircraft, and missiles. Stagnant doctrinal development did not mean stagnant weapons development. It meant, rather, an absence of criteria for making the best decision as to the allocation of resources among various weapon systems. No government can afford to produce everything that the military would like to have or to prepare for every conceivable contingency. A choice must be made between alternatives, and a system of priorities created. Choice based on an up-to-date theory of warfare is usually, but not always, better than one based on obsolete principles or on no principle at all.

Even before Stalin's death some Soviet military leaders must surely have realized that his obsolete formula hampered the procurement of the best weapon systems. As long as Stalin was alive, however, no one dared suggest the desirability, much less the necessity, of a reappraisal of doctrine.

Some months after Stalin died, the chief theoretical organ of the Soviet Ministry of Defense, *Voennaia mysl'* (*Military Thought*), carried an article by Major General Talenskii that opened the first real discussion on military theory in the Soviet Union for twenty-five years. Since 1945 this journal has been intended only for Soviet military officers.

Talenskii rejected Stalin's formula concerning the permanently operating factors, asserting that it was not a basic law of war. He advanced a basic law that, he argued, was an improvement over Stalin's formula because it did "not exclude the possibility of a decisive defeat within a limited time . . . given the existence of certain conditions." For the first time since 1945 a Soviet publication had envisaged a possible war of the future essentially different from World Wars I and II. There could be decisive defeat in a limited time. This did not mean that a single campaign with nuclear weapons would be decisive or that measures could not be taken to reduce the likelihood that the nuclear phase would be decisive. The inconclusiveness of Talenskii's article was not important. What was important was the attention it focused on a new basic issue.

The discussion, initiated at least ostensibly by Talenskii, produced ten articles of comment and forty letters combined in a single article, together with a summation and an official resolution of the issues by the editors. These writings reveal how novel was the serious consideration of these theoretical issues. Obviously no official line on the subject existed. Some argued that Stalin's idea of the permanently operating factors was still perfectly satisfactory; others said that "surprise . . . might in certain conditions even determine the outcome of the war," a clear rejection of Stalin's view that transitory factors cannot be decisive. Such diversity of views on matters of basic importance had not been possible in the Soviet Union for a generation. There seems to be no doubt that this was a real, and not a staged, discussion, for there was considerable irrelevance and some of the disputants failed to discern the main issues, concentrating on peripheral ones.

Several major conclusions emerged and the editors of *Military Thought* established these, in a sense, as a new official line in an article of April, 1955, which closed the discussion. The new line characterized the doctrine of permanently operating factors as inadequate on the whole, although valid in some contexts. The formula first dropped out of sight and then, in 1957, was explicitly abandoned as more confusing than helpful.

Talenskii's chief verbal innovation was his emphasis on the *armed conflict* as the crucial aspect of warfare. A strange innovation! Surely a law of war ought to deal with war. But the number of objections raised by Soviet commentators to this simple proposition reveals the significance of Talenskii's approach in the Soviet context. Not only did he put the armed conflict in the forefront of his treatment, but he insisted that the same principles of war affected both parties in the armed conflict. His opponents complained that it was anti-Marxist, that is, theoretically and morally wrong, to apply the same social laws to two radically different social systems. Capitalist states organized differently and seeking different goals could not command the loyalty of their own peoples over an extended period and had perforce to try for quick conclusions. The wars conducted by a socialist state were just by definition and therefore enjoyed the enthusiastic support of the population, which

besides worked within a more rational economic framework.
Talenskii and his supporters accepted the importance of these
differences but insisted on maintaining at the center of attention an armed conflict whose laws applied equally to both contending sides.

In emphasizing combat at the expense of economics and
morale, Talenskii made it possible to assess justly the role of
nuclear weapons. Once discussion was freed from the confines
of the permanently-operating-factors formula, the obvious implications of the existence of nuclear weapons followed almost
automatically. Plainly, if one country's nuclear campaign were
successful in destroying a large proportion of the armed forces,
industry, and cities of another country, the attacker might gain
an irreversible advantage. The Soviet theorists did not follow
some Western ones who have proceeded to argue that the initial
nuclear campaign itself would end the war; they contended
merely that the success of the nuclear campaign *could* mean
ultimate victory. This view, now official doctrine, puts an unprecedented emphasis on the importance of surprise. As a
corollary, the Russians argued that the advantages of surprise
might be denied to the enemy if foreknowledge of his intentions were obtained and defensive action were taken to reduce
the likelihood that his nuclear blow would decide the war.
From a defensive as well as from an offensive standpoint, the
importance of the factor of surprise had grown greatly in Soviet
eyes.

If the advantages that the offense may gain from achieving
surprise are so great, every power that recognizes this fact
must experience a temptation to pre-empt the initiative when
the outlook for peace is unpromising. Generally, Soviet writers
have gone no further than to say, and only rarely, that surprise
is a two-edged weapon, but in the more restricted columns of
Military Thought, written for officers, we find the plain statement that the Soviet Union has to be prepared to deal a forestalling blow so as to deprive the enemy of the advantage of
surprise. The image called up is that of a quick blow against
the enemy, who is poised to strike, before he can launch his own
attack. While the capacity to deliver such a blow is officially

advocated, the writers who express official views hasten to add that this policy should not be confused with that of preventive war. In this context the term "preventive war" may be taken to indicate a war initiated in order to forestall a remote possibility of enemy attack at some indefinite time in the future. In this sense, the term may be distinguished from "pre-emptive war," defined as a war initiated in order to forestall an attack that is believed to be imminent. Whatever the intention of the Soviet leaders, in public statements they would automatically deny that preventive war could be their policy. Preventive war and warmongering have become identified with each other in Soviet propaganda, and consequently it cannot be admitted that a socialist government would even consider preventive war.

The professional discussion of these matters was subsequently reflected in the public press, and it was even more obvious that the realistic military thinkers had won the day. Changes in the Soviet military posture over the next two years seemed to reflect the changes in theory. The military consequences of the new theory will be treated in more detail at a later stage. Meanwhile, what of its political consequences?

The main political result of the reappraisal of nuclear weapons was the improved prospect that the Soviet Union would not have to fight a major war unless she chose to do so. In the past, nations had often been deterred from making war because they feared that they would lose more than they gained. The experience of France and Great Britain during and after the First World War strongly suggested that in modern wars the cost of victory might be so great as to bring about a relative decline in the power of the victors. This paradox, however, could not be erected into an axiom, as the Second World War made clear. From that conflict the United States and the Soviet Union emerged much stronger than before, both absolutely and relatively, in spite of vast expenditures by the former and great devastation of the latter. In the past the conclusion that war did not pay was pragmatic rather than axiomatic. Today, however, nuclear weapons could destroy more in a few days than years of large-scale war had destroyed in the past. The belief that war did not pay would now act as a deterrent to a potential warmaker whether or not he expected to win an ultimate military victory.

Such a belief was much less likely to be held in Stalin's time, when official doctrine held that the air battle, with the use of nuclear weapons, would be more important than ever before, but still not decisive. That doctrine put a ceiling, as it were, on the potential destructiveness of nuclear weapons. As long as the enormous destructive possibilities of nuclear weapons were less than fully admitted, it was difficult to advance the hypothesis that other nations, or even one's own, would be deterred from initiating nuclear war because the costs—win or lose—would be too high.

In estimating Western intentions from the Stalinist point of view, the Soviet analyst had to assume that the capitalist powers would make a last desperate effort when they saw political dominance passing to communism. Nuclear weapons, however, introduced a fresh consideration into this old dogma. Unless the capitalists could reconcile themselves to suffer the destruction produced by nuclear weapons, they would prefer gradual decline to nuclear war. Under the Stalinist formula, the Soviet analyst might conclude that the capitalists would be deterred from making war if they felt that victory was in doubt. After the reappraisal of nuclear weapons, however, it was legitimate to argue that capitalism might be deterred from making war, irrespective of its chances of victory.

The belief that the capitalist powers would probably not attack the Soviet Union brought with it a profound modification of the traditional fear that national catastrophe was possible sooner or later. The country must continue, of course, to ensure itself against catastrophe by building up its military strength, but the constant preoccupation with impending disaster was no longer justifiable.

The Soviet analyst, however, could scarcely admit that he lived in a relatively secure new world until he was assured that the Soviet Union really had the nuclear power to deter the United States and that the United States recognized the existence of that power. Evidence on these points is presented in later chapters.

The new Soviet position rested on the possession of nuclear weapons and the ability to deliver them. It was simple enough to count the nuclear weapons in the Soviet stockpile, but it was difficult to be sure that the Soviet Union had the capacity to deliver against the United States a punishing retaliatory blow, if the latter attacked first. Nothing less than this capacity constituted an adequate deterrent. The ability to strike a first blow could constitute only a threat, not a deterrent.

In estimating the probable effects of a Soviet retaliatory blow the Soviet analyst had to consider a great many variables. He had to establish the probable weight of the American first strike, for which he depended on a knowledge of the numbers, efficiency, and strategic uses of American aircraft and weapons. He had to decide how far the weight of the American blow would be reduced by effective warning and defense measures. Having made due allowance for these factors, he had to calculate the effectiveness of a Soviet counterstrike.

The ability of the Soviet striking force to employ what power it still retained depended on many imponderables. If one assumed that the American attack aimed to reduce the size of the Soviet striking force, then the destructiveness of individual weapons became an important factor. Would the American force bring a large or a small number of hydrogen bombs? How effective would the Soviet chain of command be after an American blow?

This list of factors required for an estimate of the retaliatory capability of the Soviet Union could be extended, but it is probably clear already that it was extremely difficult for Soviet planners to determine the precise moment when the Soviet Union acquired a retaliatory capability adequate to her requirements for deterring an American attack. There seems to be little question that the Soviet Union did not have such a capability in 1950, or that she does have it in 1958. Even if one had all the facts available to both Soviet and American military planners, one could not fix with certainty a point in time when the Soviets acquired a deterrent nuclear capability. For deterrent capability is, so to speak, in the mind of the deterrer. One can, as it happens, learn within reasonable limits the period when the Soviet planners decided that their military power met the requirements of deterrence.

In March, 1954, some persons in the Soviet Union stated quite unmistakably that the Soviet Union possessed a deterrent capability. The best known of these were Malenkov and Mikoian. That they were sincere in their opinions is made probable by the fact that other persons publicly disagreed with them. Once again one has the feeling that a genuine debate was in progress. Those who opposed Malenkov's views repeated the old shibboleth about capitalist encirclement of the Soviet Union and indicated quite clearly that they did not accept the fact of Soviet deterrent capability, at least as of that moment. The most notable in this group were Khrushchev, Bulganin, Kaganovich, and Molotov. Only a directed verdict could have produced uniformity in statements of opinion on the subject, but at this early date such a verdict was not forthcoming. At this time, as we shall see, differences of opinion about military and other matters extended into the highest ranks of the Soviet leadership.

It is interesting, but by no means surprising, that the Soviet military leaders were not among the first to shout that the age of Soviet nuclear deterrence had arrived. While some civilian leaders believed that the mere possession of nuclear weapons and aircraft constituted a deterrent capability, military leaders by virtue of their experience did not make this mistake of oversimplification. Moreover, the caution and conservatism characteristic of military leaders in powerful countries must have delayed the recognition that so important a change had really taken place.

If the United States did not know that the Soviet Union could answer an air-nuclear attack in kind, she could not be deterred from making such an attack merely by fear of retaliation. It only takes one party to commit an act of aggression; it requires an unspoken agreement between two to deter such an act. For the doubters, including the military, it was extremely important to determine whether the United States was framing her policy on the assumption that an American attack on the Soviet Union would result in a level of damage to the United

States that her leaders would find unacceptable. The answer to this question was bound to make a tremendous difference in the Soviet sense of security. True, the Marxist might reason that the United States would refrain from making war on the Soviet Union because one group of capitalists wanted peace, because the population had not yet been properly prepared for war, because of contradictions in the relationships among capitalist countries, or because the capitalist military establishment was not yet ready. Under any of these hypotheses, however, the Soviet Union was secure against attack only as long as the restraining factors existed. By their very nature, these factors were transitory. Only the capitalist fear of unacceptable retaliation could be counted on to provide the desirable degree of security.

Had the United States been deterred, either transitorily or permanently, from launching war against the Soviet Union? The indicators were contradictory and confusing.

The United States had not minimized the importance of nuclear weapons while she possessed a monopoly of them and had frequently stated that these weapons constituted a deterrent to aggression. Yet during the Korean War, the only major act of Soviet-sponsored aggression in the period when the United States had a clear superiority in nuclear weapons and delivery capability, the United States exercised restraint. Far from being willing to engage the Soviet Union directly with nuclear weapons, America was clearly anxious to avoid any expansion of the war. This was true of both the Democratic and Republican administrations.

Thus far the omens were favorable to the Soviet Union, but the situation was not clear cut. While those in power in the United States were relatively cautious about committing American resources to the Far Eastern conflict, several military and political leaders urged the expansion of the war in Asia and the use of nuclear weapons against China, even at the risk of precipitating a war with the Soviet Union. The Korean War may well have forced on the Soviet military leaders a heightened awareness of how exposed they were to a nuclear attack if the Americans decided to make one.

The Korean War ended early in President Eisenhower's first term of office. The new President expressed his abhorrence of nuclear war. In a major speech of December, 1953, he began to advance his conviction that current weapons development made general war unthinkable. The leaders of the Soviet Union might well have regarded the President's remarks as evidence that their own possession of nuclear weapons was already effectively deterring the United States from making war against them.

In January, 1954, however, Secretary of State Dulles announced the latest policy of the National Security Council. The United States would meet aggression with "massive retaliation at places and times of our own choosing." Since the issue of massive retaliation in response to a massive Soviet attack was not in question, the Secretary's announcement seemed to mean that the United States might initiate a nuclear exchange with the Soviet Union if provoked by less than an all-out attack on her own positions. This interpretation implied that the United States would not be deterred by the Soviet nuclear capability from greeting local aggression with an all-out nuclear attack. But the almost instantaneous reaction of America's British ally to the Dulles statement made it obvious that the United States could not use British bases without British permission. For this and other reasons, as later chapters will show, the Soviet Union concluded that probably the United States either could not or would not use nuclear weapons against her under the provocation of limited Soviet aggression.

Since no major act of Soviet provocation comparable to the attack on South Korea has occurred since Dulles's speech of January, 1954, no real test of the readiness of the United States to execute the policy of massive retaliation has been possible.

The very idea that it was possible to count on nuclear weapons to provide immunity from attack by the United States (capitalist hostility being axiomatic in the Soviet mind) opened up many seemingly attractive vistas for the Soviet Union. First, the Soviet leaders could hope to gain parity with the United States in the newest weapons much more rapidly than in conventional armaments, where the industrial mobilization base was of prime importance. Even by optimistic estimates the Soviet Union would require decades to approach American industrial potential capacity. To achieve parity in nuclear weapons, however, might take only a matter of years.

In the months after Stalin's death, Malenkov and some others contended that possession of nuclear weapons could assure the Soviet Union of immunity from American attack, if the country concentrated on the deterrent aspects of military posture. Under such a program military expenditures could be kept at a level that would permit the Soviet Union to use its resources to raise the standard of living at home. Other Soviet leaders, notably Khrushchev, were hostile to these ideas and branded reliance on a deterrent posture as a policy of complacency which could lead to disaster. After a little time the second group prevailed.

A theoretical distinction, never precise, has long been made between a military posture that will deter the enemy from undertaking war and one designed to bring war to the enemy, destroy his forces, and occupy his territory. One might say that the second is an extension of the first. With the advent of nuclear weapons, the distinction has survived but its character has changed. Soviet military and political thinkers have addressed themselves to present-day problems with this distinction in mind. Their conclusions may be more readily understood if, at this point, a few general observations about military deterrence are introduced.

Traditional deterrents against a war of the opponent's choosing can be divided into three categories. First, an overwhelming military superiority residing in one power group will deter other powers from a calculated decision to attack that group. In 1907, France increased her ability to deter a hostile Germany by entering into the Triple Entente of Great Britain, France, and Russia, for the combined might of the three countries seemed to exceed Germany's. The existence of this alliance, however, failed to deter a German attack on France. But neither side, as it turned out, had an overwhelming superiority over the other.

In the First World War victory was believed to depend on

the rapid destruction of the enemy's military forces, an obvious maxim of war. When the front lines bogged down, the wearing effects of blockade and attrition began to play a role. Had German statesmen been faced in mid-1914 with Allied military forces unequivocally superior, and therefore clearly able to defeat an invader, one can scarcely doubt that they would have been deterred from making war. In such a case the deterrent force and the warmaking force are one and the same. The theoretical distinction between them does not apply. A marked superiority in over-all fighting capacity has been the most common deterrent to aggression on the part of the weaker powers, as it has been a frequent cause of aggression on the part of the stronger.

The second type of deterrent may be called the "sturdy rampart." For centuries England's island position, combined with an effective naval force, deterred invasion and facilitated successful military campaigns on the Continent. Similarly, the mountains of Switzerland have protected her independence for seven centuries. In each of these examples we find an excellent natural barrier supplemented by appropriate military measures. A favorable combination of geographical position and military art is required to make such a deterrent effective. Unfavorable changes in the military art may deprive a natural rampart of impenetrability, and hence of deterrent value. To be effective as a deterrent, the rampart need not discourage all attempts to breach it; it need merely prevent their succeeding. But the failure of such an attempt is likely to deter future attacks.

Where a strong natural rampart exists, the military forces required to deter a presumptive aggressor are far from identical with those required to destroy the opponent's military forces. The former are usually organized for purely defensive purposes and hence are incapable of inflicting strategic defeat on a powerful enemy. Great Britain, for example, could seldom bring war to a European enemy and defeat his land forces without the assistance of continental powers that possessed large armies.

Besides water and mountain barriers, sheer physical distance may act as a deterrent to war. Ancient Rome and China, for example, could not come to grips with each other. In this connection the transportation facilities possessed by the potential aggressor are bound to affect his decision to make war over great distances, as well as the drain on his other resources that such a war would entail.

The sturdy-rampart type of deterrent seems to be obsolete in the nuclear age. Only extraordinary developments in the art of defense seem likely to make its revival possible. At present such developments are not in sight.

The third type of deterrent is that of "disproportionate cost" and is of great antiquity. Here the presumptive aggressor is deterred because he decides that the game is not worth the candle. A potential aggressor is persuaded not to initiate a war because the cost of victory seems likely to exceed its value. As one might expect, this type of deterrent has often been used by the weak against the strong. It is, indeed, a variant of the first type. While overwhelming military superiority (the first type) will deter relatively weak powers from aggression, the latter may in turn protect themselves from strong powers by possessing and publicizing their ability to inflict an unacceptable level of damage on the attacker.

There is a certain similarity between this type of deterrent and those factors that may induce a strong power to abandon a war against a weaker one. Among such factors one may include difficulty of access to the weaker power's territory and military forces, unfavorable or strange fighting conditions, and guerrilla activity. All these factors played a part in Great Britain's abandonment of the American Revolutionary War, in spite of her obvious ability to continue it. In 1783, and again in 1814, the United States gained surprisingly favorable terms from the British. Indeed the granting of such terms by the British would be inexplicable if one were to take into account only the military forces that each contestant could muster. In view of the limited military forces that the British could transport to, or raise in, the North American Continent, however, and of the difficult fighting conditions imposed by wooded terrain on soldiers trained in the formal maneuvers of the parade ground, the Americans could exact from the British a price for continu-

ing to fight that the latter found disproportionate to what they
hoped to gain from the war.

Today the principle of disproportionate cost has become
one of paramount importance. Considerations related to this
principle have become the major deterrent to large-scale war
involving the use of nuclear weapons. In the First and Second
World Wars, though the destruction of the enemy's economic
base began to play a larger role than before, the major strategy
of the contestants was to destroy the enemy's military forces.
Today and in the future, however, a war in which nuclear
weapons are extensively employed will result in wholesale destruction of life and economic assets. Under modern conditions,
damage to the economic base of each contestant is bound to be
a major consequence of all-out war. Whether or not such destruction will be a major strategic aim of the contestants, it may
well be the consequence of an effort to destroy numerous and
widely dispersed targets in the opponent's country by the employment of megaton weapons. Such destruction is even more
likely if the delivery vehicle is a ballistic missile, for the inac-
curacy of fire of such missiles must be compensated by a large
radius of destruction if the target is to be destroyed. Hence
arises the thought that no potential aggressor can reasonably
hope for victory in general war at a cost acceptable to himself.
Thus the principle of disproportionate cost has become the
major deterrent to nuclear war. To a greater extent, perhaps,
than ever before the great powers are deterred from a head-on
clash more by the threat of destruction to their economic resources and population than by the threat to their military
forces. This historic change in the relative weight assigned to
the various deterrent factors has blurred whatever practical
significance once resided in the distinction between forces designated primarily to deter the enemy and forces designed primarily to destroy his military forces.

Before 1945 certain military arrangements were often valuable both as deterrents to aggression and in active defense
should war break out. The numerous coastal guns placed on
American shores in the nineteenth century were clearly meant
to deter a possible invader; they were certainly not meant to

carry the war to the enemy. The Dutch preparations for flooding before World War II were not intended primarily to destroy the enemy's forces, but to deter him from attempting an invasion of the Netherlands. The French fortress system built before World War I was meant to deter an invasion across the Franco-German border.

Each of these deterrent devices could be used in a defensive role in the event that deterrence failed. Although the American coastal artillery never fired a shot in anger, the flooding of Dutch lands briefly delayed the advance of the German invaders. For nearly a century before 1914 the British navy not only maintained the Pax Britannica but deterred others, at least until 1898, from attempting to compete for mastery of the world's oceans. In the First World War the navy was an essential element in Britain's fighting forces. Thus it is clear that the deterrent role of a given military arrangement is seldom, if ever, its only role. Nevertheless, the distinction between a deterrent force and a warmaking force is worth maintaining, if only as a tool for analyzing the motives behind a country's development of this or that kind of military power. Consider, for example, the case of the huge German naval program of 1900. Since Germany, from a military point of view, was essentially a land-locked power, observers supposed that the intended role of the new German navy was offensive rather than deterrent or defensive. It was not possible to detect such a distinction in the case of the British navy.

Considerations such as the above suggest that there has more frequently been an identity between the requirements of defense and deterrence than between those of offense and deterrence. Since the development of nuclear weapons, however, the relationship between offensive capabilities and deterrence has become much closer. Conversely, a large investment in defensive arrangements may very well indicate not *primarily* a desire to deter nuclear attack, but rather a form of insurance against retaliation. Where this is true, the heavy investor in defense may well be hoping to reduce the risks of initiating offensive action. As we shall see in a later chapter, the Soviet Union has invested a great deal more in measures of active and civil defense than the United States.

Why have nuclear weapons brought about this change in the mutual relationships of offensive, defensive, and deterrent capabilities? An answer has already been suggested above. The major consequence of nuclear war (and therefore the major deterrent to its initiation) is the destruction of population and economic resources; hence the tendency to devote ever more attention to minimizing this destruction, should war break out, by the development of defensive systems.

In the chapters that follow we shall present evidence indicating that the Soviet position is based on reasoning similar to the above. The group around Malenkov, which tended to rely on mutual deterrence as a guarantee of prolonged peace, was stigmatized as complacent and defeatist: complacent because they thought that Soviet nuclear weapons precluded a war not of Soviet choosing; defeatist because they did not believe in the possibility of surviving a nuclear war. The Soviet Union would suffer fearful destruction, answered Khrushchev, but it would win the war.

Khrushchev's theoretical and political victory over Malenkov had immediate practical consequences for Soviet military planning. No Soviet leader had opposed the building of long-range aircraft and missiles, weapons that were at once of offensive and deterrent value. Khrushchev's insistence on the possibility of victory in a nuclear war, however, demanded still more expensive additions to the Soviet military posture. Should deterrence fail, the country must have a defensive system capable of minimizing destruction. There is a more or less definite limit to what a country can usefully spend on offensive nuclear weapons; there seems to be no limit to the returns from added increments of expenditure on defense against such weapons. This discrepancy is a direct consequence of the unprecedented destructive potential of modern weapon systems. The great destructiveness of individual weapons requires active defense to destroy a very high percentage of the delivery vehicles. The marriage of nuclear weapons to high-speed aircraft and missiles makes a low rate of interception futile. Even an inadequate defense, however, is extremely expensive to build and maintain.

The Soviet decision to prepare to fight a war if need be, rather than to rely on the effectiveness of deterrence, involves enormous expenditures and sets severe limits on the non-military sector of the country's economy. The condition of the Soviet peoples, therefore, is directly and powerfully affected by the present military policies of the Kremlin.

* * *

Once it had been decided that the major mission of the Soviet armed forces was to fight a full-scale war if the need arose, the choice of strategies open to the planners was automatically narrowed. If war came the Soviet aim was victory, and the well-understood characteristics of nuclear weapons made it necessary to conceive of victory primarily in terms of the survival of a substantial proportion of the population and the economy. Now that nuclear weapons make wholesale devastation of the homeland an almost inescapable concomitant of war, the destruction of the enemy's military forces can no longer be *in itself* the main object of military operations. That mission has now become the means to a more fundamental end, namely the preservation of that proportion of one's own population and economic resources that one believes to be compatible with "victory." The Soviet strategy, therefore, is to destroy the enemy's military forces before those forces can destroy Soviet population and cities. This strategy has the greatest promise of success if the Soviet Union is able to initiate the use of nuclear weapons. If the Soviet leaders believe that the United States is about to attack, they must try to effect a pre-emptive nuclear assault. A retaliatory attack on their part might come too late to achieve the main object of any major war, the salvation of the Soviet population and economic wealth.

Such a pre-emptive strategy requires that the Soviet Union get timely and unequivocal warning of the enemy's intention to attack. It may be said that the cold-blooded planning of a preventive war would obviate the necessity for warning.

Soviet strategic plans, then, demand the ability to destroy

a large part of the presumptive enemy's warmaking force at its bases, to knock out such elements of this force as may reach the Soviet Union, and to minimize by civil-defense measures the effects of the weapons that get through the active defenses. Such requirements necessitate a striking force able to hit with considerable precision. The more the targets to be destroyed have been "hardened," the greater the required precision of delivery. Underground installations protected by thick concrete must receive near-direct hits.

An important role in this over-all strategy has been assigned to ground forces, at least for the next decade. If the main object of the war is to protect the Soviet population, enemy missiles moved to new bases in Western Europe after the initiation of hostilities will constitute a major menace. The surest way of eliminating them is to occupy the ground. A rapid Soviet advance across Europe is therefore essential for the successful execution of the whole Soviet strategy.

The present Soviet strategy, as outlined above, is designed for a period when the Soviet Union has no retaliation-proof capability. But if that country should continue to develop its warmaking capability to the point where its high-yield weapons have great accuracy and reliability, and if its presumptive opponents should fall behind, the strategy of the initial blow may become much more attractive to the Soviet leaders than it is now. As soon as such a blow seems to promise immunity from retaliation, the Soviet planners will have greater freedom in making major military decisions.

At present, however, the planners must rely on the least of several evils, namely their ability to get in a first blow upon receipt of warning, though not necessarily with the hope of eliminating retaliation. At best this means, for the Soviet Union, that the enemy chooses the time for initiating hostilities; at worst it means that the Soviet homeland may be devastated if warning comes too late. Nevertheless, the Soviet Union has to aim for the expected advantages of getting in the first strike, should war threaten. Without the power to obliterate the enemy's striking force by a single, all-out blow, the Soviet Union would court destruction by launching a nuclear strike "out of the blue." Such a strike would be insane, and we have no reason to think that the present Soviet leaders are anything but shrewd and calculating. For this very practical reason, their professed abhorrence of "preventive war," that is, of the cold-blooded planning of all-out war, is no doubt sincere.

Should the Soviet Union ever acquire what her leaders consider a retaliation-proof capability, the world situation will alter radically. One need exercise little imagination to visualize the dangers inherent in such a development. No one can say that the acquisition of such a vastly improved capability would induce the present Soviet leaders to plan a cold-blooded "preventive" war. In such circumstances, however, the United States would have to fear constantly that the Soviet Union might be tempted to initiate war in the conviction that the first blow would decide it.

For a few years the United States possessed a monopoly of both nuclear weapons and delivery vehicles. Yet there was no general war. This seemingly hopeful analogy departs from the hypothetical situation just described in two important respects. First, for much of the earlier period the Soviet leaders did not really believe that the employment of nuclear weapons could decide the outcome of war. Second, in this period the Soviet Union did not possess the capability of making *any* kind of nuclear strike against the United States. This fact emphasizes the principal danger in one power's gaining a retaliation-proof strategy. That power's presumptive enemy will possess the capability of making a first nuclear strike. The weaker power is bound to consider that making a first strike, in its own time and without specific provocation, may well be the best insurance against national extinction. Hence an imbalance of this unprecedented kind is likely to lead to an unprecedented danger of all-out war.

Should the Soviet Union ever acquire a retaliation-proof capability, she would have to consider the possibility that any small international crisis might be the occasion for the execution of an American nuclear strike. For the Russians would surely argue that a desperate American attempt to reap the benefits of surprise and priority was more likely now that the United States lacked the power to recover from an initial Soviet blow. Hence, the Soviet leaders would feel tempted, on grounds of reason and prudence, to plan an obliterating strike in their own time and without any specific provocation.

CHAPTER TWO

BREAKING THE OLD MOLD

In this chapter we shall examine in detail the revolution in Soviet military doctrine that occurred between the latter part of 1953 and the spring of 1955. The influence of this revolution on Soviet strategic posture will be considered in a subsequent chapter.

First, let us consider Soviet military history in the fifteen years before Stalin's death. One can detect a pattern in the wars initiated by the Soviet Union in this period: the attack on Poland in 1939; the Finnish war of 1939-1940; the war against Japan in 1945; and the war against South Korea through the agency of the North Koreans in 1950-1953. In all these cases the Soviet Union hoped that the employment of limited means would achieve ends proportionate to the effort expended. The Soviet Union expected to, and did, obtain important objectives by occupying Eastern Poland in 1939 and Manchuria in 1945, with a negligible expenditure of resources and with little risk of an expansion of the conflict beyond what was justified by the expected gains. In the wars against South Korea and Finland the Soviet Union was unable to obtain her planned objectives in the time allotted and therefore abandoned the original objectives rather than risk an expansion of the war and an expenditure of resources incommensurate with the ends desired.

The defensive campaigns against Japan in 1938 and 1939 also demonstrated the Soviet willingness to fight a limited war for limited ends. Numerous border incidents had occurred along the Manchurian-Russian and Manchurian–Outer Mongolian borders. In 1939 these culminated in a series of full-scale military engagements. In all cases the Japanese took the initiative, successfully advanced across the Manchurian border, and were then beaten back by the Russians. The Russians' primary object in fighting these engagements was obviously to defend their territory, but in doing this successfully they demonstrated their strength and determination to the Japanese. The latter were thereby put on notice that they could hope neither to expand piecemeal, after Hitler's example, nor to win a cheap victory over the Soviet Union. The Russians, however, did not push their advantage beyond the limited requirements of defense. By limiting the geographical scope of their operations, when they had won the power to extend it at Japan's expense, and by their care to avoid even the suggestion in their propaganda that their actions presaged a large war, the Russians made it clear that they sought only the limited objectives of throwing the Japanese back into Manchuria and deterring them from further aggression.[1] In all the wars so far initiated by the Soviet Union the objective has been limited, both in the planning stage and in the aftermath. The temptation to expand the conflict when the resources needed to attain the original objective turned out to be excessive has always been resisted.

In the only war imposed on the Soviet Union since 1921, the Russo-German war of 1941-1945, the German aim was to conquer the Soviet Union. The latter was obliged to seek the complete defeat of the enemy and whatever further advantages might accrue from victory. Since this war has been the major military event in the life of the Soviet Union, its course is worth considering briefly.

As in most wars, the period of preparation was crucial in determining the course of the conflict. It was for such a war with a great power that the Red Army had been prepared and trained in the thirties. The resources of personnel and materiel available to this army were limited by the political and economic facts of Soviet life. The Soviet Union's industrial establishment, on the whole, could not produce goods of quality comparable to that of its likely enemies, although some items of military equipment compared favorably with their German and British counterparts. To compensate for these deficiencies the Soviet Union gradually built up vast quantities of military equipment. By the time the desired quantity of certain items was reached many of them were obsolete. Hence a relative superiority in the numbers of such items was not necessarily of any military significance. As events proved, however, the very great numbers of tanks possessed by the Soviet Union compensated in some degree for their obsolescence.

Besides great masses of military equipment the Russians had great masses of men in their armed forces. No other sovereign state except China could equal the reserves of population possessed by the Soviet Union. The efficiency of the huge Russian military machine was relatively low. Though they might not admit it, many Russians probably knew that their officers were not to be compared with German officers, as the course of the war was to demonstrate. While some individual generals and officers proved competent, the Army command as a whole was lumbering and clumsy.

The military weaknesses of the Soviet Union in the nineteen-thirties put rather stringent limits on the foreign aims that it was prudent to pursue. It was obviously risky to become embroiled in war with one of the great powers, especially with the most likely antagonist, resurgent Germany. Soviet diplomacy, therefore, was mainly directed toward avoiding war with Germany. There can be no doubt that in 1939 it was the Soviet Union that made overtures to Germany for a *rapprochement*. There is evidence that since 1935 she had made repeated but vain efforts of this kind.

With the advantage of hindsight it is now easy to see what few Westerners realized in the late thirties: that Soviet policy was to further the "natural" tendency of capitalist nations to make war on one another, leaving the Soviet Union as *tertius gaudens*. Once we accept the fact that Stalin had no preference for "democratic capitalism" over "fascist capitalism," we can understand why the Soviet Union used its not inconsiderable influence in German domestic politics to help bring Hitler to power in 1933. Having no ideological preference for Western democracy, Stalin hoped and believed that the rise of German fascism would mean war among the capitalists rather than a capitalist war against the Soviet Union. When the Nazi-Soviet pact was signed in 1939, it seemed as if Stalin's policy had been crowned with success. As we know, however, the triumph was short lived.

The same inadequacy which made it advisable for the Soviet Union to avoid war with a great power affected whatever preparations the country might make for a war imposed on her. It did not matter what kind of defenses the Soviet Union wanted; she could have only what her resources permitted.

In the twenties and thirties some Soviet theoreticians had made radical proposals for the reorganization of the armed forces. They emphasized the value of airborne troops, the high mobility of tanks, and the usefulness of other "team-operated" weapons. But by 1937 the Soviet leaders had decided that infantry ruled the battle and that the army must consist primarily of great masses of individual fighting men. They may have reached this conclusion partly as a result of misinterpreting the "purely localized experience of the Spanish Civil War."[2] In the nineteen-thirties, however, it would have been pointless to impress on the Soviet leaders the theoretical superiority of a small, mobile, concentrated force over a mass army, for the Russians had no choice but to rely on the latter. The state of technical expertness in the society as a whole and the unwillingness to permit commanders to exercise initiative determined the dependence on a mass army. It would have been preferable, of course, to have an army as efficient as the German and as large as their own, but this was not a practicable alternative.

Within limits the Russians were free to vary their military posture. They could disperse their tanks through the infantry units, as they did at the beginning of the war, or concentrate them in special armored units, as they did later in the war. No matter how they arranged the elements of their massive army, however, the only basic strategy open to them was to use superiority in numbers of men and amounts of equipment to smother the Germans. Such a strategy, though the only practicable one, was far from a guarantee of victory. The Russians could not wear down the Germans unless they could first deny them a quick victory. Here Hitler's rashness played into Russian hands. Hitler failed to mobilize the German economy as thoroughly as the Russians did their own. He expected to gain victory over the Russians with less than the utmost effort. The success of German mobilization measures in 1943 and 1944 when the situation had deteriorated demonstrated that fuller mobilization would have been possible in 1941, when it might have saved the day for the Germans. In 1943 it was too late, for the Red Army continued to outnumber the German forces, and Soviet command, weapons, and morale improved, while German strength declined. German units had to be taken away from the Russian front in increasing numbers as the Western allies advanced across North Africa and into continental Europe. By 1943 it was possible for the Soviet Union to win by employing the strategy of massive attack and attrition.

Because the German blitzkrieg strategy failed in 1941, the Russians were confirmed in their belief that surprise could not determine the outcome of wars and that no single arm in warfare could be decisive. If the Russians had been more cautious they might have concluded merely that the inferior manpower of the Germans, coupled with the onset of a Russian winter, had outweighed the advantages obtained from surprise. This more modest interpretation would have left the Russians free to recognize that surprise might have been successful in somewhat different circumstances. If the Russians had been followers of Clausewitz, they would have tried to analyze surprise in relation to other factors bearing on the issue of victory or defeat, balancing one against another. Instead, they laid it down virtually a priori that surprise could never succeed without superiority in every major aspect of military strength. The Soviet tendency was to elaborate rigid rules of warfare, rather than to develop a pragmatic approach to particular military problems. They asserted that the strategy they had successfully employed against the Germans in 1941 would always be a winning strategy. That the only strategy open to the Russians turned out to be a winning one served to bolster their conservative prejudices.

The lessons the Russians drew from World War II may readily be traced in Soviet published materials. In the second edition of *Bol'shaia Sovetskaia Entsiklopediia (Great Soviet Encyclopedia)* an unsigned article on the military art postulated that "bourgeois military science [has] sought the secret of victory in the use of surprise and other transitory factors which could only have given temporary successes."[3] This statement was consistent with the view that in World War II the Germans depended on deciding the issue at the outset of the war and lost the war because they were not strong enough to do so. It did not necessarily imply a universal rule that initial successes deriving from surprise can only have temporary effects.

Another article on military science in the same encyclopedia makes it clear that about 1950 the merely temporary importance of surprise was viewed as a universal principle. In commenting on the significance of Stalin's formula concerning the permanently operating factors (the stability of the rear, the morale of the armed forces, the quantity and quality of divisions, the equipment of the fighting services, and the organizational abilities of the military commanders), the encyclopedia article characterized factors such as surprise as "transitory" and the permanently operating factors as "decisive."[4] This contrast made it quite clear that transitory factors, in the Soviet view, could not be decisive. The same article insisted that the Soviet Union would always be superior in the permanently operating factors: "The military science of the Soviet socialist government assumes the invincible superiority in economic and morale potential of the Soviet Union over any coalition of possible opponents from the imperialist camp."[5]

One military writer, in a book published shortly after Stalin's death in 1953, showed that little had changed in the Soviet view of war since 1951, the date of the article cited above:

> Soviet military science rejects the bankrupt position of bourgeois military theory which exaggerates the importance of temporary factors for the outcome of war and thereby relies on the triumph of the transitory elements. Recognizing the limited role of transitory factors in the

course of military events, Soviet military science considers that the main elements determining the course of war according to the rules are the permanently operating factors. The adventuristic and anti-scientific theories of "atomic blitzkrieg," "lightning," "aerial" wars, etc., are alien to the military science of a socialist government. It [military science] realistically takes into account and utilizes all factors assuring victory in warfare. It is this that constitutes the invincible strength of Soviet military science and its indubitable superiority over bourgeois military science.[6]

This theory, in characteristically Soviet style, insists that the course of events in a given historical period follows definite laws and rules. The author, in a manner typical of those years, asserts that bourgeois theory is bankrupt because it says that a blitzkrieg or an atomic strike can win wars.

The old Soviet formula was not content to say that in the conditions of 1941 a blitzkrieg could not win the war, or that in 1953 a nuclear strike would not be decisive. Soviet theory, before the modifications to be discussed, held that in the machine period (as opposed to the period before World War I) blitzkriegs and atomic strikes did not win wars in any circumstances. Such an attitude is consistent with the Soviet application of Marxian determinism. Soviet Marxians have believed that human events can be predicted because laws govern their unfolding. Marx predicted the coming of socialism on the basis of his scientific analysis of the laws of historical development. Most present-day Russian thinkers probably believe in the validity of the Marxian analysis of historical change. We in the West would say that Marx based his analysis of history on a minute examination of mid-nineteenth-century British capitalism, whose tendencies as he discerned them, he projected into the future and into other countries. According to Marx, capitalism was bound to become more oppressive and, by creating an ever larger proletariat, to generate the conditions for its own destruction. One may wonder if a knowledge of the next hundred years of capitalist history might not have caused Marx to modify his predictions, as many Marxians have

since done and as the Bolsheviks have conspicuously avoided
doing. The Bolsheviks believe Marx's prediction of the doom
of capitalism to be as reliable as Newton's Law of Gravitation.
In the materialist view of the world, it is sacrilege to suggest
that large-scale human events cannot be predicted by using the
"laws of history."

The Bolsheviks have clung desperately to their belief in the
predictability of the future. When we recall how much the
Bolsheviks wrote about the danger of their own destruction, the
importance of being able to predict the future becomes understandable.[7] Those who feel secure are confident of their ability
to cope with whatever the future brings; those who are uncertain of their strength need to reassure themselves about the
future. For example, Churchill's optimism about the outcome
of the First and Second World Wars sprang from the self-confidence of the man himself and of the society in which he grew
up, not from any conviction that the future was predictable and
therefore manageable.

While all statesmen are concerned in varying degrees with
the probable course of future events, the Bolsheviks fear that
a failure to predict accurately the broader trends of history
means catastrophe. This attitude has pervaded Soviet military
thinking. The following is typical of hundreds of quotations
from Soviet military writers:

> The demonstration that the laws of economic development
> are objective laws expressing the process of economic devel-
> opment and that people can discover these laws, compre-
> hend them and employ them in society's interests, but that
> they cannot destroy old or create new economic laws—has
> great significance for the comprehension of the rules of war
> and military affairs and furnishes an opportunity for the
> scientific understanding of the superiority of Soviet mili-
> tary science (which rests on the unshakable foundation of
> materialistic theory) over bourgeois military science, which
> is permeated with the spirit of idealism. . . .
>
> Soviet military science, built on the theoretical foundation
> of Marxism-Leninism, assumes that the phenomena of war,
> as of other spheres of the life of society, are completely

knowable, and that our knowledge of the rules of war,
based on experience, is trustworthy knowledge which has
the importance of objective truths. A knowledge of the
rules of war is a necessary condition for the scientific prediction of the events of war and the successful leadership
of troops on the field of battle.[8]

Here is an instance of anxiety to control the future by following the laws governing it, which are "completely knowable."
No wonder Stalin felt it necessary to attack Clausewitz, who
was essentially the proponent of a pragmatic approach to military science.

After Stalin died, many long-established formulas were re-
examined. The most dramatic episode in the revision of Stalinism was Khrushchev's speech at the Twentieth Party Congress
in 1956, but by then certain less obvious modifications of
Stalinist principles had already occurred. One of these was the
revision of military doctrine.

Before the principles of war enunciated by Stalin in 1942
could be applied to the conditions of the early fifties it was
necessary, at the very least, to subject them to a critical review.
Stalin's formula concerning the permanently operating factors,
which were said to determine the outcome of wars, had been
put forward when a qualitatively inferior but quantitatively
superior Soviet force had been forced to fight a German army
with the converse attributes. Stalin's concept of war, with its
emphasis on morale and war production, prescribed a strategy
of attrition. By 1953, when there was no great rival land power
on the Continent, when the most powerful putative enemy, the
United States, was superior in airborne nuclear weapons, it
was no longer certain that a Soviet strategy of attrition could
be put into practice, or that if practicable it would lead to
victory.

The Soviet military, realizing the need for a revision of
doctrine, employed old terminology to ease the transition to a
complete revolution in military thought. The seeds of this
revolution were sown in a discussion ostensibly initiated by
Major General Talenskii, who had been editor of the daily
organ of the Ministry of Defense, *Red Star,* and who was then

editor of *Voennaia mysl'* (*Military Thought*), the monthly organ of the Ministry of War. These high positions guaranteed that he was not speaking lightly and suggested that he had powerful official backing.

In the September, 1953, issue of *Military Thought,* a periodical written for Soviet officers, Major General Talenskii took the first step toward a revision of the Soviet view of warfare. The discussion that ensued extended to other military journals, which were intended for all ranks. Talenskii's article bore the title "On the Question of the Laws of Military Science."[9] It began with the statement that objective laws govern wars as they do all human activity. In order to win wars one must understand these laws. Military science has as its purpose the establishment of the rules which govern the armed conflict, the conduct of the war in accordance with these rules, and the organization of a military establishment capable of meeting the demands imposed by the laws of war.

The laws of war will reflect two distinct but related tenets. On the one hand, both capitalist and socialist societies have similar military equipment, and the character of the equipment is an important factor in determining the methods used in the armed conflict. On the other hand, the difference between the two great social systems is such that there exist two incompatible sets of laws governing human society. The socialist laws of society alone are objective and realistic. Upon this foundation Marxism-Leninism has built certain laws of war that only socialists can understand and only socialist states exploit. Military science, in the technical sense, reveals that over time wars have been expanding in scope and intensity; but only Marxism, with its understanding of the nature of capitalism in its imperialist stage, can explain why this has happened.

Soviet military science assumes the "objective" character of the laws of war. As a rule, however, capitalist military science fails to do this, built as it is on an "idealistic" basis. (Idealism, in Soviet terms, is that theory of history which explains major events in terms of individual leaders who embody a world idea; whereas materialism explains history in terms of broad social classes.) Clausewitz, according to Talenskii, is idealistic because he puts so much stress on accidents in war and on the personality of the military leader.

As an example of what he means by an objective law of war, Talenskii offers: victory is gained by advance and not by retreat. Another such law is that modern war cannot be won by one arm such as the air force, since the means by which war is waged have become steadily more complex. There has been no case, for example, where a new weapon, such as the airplane, the tank, poison gas, or the recoilless gun, has won a war. This applies to atomic weapons too. The objective rule is that only the employment of a whole complex of weapons can secure victory. Armed with such objective laws, Soviet military science can foresee future military developments.

To posit a Marxist law does not mean to lay down an eternal and absolute rule. These laws apply to concrete but changing historical situations. For example, when muskets and guns had smooth bores and a range, accuracy, and rate of fire far below present standards, it was cold steel rather than firepower that was decisive. This law has lost its force in a later historical era.

Military science has not completed its task when it has discovered the rules of war. These rules have to be applied to specific situations, in some of which they have to be modified. For example, the rule that it is impossible to win a war with only one type of force has to be qualified for countries having common land borders or great expanses of ocean in between. (The probable implication is that in the first case the armies will be preponderant and in the second, the navies.)

It is possible, says Talenskii, to arrive at a basic law of war, but he ventures his own opinion that the statement about the permanently operating factors determining the outcome of wars is not such a law, because it does not allow sufficient importance to the armed conflict or say how a war should be waged. Though the permanently-operating-factors formula is important, argues Talenskii, it is not basic. There can only be one basic law of war and it must be concerned primarily with the armed conflict. Stalin's permanently-operating-factors formula had not usually been described as a law, so that technically Talenskii was not rejecting Stalin's theory when he denied that it constituted a law of war. Since the political goal of war is achieved through victory in the armed conflict, the basic law should provide the key to victory.

Talenskii offers the following as his statement of the basic law of war:

> Victory in modern war is attained by the decisive defeat of the enemy in the course of the armed conflict through the employment of successive blows accumulating in force, on the basis of superiority in the permanently acting factors which determine the fate of war, and on the basis of a comprehensive exploitation of economic, moral-political, and military potentialities in their unity and interaction.

This formulation, argues Talenskii, meets the criteria he has established for a satisfactory law of war. In concluding his own evaluation of it, he adds a capital qualification that, with the tentativeness characteristic of the whole article, is not made part of the definition:

> While taking as a point of departure the concept of contemporary world wars as extended wars, the basic law in the above-cited formulation does not exclude the possibility of a decisive defeat in a limited time of one or another opponent, given the existence of certain conditions.

We shall return to this key idea later.

According to the unqualified basic law, not a single blow, but a series of blows of cumulative force, is required for victory. Under some conditions, however, it will be possible to win strategic victory without recourse to such extended operations. These conditions will be exceptional and the special case in which they arise will not affect the essence of the military art.

The armed conflict is a two-sided process, and the activity of both sides is governed by the same set of rules, but both sides do not have the same opportunities under these rules. The leaders of capitalist states, who by definition do not have just war aims, cannot exploit the moral force of their people, and this limits the extent to which they can exploit the basic law of war on which victory hinges. As Talenskii's qualifica-

tion of the basic law indicates, Soviet military science does not
deny the importance of chance in military affairs. Chance is
thought to be more prominent in warfare than in other social
phenomena. A commander who knows the laws of war can fail
in an operation because of an accident, and a skillful one can
turn an accident to his advantage, "but not a single commander
has attained victory in war despite the laws of the armed conflict using accidents only."

Denying the objective laws leads to adventurism, that is,
taking unjustified risks; but denying the subjective factors
leads to passivity and to collapse in the face of an active enemy.
The objective law of the armed conflict declares that, other
things being equal, the side superior in strength wins. The
operation of this law, however, does not reduce the weaker side
to helplessness. It can

> . . . find means for neutralizing "the negative" aspect of this
> law. . . . History shows examples, when as a result of skill-
> ful action by military leaders and troops, this general law
> was neutralized and an opposite result was achieved—the
> side with inferior forces won. . . . In the light of this propo-
> sition the aphorism "not numbers, but skill wins" has as
> good a claim as the other aphorism, "the biggest battalions
> win."

Another example of the modification of the rules governing
warfare is presented by Talenskii. A surprise enemy attack,
which theoretically should yield gains to the attacker, can be
more or less paralyzed by a system of measures developed by
Soviet military science.

As Stalin pointed out, attacking nations are usually better
prepared to fight, as well as having the advantages of the initiative. Once more Talenskii could discern a loophole in the law
of war:

> The action of this law can also be neutralized or weakened
> by a system of international political measures as well as by
> appropriate organization in governments threatened by an
> aggressor's attack, by a system of organization and military
> service, by the preparation of the country for war, by the

organization of the anti-air defense of the country and the
troops, by a skillful and vigilant intelligence, etc.

Knowing the objective laws, it is possible to foresee events, to
prepare for them as much as possible, and to direct them.
Therefore the great military leaders are those who have understood these laws.

Talenskii concludes by saying that he does not pretend to
have given a comprehensive elucidation of the laws of war, and
he calls for discussion.

Various deductions can be made from Talenskii's article,
which opened the Soviet discussion on the character and content of the laws of war. Obviously Talenskii was dissatisfied
with the state of Soviet thinking on the nature of war, and just
as obviously he failed to make a clear, logically consistent statement of what the laws of war should be. In his thrashing about
for a solution, however, he laid the foundation for a new Soviet
conception of war.

In the same breath Talenskii talked of the permanently
operating factors and of the possibility of the "decisive defeat
in a limited time of one or another opponent." The permanently-operating-factors formula had been so long associated
with Soviet strategy in World War II that it almost automatically implied an extended war of all-out mobilization, in which
morale on the home front and the ability to command vast resources would tell in the end. Yet Talenskii also asserted the
possibility of defeat in a limited time. In other words, he implied that in certain circumstances the Soviet Union might be
unable to utilize her power to mobilize vast resources. This, in
turn, implied that the permanently operating factors had lost
a good deal of their former importance. Talenskii, however,
approached the weaknesses of the Stalin formula obliquely
rather than directly. First he stuck to a quasi-religious faith in
"the laws of history" and the existence of a basic law of war;
then he advanced the idea that the action of these "objective"
laws could be paralyzed by an intelligent regard for "subjective" factors. Clearly Talenskii was attempting to pour new
wine into old bottles.

It appears that Talenskii appreciated that the pragmatic approach to military problems was genuinely objective. At the same time, he seems to have questioned the objectivity of Stalinist dogma. Traditionally, however, dogmatism had been officially characterized as "objective" and pragmatism as "subjective." Talenskii's first article seems to have been an awkward attempt to dignify the pragmatic approach, at the expense of the dogmatic, by reversing the definitions of the terms "objective" and "subjective." Moreover, he had to perform this *volte face* without appearing to move. Hence he found himself postulating the existence of basic laws, the knowledge of which was essential to victory, and simultaneously suggesting that a little human ingenuity could readily evade these laws.

In any case individual thinkers rarely come up with a set of ideas entirely new in content and terminology. The guiding ideas in human societies tend to change very gradually, and by the efforts of many. Perhaps these generalizations alone are enough to explain the peculiar mixture of tradition and innovation in Talenskii's article.

The most obviously traditional feature in Talenskii's treatment was his insistence that war is governed by the action of "objective" (that is, dogmatic) laws. Here he used as his authority Stalin, who a year before in his *Ekonomicheskie problemy sotsializma v SSSR (Economic Problems of Socialism in the U.S.S.R.)* had issued a dictum on the subject and admonished those who were then deviating from it:

> Some comrades deny the objective nature of scientific laws, in particular the laws of political economy under socialism. They deny that the laws of political economy cover processes governed by objective law which occur independently of the will of man. In view of the special role allotted by history to the Soviet state, they hold that the Soviet state and its leaders can negate laws of the existing political economy, can "establish" new laws, "make" new laws.
>
> These comrades are profoundly mistaken. . . . Men may discover these laws, may learn them and, relying on them and applying them in the interests of society, may impart a

different direction to the destructive operation and allow
fuller scope to other laws which are forcing their way to
the forefront; but men cannot negate nor make new economic laws. . . .

The laws of political economy under socialism are objective laws which reflect the fact that the processes of economic life have their own rules and proceed regardless of
our will. Those who deny this thesis are really rejecting
science, and in rejecting science are denying the possibility
of prognosis and therefore any possibility of guiding economic life.[10]

Stalin is here dealing with one of the recurrent problems of
Western civilization. Determinism, whether it be Calvinist,
Marxian, or Freudian, automatically raises a question as to the
existence of free will. If God, history, or parents have predetermined the fate of an individual, class, or nation, can there
be any such thing as free will? In each case the danger of
fatalism and passivity has been overcome by a feat of intellectual legerdemain.

The Marxians worked out this dilemma as it applied to
historical changes in class relationships. No one could accuse
Stalin or the Bolsheviks of being fatalistic or quietistic. Stalin's
passage, quoted above, embodied the standard Bolshevik rationale of activism. History is a juggernaut that will roll forward in its prescribed course no matter what men do to oppose
it. It is man's role to discover and accept the laws of history,
and to push the juggernaut in the direction that these laws have
given it. Thus it is possible at once to be certain of the ultimate
future and to enjoy a sense of power and importance in speed-
ing the juggernaut on its predestined path.

If you deny that the course of history obeys objective laws,
you are, in Stalin's words, "really rejecting science, and in
rejecting science are denying the possibility of prognosis and
therefore any possibility of guiding economic life."

The Bolshevik emphasis on the necessity for accurate prediction reflects the belief that mistakes by the human agents
of history can cause a very long, or even indefinite, postponement of the earthly heaven of worldwide communism. Talen-

skii adopted this point of view in his treatment of the laws of war. His insistence that the laws of war are knowable and that the Marxists know them better than the capitalists, who follow a false idealistic philosophy of history, is standard Bolshevik theory that has been reiterated a thousand times, both before and since Talenskii's article.

This article, however, also contains viewpoints that are completely incompatible with the traditional view of the world, and states them matter-of-factly as if they followed naturally from the old premises. When Talenskii says that the action of fundamental laws can be paralyzed, he is breaking with Marxism as it has been interpreted in the Soviet Union. Stalin allowed that human activity could limit the scope of the action of a law and that when one historical era was giving way to another, human activity could "allow fuller scope to the other laws which are forcing their way to the forefront," but he was completely opposed to the idea that human beings can paralyze the action of a law and regarded it as a contradiction of Marxism.

It is not clear that Talenskii consciously set out to revise Marxism, but the numerous important exceptions that he cites to the operation of basic laws suggest some such motive. Although he assumes that modern wars will be extended wars, Talenskii "does not exclude the possibility of a decisive defeat in a limited time of one or another opponent, given the existence of certain conditions." It is a law that the stronger side wins, but the weaker side does not have to lose. Surprise is known to yield important advantages to the attacker, yet "the effect of an enemy surprise attack can be more or less paralyzed by a system of measures worked out by Soviet military science. . . ." An aggressor attacks first and thereby gains the advantage of surprise, but "the action of this law can also be neutralized" by good preparations, particularly in air defense and intelligence. It is a law that strategic victory is won not by a single blow but by the development of a series of blows, but "perhaps in certain conditions and situations it will even be possible to win a strategic operation without recourse to consecutive operations."

All these statements are in the pragmatic spirit of Clause-witz, who is condemned by Talenskii as "idealistic." Gone is the old refrain that the Soviet Union is bound to win wars because their outcome depends on permanently operating factors such as morale and industrial potential. This sober evaluation of the risks and hazards of an uncertain future testifies to a growing Soviet self-confidence far more than the loud boasting of an earlier period. Now that the Russians feel strong, they are ready to face the future without wishful thinking. Talenskii's arguments imply a spirit of self-confidence without ever explicitly appealing to it.

It seems that Talenskii's confidence in Soviet strength and his realism about the effects of the new weapons helped him to break the mold of the "laws-of-war" framework without his being fully aware of how much he had weakened the older arguments. As we shall see shortly, some of his critics pounced on the fact that he had broken the older framework, but his viewpoint, with all its contradictions, was nevertheless generally accepted.

Talenskii was, as far as can be ascertained, the first Soviet official to say that the permanently-operating-factors formula is not adequate as a law of war. Even without taking into consideration the complaints against his bold statement (as we shall do shortly), it is obvious that Talenskii seriously questioned whether the strategy demanded by this formula was the only possible one for the Soviet Union.

In 1953 Russia did not have to expect that she would once again fight a numerically inferior but better-equipped and more skillful opponent with contiguous land borders. It seemed more likely that the opponent of the future would be separated from her by an expanse of ocean. This Talenskii specifically pointed out, suggesting that the strength of the rival "forces in being" at the outset of the war might not be significantly disparate. This would apply more to the air forces, of course, than to the ground forces. Therefore it was neither necessary nor sensible to concentrate only on the strategy of wearing down the enemy over a long period by superior weight of numbers. Hence the concentration of attention on the armed conflict.

Talenskii also specifically raised the possibility (not the probability) that the armed conflict might not be extended, and that under certain conditions the decision could be reached in a short time. Later writings made it clear that this was a reference to nuclear weapons. Talenskii implied a relationship between surprise and the possibility of a war being decided in a short time, when he wrote that the effects of surprise, great as they potentially were, could be more or less paralyzed by suitable active air defense and intelligence. When the connections that he fails to make are made, his position would be this: given the use of nuclear weapons, a surprise strike against an opponent who has not adopted the proper measures in advance may be decisive. Such a strike against the Soviet Union is possible but not likely, since Russian leaders know what the proper measures are.

Talenskii struck out against the statement often made that the Soviet Union, as a socialist country, was subject to laws of war different from those applying to capitalist countries. This statement had some significance in the context of the kind of war that the Russians had fought with the Germans. The argument derived from it fell into two parts, of which the first part was better grounded than the second. The first part of the argument was that the superior economic organization of the Soviet system (a euphemism for the ruthless pressure on civilians) made it possible for Soviet industry to convert to a war footing more quickly and completely than the industry of capitalist countries. In the Russian view, this generalization held in a comparison of German and Russian mobilization, and presumably would hold in any future comparison of American and Russian war mobilization. The second part of the argument was that civilian morale was much better in socialist countries than in capitalist. The Russo-German conflict hardly furnished unequivocal proof of this assertion. In fact a good case can be made for the belief that German morale on the whole was better than Soviet, while it is very difficult to make a case for the contrary. Every government, of course, is constrained to assert publicly that its country's morale is superior to the enemy's.

By insisting that the same laws of warfare applied to both capitalist and socialist states, Talenskii questioned the inevitability of Soviet superiority in mobilization and in morale. To minimize these "permanently operating factors" is to imply that the outcome of wars may be determined by the forces in being at the outset. Talenskii, however, granted only that the outcome might be so decided in an exceptional case. By making the victorious surprise attack an exception to the rule, Talenskii returned by implication to the position that he had just abandoned, namely, that the permanently operating factors are of fundamental importance in deciding the outcome of wars. In effect what he has done is to challenge the determining role of the permanently operating factors while leaving open the question as to how much weight should be added to the factors of surprise and "forces in being." In challenging the old formula he clearly abandoned the tenet that the strategy of attrition is the only strategy open to the Soviet Union.

The last point on which Talenskii overtly diverged from the standard formula was his emphasis on the skillfulness of commanders. While recognizing the paramount importance of basic, "objective" factors, he cautioned against neglecting the "subjective" factors, in particular the skill of the commanders. He assigned much more importance to the qualities of the individual general than had been customary. From one point of view this may have been a foretaste of the later campaign to deny Stalin the exclusive credit for winning the war and to give the generals their proper due. At the same time, however, Talenskii was justifying his own emphasis on the armed conflict. If the battle is the thing, the general must be more than a pawn of his superiors.

The critical discussion aroused by Talenskii's article shows that his professional readers realized whither his ideas were tending. There can be no doubt that many felt Talenskii's formulations to be both radical and pernicious. The feeling that Talenskii threatened to subvert the whole framework of accepted thinking was expressed in several different ways. One line of rebuttal was the flat assertion that military science did not require the kind of basic law that Talenskii sought to frame for the first time in the Soviet Union. A Colonel M. Shvarev characterized the attempt to find a law of war as contrived and artificial. Every science did not need to have its basic law: "For military practitioners and theoreticians what is important above all are those factors determining final success in war. The thesis on the permanently operating factors gives an exhaustive answer to this question."[11]

A Major Balashov sought to demonstrate the futility of the search for a basic law of military science. There could be no special law for the "armed conflict"; the only basic law was the general one governing the development of society.[12]

Not only majors and colonels contended that the proposition on the permanently acting factors was the be-all and end-all of Soviet military doctrine; no less a personage than Marshal Vasilevskii, in an article written for the widely circulated *Red Star* in February, 1954, asserted that Soviet military science "is based on the permanently acting factors determining the fate of a war. . . ."[13] In May of the same year, Vasilevskii reiterated his stand that the old formula was adequate by quoting Stalin approvingly to the effect that "the outcome of a war is determined not by transitory factors but by the permanently operating factors."[14]

Other statements in the open press made it clear that Talenskii did not represent official opinion when he described the permanently-operating-factors formula as insufficient. Colonel V. Petrov, in an article that appeared in a collection on Soviet military science, argued that the formula was adequate for both wartime and preparation for war. The following excerpts from his article convey its tone:

> The proposition on the permanently operating factors gives an exhaustive, scientific answer to one of the most important questions of military science, to the question of which of the numerous and varied factors influencing the course and outcome of a war are the chief and decisive and which are transitory and temporary. . . .

These transitory factors could have a positive influence on the course of the whole war only if they rested on a secured superiority over the opponent in the permanently operating factors. . . .

An investigation of the role of the permanently operating factors in the Great Fatherland War reveals the wisdom and genius-like prophetic power of our Communist Party, which long before the war with its profound comprehension of the rules governing contemporary war had shown ceaseless concern for the comprehensive strengthening of the Soviet rear and for the broad expansion of our economic, politico-moral, and military potentialities. . . .

This proposition [on the permanently operating factors] shows the people of the U.S.S.R. and the toilers of the countries of the people's democracies the only correct and reliable way to the further strengthening of their defensive capability.[15]

The collection of articles in which these words appeared was published by the Ministry of Defense. Talenskii's views, then, did not at this time represent ordinary official opinion, but at some later point they were adopted as the official view.

The first publicly expressed modification of the permanently-operating-factors formula occurred in an article written by General Rotmistrov in March, 1955. Rotmistrov did not reject the formula out of hand. It would have been unreasonable to insist that the country with the larger, better-equipped, better-led forces, with better morale, and a better industrial base did not enjoy great advantages. Rotmistrov repeated, as many had done before him, that superiority in the permanently operating factors was a condition of victory. His assault was on the narrow and unimaginative use of this formula that precluded further thought about the conditions of victory. The victims of his scorn were M. Taranchuk and V. Petrov, whose words were quoted above.

Rotmistrov complained about Petrov's conclusion, on the basis of some "verbose talk about the permanently operating factors," that surprise attack "had no significance."[16] Rotmistrov felt that a surprise attack might even have decisive significance.

He quarreled with complacent reliance on the permanently
operating factors and with the futile argument that the Soviet
Union would win wars because she would win wars.

Rotmistrov objected to the writers who said, in effect, that

> . . . only Soviet military science understands the perma-
> nently operating factors of war, and that this is not the case
> for bourgeois military science. And, if this is so, we can be
> untroubled: we, they [Taranchuk and Petrov] say, under-
> stand the permanently operating factors, the socialist sys-
> tem permits us to secure a lasting superiority in them, and
> this will have its results in any war.
>
> It is impossible to agree with this of course. . . .
>
> In the past many strategists in the pursuit of victory also
> took into account the permanently operating factors as de-
> termining the outcome of war to a greater or lesser ex-
> tent. . . .
>
> M. Taranchuk takes the well known and incontrovertible
> position that he who seeks to attain victory using tempo-
> rary factors and not taking into account permanently act-
> ing factors suffers defeat. But who is that "he"? There are
> no military leaders, as there were none in the past, who do
> not take into account the stability of the rear, the quantity
> and quality of divisions, the weapons of the armies, and the
> organizational abilities of the leaders on the staff level.[17]

Rotmistrov, however, agreed that there was a difference
between bourgeois military science and Soviet military science.
First, Soviet military science understood the laws of warfare
and military affairs better; second, only bourgeois military
science furthered the goals of the capitalist system:

> In all this, indubitably, one has to see the basic difference
> between Soviet military science and bourgeois military sci-
> ence. But what is not understandable is that M. Taranchuk
> when he comes to the examination of the question of the
> permanently operating factors suddenly asserts that it is
> precisely on the question of these factors that "the radical
> difference between Soviet military science and bourgeois

military science is expressed." Such an assertion cannot but
leave the reader at a loss.[18]

Rotmistrov apparently believed that the permanently-operating-
factors formula, while sound enough in general, had proved to
be more of a hindrance than a help in dealing with the vital
question of surprise attack with the employment of nuclear
weapons.

The inadequacy of the formula was proclaimed even more
unequivocally by the editors of *Military Thought* in the article
that concluded the discussion of Talenskii's article:

> Can one really accept the adequacy of an argument such as
> the following? "For military theoreticians and practitioners
> it is most important to know what factors determine the
> final outcome of the war; inasmuch as the thesis on the
> permanently operating factors determining the fate of a
> war gives an exhaustive answer to this question, it is not
> necessary 'to discover' a basic law of military science."
>
> It is easy to see that in the best case this avoids a solution
> of the problem and is not a solution, and in the worst case
> it is a voluntary or involuntary withdrawal from the posi-
> tion of Marxist materialism. Indeed, this style of analysis
> can lead one unwittingly to conclude that there is neither
> "necessity" for a basic law of military science nor for other
> laws, general and special, since in every general and par-
> ticular case it will be permissible to substitute some factors
> or other for a law, saying each time that the law is not im-
> portant. . . .
>
> The assertion was also made that, since the thesis on the
> permanently operating factors determining the fate of a
> war "helps the leading organs of our society to mobilize the
> forces of the people for the solution of the basic problems
> on which the course and outcome of the war depends, mili-
> tary science does not need a basic law and there is no such
> thing in nature." What! The understanding of the objec-
> tive laws of the armed conflict makes more difficult rather
> than helps the leading organs of our society to mobilize the
> forces of the people for the solution of the basic problems
> on which the course and outcome of war depends?[19]

In writing these lines the editors of *Military Thought* gave official approval to the position that Stalin's permanently-operating-factors formula did not meet present-day requirements. In reducing the importance of Stalin's formula the editors referred to it merely as "some factors or other" that tended to obscure the true laws of military science. The underlying tendency of Talenskii's argument was in the direction of considering each case on its merits, and the editors saw in that approach the royal road to an "objective" law of war. In this context the term "objective" has shifted its meaning and come closer to Western usage.

The editors of *Military Thought* did not admit specifically that the permanently-operating-factors formula had hitherto been treated as the basic law of Soviet military science. They simply said that the formula was no substitute for such a law. In other words, the true law was to be found outside the Stalinist frame of reference.

After April, 1955, the Soviet press carried but a few scattered references to the permanently operating factors and in 1956 none at all. In 1957 the old formula concerning these factors was specifically proscribed as leading to rigidity and complacency. Reviewers writing in *Red Star* objected to a book by P. A. Chuvikov that repeated "the old propositions."* The tone of condemnation was that customarily reserved for effete doctrine:

> In a number of cases, he [the author] almost literally repeats old propositions which at the present time are treated differently in the Soviet military-theoretical literature. . . . Thus, questions concerning the conditions for the attainment of success in modern war are presented in the book in the old way, as the question of the five permanently operating factors. It would have been more correct to talk about the moral-political, economic, and military factors and seek a comprehensive elucidation of their place in securing victory in war. . . .

* By the time a book is published, of course, it may reflect viewpoints that are already outdated.

The question of the role of such a factor as surprise is treated in a one-sided fashion in the book. The book talks about the growing role and potentialities of surprise in modern war but does not indicate that it obligates the Soviet military cadres to [accomplish] much in their practical work of perfecting the military readiness of our troops.

The critics also took the hapless writer to task for following Stalin in translating the rules of political struggle to military affairs. In political life, they said, it may be necessary to stick to a course of action once adopted, but the execution of a military plan "cannot but change in dependence on the actual situation."[20]

A month later another writer in *Red Star*, addressing students and teachers of Marxian theory, was for improving on Lenin's dicta as well as Stalin's:

We have had attempts to reduce all military theory to I. V. Stalin's propositions on the permanently operating factors determining the course and outcome of war. This proposition essentially reproduces Lenin's ideas on the conditions of victory over aggressors. However, it does not completely exhaust the question of the factors determining the course and outcome of modern war. It would be possible for example, to show that it does not include such important factors as the preparation of troops, their organization, the military art, the state of the military theory of the warring armies, and others. It is impossible also not to note that in present conditions the significance of the surprise factor has grown.

Basing itself on the unshakable foundation of Marxism-Leninism, Soviet military science makes a searching generalization of the experience of past wars and the latest developments for the preparedness of the Soviet Armed Forces.[21]

In 1953 Talenskii had stated that the permanently-operating-factors formula was correct but not exhaustive; three years later it was officially rejected as old fashioned. Dismissing the Stalin formula was a prerequisite for the re-examination of the problems of war in the nuclear age. The next important step, taken by Talenskii, was the argument that the laws of war were the same for both contending sides. Here, of course, he was striking directly at the comforting theory that a socialist society at war with a capitalist society must win because, being socialist, its cause alone is just and imparts high morale to its citizens; because it mobilizes more efficiently; and because it better understands the laws of war.

It is natural to insist that victory in war will somehow be a consequence of the very character of one's society. Naturally one does not go about voicing fears of defeat. But when a litany of inevitable victory prevents one from taking the necessary steps to avoid defeat, it is time to call a halt.

By insisting that the laws of war were essentially the same for both sides, Talenskii focused attention on the battle, "the armed conflict," and made it more difficult for the Soviet Sir Galahad to say:

> My strength is as the strength of ten,
> Because my heart is pure.

Talenskii's argument that the armed conflict was subject to its own laws, and not to social laws that differed in different societies, aroused the most violent objections. Talenskii was clearly felt to be striking at the *mystique* that insisted that the Soviet Union would win any war she fought because she was bound to do so. As one Soviet officer wrote:

> The conditions of socialist and capitalist society are qualitatively different and the objective laws of military science, which are the expression of these conditions, must also be different. . . .[22]

Colonel V. Vronin objected to the concept of a general law for war applicable to both socialist and capitalist states. Only a socialist government, he argued, could really transform a national economy to a war basis. Talenskii spoke of victory achieved by consecutive blows, growing in strength. Germany's blows had diminished in strength, partially because of the anarchy of production in capitalist countries, and because the popular masses could not be made to wage an extended war that was not in their interests. Germany, therefore, was unable to employ Talenskii's formula for victory because she was a capitalist state. It followed that there were special rules for each side in an armed conflict between socialist and capitalist governments.[23]

Colonel R. Gusakov also gave reasons for the unacceptability of a universal law of armed conflict.[24] Leninism taught that the goals of the warmakers influence the course of the war: "One of the immutable objective laws of the conduct of war is that a just war furthers in the highest degree the development of the military art and an unjust war hampers it."[25] That is why the Germans followed stereotyped tactics.

Others adopted the same line of criticism. Their arguments boiled down to the assertion that in the nature of things the same laws of warfare could not be applied to different social systems. Colonel A. Kapralov carried the argument against Talenskii to its ultimate: "The law of victory formulated by Talenskii differs very little in principle from the well-known theories of bourgeois military theoreticians such as Douhet, who asserted in his time that victory in modern war could be attained by crushing aerial blows, and Fuller and many others who sought to find the means of victory beforehand [that is, in the forces in being at the outset]."[26] It is a measure of the emotions that Talenskii aroused in his opponents that they likened him to a Douhet or a Fuller. This was fully equivalent to calling an American general officer a communist.

Some of his critics, mostly younger men nurtured in the Soviet system, were quite willing to accept that there could be a basic law of war valid for all social systems, but they insisted that there must also be special laws applicable in different degrees and ways to the capitalist and socialist systems. Colonel Chalik argued that there were universal laws governing war as a social phenomenon, its outbreak, development, and outcome; but that the attitude of the popular masses in a capitalist society toward war belonged to a special law of war applicable only to capitalist society.[27] Although Chalik was willing to ac-

cept the existence of a universal law of war, he still wanted the
Soviet Union to be in a special category with better prospects
than any potential capitalist enemy.

The editors of *Military Thought*, in the article that summed
up the doctrinal discussion and laid down the new line, took
Talenskii's side: "One cannot consider as well founded the
assertion of some participants in the discussion that the recognition of the 'generality' of objective laws is incorrect and unacceptable since it supposedly would lead to the denial of the
difference in principle between Soviet and bourgeois military
science. . . ."[28] The editors of the magazine agreed, however,
that capitalist military scientists could not understand and interpret the laws of science as well as Marxists and that a country
waging a just war was superior in morale to a country waging
an unjust war; they even claimed invincibility for a people
conducting a "war in the interests of their socialist Motherland."[29] Unquestionably, two military sciences exist, they said,
but this "does not demonstrate the existence of two different
kinds of objective laws."[30]

Upon first examination the controversy about a general
objective law of war seems futile. The purpose of all this
theorizing was to arrive at some satisfactory picture of the war
of the future and, as a consequence, to make the proper military dispositions to wage the war to the best possible effect, if
they did not actually deter its outbreak altogether. However
similar the military doctrine and the outlook of two warring
states, the differences between their social systems would be
reflected in diverging reactions to attack and recovery. Did it
really make any difference whether the socialist protagonist
believed that there was a universal law of war governing the
armed conflict or a separate body of law for each society participating in the armed conflict?

The Soviet problem was not simply one of developing a
more rigorous mathematical and scientific analysis. In the past
the grand strategy of wars has not been worked out with slide
rules. Although rigorous scientific methods had become increasingly necessary for planning particular segments of war
activity, the greater complexity of warfare demanded sound

subjective judgment as much as ever. Rigid procedures could not deal with imponderables such as the adaptation of habits and practices suited to a tried weapon system to systems yet untested in combat. Sound judgment depended on more than comprehensive information and close reasoning; an essential component was detachment, a state of mind difficult to attain when one's firmest prejudices were called in question. Before 1953 one of the most deeply rooted Soviet prejudices was that socialist and capitalist states operated under different sets of social laws. War was a social phenomenon. Therefore a universal law of warfare could not exist. These views were incompatible with the detachment that must enter into reliable military calculations. After 1953 a spirit of genuine objectivity began to invade Soviet military writings and made possible a rapid advance toward the recognition that all societies are affected by the same laws of warfare.

How did the changing Soviet outlook affect views on the significance of nuclear weapons in surprise attack? It was quite clear, especially after the American hydrogen bomb tests of March, 1952, that the physical effects of nuclear weapons were vastly greater than those of the weapons available to, say, the Germans in 1941. The Russians naturally wanted to know what these effects meant for the future of warfare.

The believers in two separate laws governing the military behavior of two contending societies inevitably stressed the difference in the responses of the societies to the effects of these weapons. The Soviet analyst, intent on the imperative of victory, pointed to the high level of Soviet morale, which derived from the superiority of Soviet society and from the feeling of fighting for the right; to the superior endurance and performance of the Soviet people in adversity; to the more rational organization of Soviet society and its ability to mobilize faster and more thoroughly than the capitalists. For these and many similar reasons the Soviet Union could sustain a surprise nuclear attack better than the capitalists and would win any war that began with such an attack. It was the old Soviet theme: we will win because it is in the nature of things.

The exponents of a universal law of the armed conflict argued quite differently. They accepted that the Soviet Union was a superior society and that its prospects in war were therefore brighter, but they refused to concede that the outcome of the armed conflict would be determined by such considerations. If other things were equal, the side with the larger forces would win the war; if other things were equal, the side with the superior morale might well have a determining advantage; under favorable conditions a surprise attack employing nuclear weapons might be decisive. These views were clearly incompatible with the proposition that separate social laws determine the fate of contrasting societies, for these statements applied equally to all societies.

A group of Talenskii's critics perceived that his concept of the content of military science differed greatly from the prevalent one and took issue with him in very sharp language. Colonel A. Pshenichkin thought it impermissible to ignore the social and political aspects of war as Talenskii did. He therefore categorically opposed limiting military science to the problems of the armed conflict. Such circumscription of the subject would contradict "the Marxist-Leninist teachings on war and the army."[31] Colonel S. Pekarskii viewed this limitation as "the intrusion of idealism into military science," which "should concern itself simultaneously with all the laws of war, both the social-political and those of a special character, since they are all indivisible from each other."[32] Colonel M. Marienko held a similar opinion:

> Military science should investigate the rules of war not only as the armed conflict but also the rules of war as a social phenomenon (the rules of the social-political aspects of war) and not be limited to a passive recital of these rules in the form given by Marxist-Leninist science. But this means that General N. Talenskii's proposition on what the subject matter of military science should be and his definition of the military science evoke doubts.[33]

Colonel R. Zverev was less restrained in his criticism. Talenskii, he wrote, views

... the armed conflict apart from its dialectical inter-
dependence with the social and political aspect of wars,
and this leads to a non-Marxist, non-scientific point of view
on the nature and character of war, and on the nature and
character of the rules of military science, and reduces military science to a mere military art. . . .

He [Talenskii] thinks that the armed conflict exists in general without a human being as the representative of a definite social structure, of definite classes, that a bare military
science exists, a naked strategy, a naked operational art, a
naked tactics, naked, eternal military rules which are the
same for all. Such things do not exist in nature. This attempt to "work out" "a pure military science, one and the
same for all times and peoples" is idealistic in essence and
should be decisively rejected.[34]

Colonel R. Gusakov criticized Talenskii along much the
same lines:

Following Marx and Engels, Lenin always viewed the
armed conflict in its interconnections with social and political questions. He placed the revolution in the military art
in direct dependence on revolution. The most striking
demonstration of the influence of revolution on the military art was the great October Revolution . . . which created
immeasurably more profound and greater transformations
in military affairs than did the bourgeois revolution. Therefore in investigating the laws of military science the question of the connection of science with economics and
politics should occupy a most prominent place. In the
article under review it obviously occupies a most modest
role.[35]

Talenskii also had defenders for his attempt to focus military thinking on the battle. Colonel G. Sapozhkov wrote that
military science should certainly take into account the difference in economic potential and morale between the contending
sides, but this was the proper concern of the Communist Party
and the Soviet Government: "It is impossible to convert military science into a science without boundaries and to set inappropriate tasks for it."[36]

Colonel E. Chalik, who it will be remembered differed with
Talenskii on some points, agreed with him as to the appropriate content of military science. While recognizing completely
the influence of economic, social, and moral factors on Soviet
military prospects, Chalik found it impossible to agree with
"some comrades who seek to reduce Soviet military science to
a popularization of these factors. This leads to a diminution of
the role of the military art." Military science properly took
into account questions of morale and the economies of warring
countries, but "subordinated all this to the chief and basic
thing—the elaboration and perfection of the military art on
the basis of Marxist-Leninist teachings." The tasks of strengthening the government economically and politically and of
building up the armed forces were "the function of the government and its apparatus as a whole."[37]

On the subject of the content of military science the editors
of *Military Thought,* in their resolution of the discussion, took
Talenskii's side of the argument without any equivocation.
They criticized those participants in the discussion who included too much within the bounds of military science. They
could not agree to the inclusion of "the whole complex of
questions of war as a social and historical phenomenon."
"Some partisans of this [inclusive] view even assert that military
science includes the Marxist-Leninist teachings on war and the
army, which go into the question of the origin and nature of
wars as a continuation of politics. Such an expanded conception of the subject matter of military science cannot be recognized as correct." Lenin, wrote the editors of the journal, described the armed uprising as a special kind of struggle with
special laws of its own. Special laws are all the more applicable
to a war between governments:

> The subject of military science is above all the investiga-
> tion of these very special laws of . . . the armed conflict.
> But the expanded interpretation of the subject matter of
> military science leads away from the resolution of its spe-
> cific tasks. . . . Therefore to include in military science
> questions going beyond the limits of its competence means
> to doom military science as a special branch of knowledge.

Military science, however, properly has to take into account matters other than the strictly military:

> Military science in investigating the cause of the armed conflict and the methods of its conduct does not disengage itself from the economic, moral, and political factors, but examines them and studies them in the interests of the attainment of victory in the armed conflict and in the interests of the military art.

Naturally an advanced military science can only be created on the basis of Marxist-Leninist theory.

The absence of proper attention to the problem of basic doctrine, the editors continued, has been a serious deficiency of Soviet military science. The true basic law should express that aspect of the armed struggle which relates directly to military operations, as well as to morale and politics. Talenskii's formula is to be recommended in that it comes close to a correct understanding of the subject matter of military science, since it includes the particular and specific matters peculiar to the armed conflict. Some topics examined by Talenskii, however, require explanation or support; for example, "the essence of consecutive blows growing in force, the place in war of other combinations of blows or other means of pursuing the armed conflict, the relationship of the various factors determining the fate of war. . . ."

Perhaps as revolutionary as any statement in the summing up was the following:

> The editors [of *Military Thought*] suggest that it is not yet possible to propound any final and definite formulation of the basic law.[38]

This matter-of-fact recognition that there was no guiding dictum, no last word, contrasted sharply with the older atmosphere in which it was assumed that everything fundamental was known.

In April, 1955, when the editors analyzed the results of the discussion opened by Talenskii and gave their own views, official Soviet ideas about the nature of war and the functions of military science had already changed radically. The editorial

comment, as the above quotations show, was in sharp contrast
to the official line of 1951, when the *Great Soviet Encyclopedia* started its article on military science with the following
four paragraphs:

> MILITARY SCIENCE is the system of knowledge about
> the rules governing warfare, the methods of preparing for
> it, and its conduct in a given historical situation. Military
> science encompasses the *military art* [q.v.], the questions
> of the organization and preparation of the armed forces,
> and the questions of the economic and morale potential-
> ities of one's own country and that of the opponent.
>
> The rules governing war arise from the rules governing the
> development of class society; therefore military science is
> a social science. Military science assumed those views, ideas,
> and concepts which comprise the military ideology of a
> given class. The contemporary military science of the im-
> perialist governments is identified in the best case with the
> military art and being basically reactionary serves the in-
> terest of the bourgeoisie and their aggressive aspirations.
> Soviet military science serves the interests of the Soviet peo-
> ple and is a powerful weapon of the socialist government
> and its Armed Forces.
>
> Bourgeois military science, which expresses the idealistic
> and metaphysical views of the bourgeois military ideo-
> logists and which believes in the existence of eternal and
> unchanging principles of war, is incapable of discovering
> the rules governing it and correctly determining the con-
> tent of true military science. . . .
>
> The only real military science is Soviet military science,
> since it is built on the firm foundation of Marxism-Lenin-
> ism and relies on the Leninist-Stalinist teachings on war.[39]

By 1955, the whole atmosphere had changed. No longer
were the permanently operating factors the sacred limits of
Soviet military thinking. No longer did a statement on the
laws of war have to include the conclusion that the Soviet
Union would win wars because it possessed a more advanced
political system. No longer did every statement about capitalist

military science have to say it was bankrupt because it was only interested in the battle itself. For the first time Soviet military thinkers could openly discuss the possibility of the defeat of the Soviet Union. That country was now strong enough militarily, and conscious enough of her strength, to consider the chances of defeat in an objective way. Her leaders had lost the need to comfort themselves by repeating the formula: we will win because we are we.

NOTES

1. Clark W. Tinch, "Quasi-war between Japan and the U.S.S.R., 1937-1939," *World Politics*, January, 1951, pp. 174-199.
2. N. Galay, "The Problem of Quantity and Quality in the Soviet Armed Forces," *Bulletin,* Institute for the Study of the U.S.S.R., Vol. 3, No. 10, October, 1956, pp. 3-14. An excellent treatment of this point.
3. "Voennoe iskusstvo" ("The Military Art"), *Bol'shaia Sovetskaia Entsiklopediia (Great Soviet Encyclopedia)*, 2d ed., Vol. 8, Leningrad, 1951, p. 439.
4. "Voennaia nauka" ("Military Science"), *Bol'shaia Sovetskaia Entsiklopediia*, 2d ed., Vol. 8, Leningrad, 1951, p. 409.
5. *Ibid.*, p. 410.
6. Colonel I. V. Maryganov, *Peredovoi kharakter sovetskoi voennoi nauki (The Advanced Character of Soviet Military Science)*, Moscow, 1953, p. 37.
7. See Nathan Leites, *A Study of Bolshevism,* The Free Press, Glencoe, Illinois, 1953, pp. 399-404.
8. Maryganov, *op. cit.*, pp. 19, 20.
9. N. Galay, "New Trends in Soviet Military Doctrine," *Bulletin,* Institute for the Study of the U.S.S.R., Vol. 3, No. 6, June, 1956, pp. 2-12, contains an account of the article and of one critique of the article.
10. I. Stalin, *Ekonomicheskie problemy sotsializma v SSSR (Economic Problems of Socialism in the U.S.S.R.)*, Moscow, 1952, pp. 10, 11, 15, and 24; Leo Gruliow (ed.), *Current Soviet Policies,* New York, 1953, pp. 2, 3. This is a convenient translation, from which the present one differs only in minor details.
11. "On the Question of the Character of the Laws of Military Science," *Voennaia mysl' (Military Thought)*, No. 11, November, 1954, p. 30. Review of comments on Major General N. Talenskii's article "On the Question of the Character of the Laws of Military Science," *Voennaia mysl'*, No. 9, 1953.
12. *Ibid.*
13. Marshal of the Soviet Union A. Vasilevskii, "On Guard over the Security of Our Soviet Motherland," *Red Star,* February 23, 1954. (An exception to the general practice of citing Soviet publications in the Russian will be made for the well-known *Red Star*.)

14. Marshal of the Soviet Union A. Vasilevskii, "The Great Lesson of History," *Red Star*, May 7, 1954.
15. Colonel V. Petrov, "On the Permanently Operating Factors, Determining the Fate of a War," in *O sovetskoi voennoi nauke (On Soviet Military Science)*, Moscow, 1954, pp. 96-97. Delivered to the printer on April 25, 1954; galleys approved by the censor on June 30, 1954.
16. Tank Marshal P. Rotmistrov, "For Creative Examination of the Questions of Soviet Military Science," *Red Star*, March 24, 1955.
17. *Ibid.*
18. *Ibid.*
19. "On the Results of the Discussion on the Character of the Laws of Military Science," *Voennaia mysl'*, No. 4, April, 1955, p. 20.
20. Colonel V. Gorynin, Candidate in the Philosophical Sciences, Colonel P. Derevianko, Candidate in the Historical Sciences, Colonel V. Seregin, Candidate in the Historical Sciences, "Inadequacies of a Book on an Important Subject," *Red Star*, February 19, 1957.
21. Colonel N. Baz', "V. I. Lenin on the Basic Factors Determining the Course and Outcome of War," *Red Star*, March 6, 1957.
22. "On the Question of the Character of the Laws of Military Science," *Voennaia mysl'*, No. 11, November, 1954, p. 38.
23. *Ibid.*, p. 40.
24. Colonel R. Gusakov, "A One-sided Approach to the Study of the Laws of the Armed Conflict," *Voennaia mysl'*, No. 9, September, 1954, pp. 33-36.
25. *Ibid.*, p. 35.
26. "On the Question of the Character of the Laws of Military Science," *Voennaia mysl'*, No. 11, November, 1954, p. 39.
27. Colonel E. Chalik, "On the Question of the General and Special Laws of War," *Voennaia mysl'*, No. 9, September, 1954, pp. 26-32.
28. "On the Results of the Discussion of the Character of the Laws of Military Science," *Voennaia mysl'*, No. 4, April, 1955, p. 18.
29. *Ibid.*
30. *Ibid.*, p. 19.
31. "On the Question of the Character of the Laws of Military Science," *Voennaia mysl'*, November, 1954, p. 33.
32. *Ibid.*, p. 34.
33. *Ibid.*
34. *Ibid.*, pp. 33, 34.
35. Colonel R. Gusakov, "A One-sided Approach to the Study of the Laws of the Armed Conflict," *Voennaia mysl'*, September, 1954, p. 34.
36. "On the Question of the Character of the Laws of Military Science," *Voennaia mysl'*, November, 1954, p. 36.
37. Colonel E. Chalik, "On the Question of the General and Special Laws of War," *Voennaia mysl'*, September, 1954, p. 26.
38. The passages quoted and paraphrased are from "On the Results of the Discussion of the Character of the Laws of Military Science," *Voennaia mysl'*, April, 1955, pp. 16, 17, 20, and 21.
39. "Voennaia nauka" ("Military Science"), *Bol'shaia Sovetskaia Entsiklopediia*, 2d ed., Vol. 8, Leningrad, 1951, p. 406.

CHAPTER THREE

IS DETERRENCE RELIABLE?:
THE SOVIET VIEW

After the first employment of atomic weapons many Western commentators wrote that war had abolished itself because it had become too horrible. They knew full well that their predecessors had greeted other new weapons, such as high-explosive projectiles, with similar hopes, only to see those hopes dashed by wars of unprecedented severity. The destructiveness of nuclear weapons, however, seemed to promise that at last, war had become so fruitless that all must avoid it. This kind of comment was still, as in the past, a product of wishful thinking rather than of careful analysis.

Would the same writers have made statements about war having abolished itself if only the Soviet Union had possessed nuclear weapons? What they meant was that the United States would not use nuclear weapons to initiate war, and that no other country would risk starting a major war while the United States had a monopoly of atomic weapons. Western writers were saying in effect that the West was peacefully inclined, so that terrible weapons in its hands virtually assured the continuance of peace. To the Soviet leaders, however, capitalist states were aggressive by definition, and the more powerful their weapons, the more probable their aggression. This position was not immediately affected by the Soviet acquisition of nuclear capabilities. It is therefore all the more striking that soon after Stalin's death, when the Soviet Union possessed fission bombs but a poor delivery system, a few Soviet leaders cautiously expressed the hope that mutual possession of nuclear weapons made it reasonable to count on peace.

In his last published work Stalin had said that war was inevitable as long as imperialism existed, but he limited his whole discussion to the question of war among "imperialists." The popular peace movements might prevent a specific war, but sooner or later war among the capitalists was inevitable. Stalin clearly meant, and was read in the Soviet Union to mean, that as long as capitalism existed, war involving the Soviet Union was inevitable.[1]

This viewpoint did not long survive the death of the old dictator. At the end of 1953 and the beginning of 1954, the Chairman of the Council of Ministers, Malenkov, and other by no means unimportant persons advanced the idea that perhaps there would be peace in their time. Obviously the elevation of such a hope to the status of a prediction would have had far-reaching consequences for Soviet military posture, foreign policy, and domestic conditions. Shortly Malenkov's power declined and his optimistic views were proscribed. The official Soviet analysis became that of Khrushchev and others, who asserted that war initiated by the capitalists was always possible, and that the military posture, foreign policy, and domestic arrangements of the Soviet Union should be shaped accordingly. The dismissal of Malenkov from the premiership did not in itself guarantee the ascendancy of the less optimistic policy. As recently as June, 1957, it was necessary to demote Malenkov still further and charge him with having jeopardized Soviet security. The persistence of the rejected ideas makes it all the more important to understand their history.

For years before 1953 all Soviet writers had repeated the familiar theme that the natural aggressiveness of capitalism made war inevitable. This theme furnished the permanent background to all Soviet discussions on international politics. The premises of what we may call the Malenkov argument were initially stated by little-known persons. The first to make a change in the monotonous litany of Stalinism was an obscure writer, **M. Gus.**

Following the style required of Soviet writers who consciously depart from official doctrine, Gus started with a low
bow to orthodoxy: Lenin made the great discovery that capitalism suffers from uneven development; as one capitalist nation outstrips others, the economic balance of all is upset; capitalism knows no way to right the balance without economic
crises and war. Thus far Gus's doctrine was unexceptionable to
the orthodox, since it had been propounded in almost the
identical phrases thousands of times in the Soviet press. But
only a taste cloyed by the endless repetition of this formula
could have found Gus's next paragraph palatable:

> Experience has shown and proved that we are in a position
> to prevent war, and to paralyze the action of this law [of
> the inevitability of war]. As one bourgeois radio com-
> mentator expressed it, in previous years people looked at
> their calendars anxiously as the pages came nearer and
> nearer to August, the classic month for the beginning of
> world wars, but in 1953 for the first time people drew an
> easy breath in the certainty that such an obvious threat of
> war had been significantly reduced this year, and had con-
> siderably receded.[2]

Although Gus began by appealing to Lenin's authority, he went
on to deny one of the latter's most important theoretical formulations, namely that capitalism inevitably breeds war. If the
law of the inevitability of war could be paralyzed, in Gus's unprecedented phrase, one or both of two heterodox propositions
had to be true: first, capitalism had changed its nature; second,
now that war had become so destructive to all participants, the
fear of its consequences outweighed the capitalists' aggressive
propensities. The acceptance of either of these propositions
meant a radical revision of the prevalent doctrine.

Other Soviet writers immediately apprehended the implications of Gus's remarks and refuted them in no uncertain
terms. No less a personage than V. Kruzhkov, then chief of the
Agitation and Propaganda Section of the Central Committee
of the Communist Party, attacked Gus's theory but without
mentioning him by name. Kruzhkov recalled Stalin's criticism

of those Soviet philosophers, economists, and historians who
wanted to formulate or create new laws. The incidence of such
mistakes had declined, but it was still necessary to direct attention to them when they appeared. Talk about the possibility
of paralyzing the laws of the development of capitalism was not
Marxism-Leninism.[3]

Other writers differed with Gus's view but did not always
mention his name.

Colonel G. Fedorov, writing in *Red Star* for January 6,
after echoing Stalin's dictum that the popular masses could
prevent a particular war or delay its outbreak, specifically reaffirmed the standard formulation that Gus had challenged.
Fedorov said:

> In this connection it must never be forgotten that as long
> as capitalism exists wars are absolutely inevitable. Only
> with the destruction of the last system of exploitation—
> capitalism—will wars become impossible.[4]

Stalin had been satisfied with the epithet "inevitable," but
Fedorov insisted that wars are "absolutely inevitable." Any
informed Soviet reader who had seen Gus's original deviation
from the old formula would realize that the redundant term
"absolutely" pointedly contradicted the idea of the paralysis
of this law.

Gus's thesis was refuted, in the journal that published it,
by a V. Tereshkin, who accused Gus of taking a capricious
attitude toward the laws governing the historical development
of society. Tereshkin argued that even under the conditions
prevailing since 1945 the law of the inevitability of war held
true and would do so as long as capitalism existed. Only the
destruction of capitalism could remove the inevitability of war.
It was impossible to speak of the paralysis of a social law, although once a specific historical period had passed, the laws
applicable to that period gave way to new ones:

> But, according to Gus, if a law cannot be destroyed then
> it can be, it seems, paralyzed and thus voided. But a para-
> lyzed law is no longer a law; it is in the situation of a
> paralytic and cannot move. Either it is a law or not a law.[5]

Colonel Piatkin, writing for officers in *Military Thought*, without referring specifically to Gus, also declared that in contemporary conditions capitalism was still giving birth to wars and that the Leninist proposition on the inevitability of war had not lost its force. "Imperialism cannot live without force and bloody wars."[6]

In the traditional Bolshevik view, since a capitalist-made war was inevitable, the Soviet Union must be fully prepared for war. The problem was how best to prepare.

Gus, who probably had supporters in Soviet higher circles, also received some support from the other side of the Atlantic. The President of the United States himself, in an address to the United Nations on December 8, 1953, indicated that war might not be inevitable. President Eisenhower had insisted that the United States then had a great superiority in nuclear weapons, but even that was no guarantee against "fearful material damage." As consequences of a nuclear war he foresaw "the probability of civilization destroyed . . . and the condemnation of mankind to begin all over again the age-old struggle upward from savagery." Here indeed was an argument supporting the thesis that the United States would not initiate a war because it abhorred the consequences. Little more than a month after the President's speech his arguments were employed by an anonymous retired general writing in *Izvestiia*, the Malenkov organ. The general "agreed completely with the appraisal of the danger contained in present-day atomic weapons which was expressed by Eisenhower." This strongly suggested that Malenkov and his group stood behind Gus.

The article drew attention to the fact that American military theoreticians, commentators, journalists, and occasionally people in high positions had been in the habit of describing an easy atomic war against the Soviet Union, since they believed they had a monopoly of atomic weapons. Looking into the past for the source of this American attitude, the author first observed that there had been a time when great powers could participate in wars without subjecting their own territories to destruction and devastation. Great Britain was able to do this in the eighteenth and nineteenth centuries because the English

Channel was then an insuperable barrier. Even in the First World War Great Britain suffered air raids, and the Second World War demonstrated England's high vulnerability to air attack. The United States had hitherto benefited from a more favorable geographical position, but times were changing:

> The postwar development of the technical facilities of warfare has advanced so far that now the ocean is no longer a reliable protection against blows in war. The contemporary development of aviation, missiles, and the submarine fleet makes it possible to deal crushing blows across a distance of many thousands of kilometers. . . . Why, there are already appearing even in the American press sufficient admissions of the fact that the age of invulnerability of overseas states is a thing of the past.

The author of this article did not say specifically that new Soviet weapons made the United States home territory vulnerable or that this fact would deter the United States from making war; but for the first time the Soviet general reader was given such optimistic hints about new Soviet technical capabilities that he might make them the foundation for a theory of deterrence.[7]

On January 21, 1954, two days after the general in retirement published his article in *Izvestiia*, a fairly high-level person, P. N. Pospelov, a secretary of the Central Committee of the Communist Party, made a major speech on the thirtieth anniversary of Lenin's death, in which he said that the Soviet Union was seeking ways and means of employing atomic energy for the good of mankind and not for the "destruction of the peoples or the annihilation of world civilization." Rather indirectly Pospelov was echoing Eisenhower's warning of December 8 that a nuclear war would destroy both sides. He touched upon the possibility of deterring the United States from war, taking comfort from the technical and economic might of the Soviet Union, which had sobered some of the more vigorous capitalist proponents of a crusade against the Soviet Union.

On the whole, the speech was one of the mildest major Soviet speeches in years, without a single reference to the possibility of war. Furthermore, after the standard analysis of the contradictions of capitalism in its imperialist stage, the standard conclusion that war was inevitable was missing. Pospelov said merely that imperialism was vulnerable and the general crisis of capitalism was intensified by the widespread opposition to imperialist policies.[8]

In a speech on March 12 Premier Malenkov pointed out that it was not necessary for mankind to choose between a new world war and the so-called cold war. The Soviet government, he said, resolutely opposed the cold war, "for this policy is a policy of the preparation of a new world holocaust which, with the present means of warfare, means the destruction of world civilization."[9]

What Malenkov hinted in a few phrases was elaborately spelled out by Mikoian on the same day in a speech at Erevan, Armenia. The following paragraphs from the Erevan speech were not published in the Moscow press and appeared only in the Erevan party newspaper:

> The danger of war has receded to a large extent in con-
> nection with the fact that we now have not only the atomic
> but also the hydrogen bomb. These successes of the Soviet
> Union are striking evidences of the fact that our physics
> and chemistry have attained the heights of modern human
> knowledge and that the U.S.S.R. has reached tremendous
> industrial might.
>
> In the course of the last four or five years the ruling circles
> of the U.S.A. have declined negotiation with the Soviet
> Union, while trying to convince public opinion that these
> negotiations were useless and that it was not even worth-
> while to initiate them. It is quite instructive therefore that
> after the Soviet Union made the hydrogen bomb, and it is
> not yet known whether the United States of America has
> such a bomb, the government of the United States of
> America proposed to the Soviet Union the initiation of
> negotiations on questions of atomic energy. We agree to
> this because our principle is to resolve all international
> questions by the method of negotiation. Such negotiations
> are in progress and the fact of these negotiations speaks
> for itself.

. . . Atomic and hydrogen weapons in the hands of the Soviet Union are a means for checking the aggressors and for waging peace.

If former wars in which the United States participated did not spread to the territory of the United States of America and not one of their factories, not one of their homes was destroyed, now the situation would seem to be different.

Hence a new tone in the American press:

If, not so long ago, the American bourgeois press printed insolent articles illustrated with maps showing Soviet cities as targets of atomic bombings, so now the very same newspapers and magazines describe the destruction of American cities in the future atomic war.[10]

The group of leaders who had less confidence in Soviet deterrent power was able to prevent the dissemination of Mikoian's arguments. Manifest differences of opinion on what would deter the United States from war indicated a major political dispute in the Soviet Union. The opponents of the policy of relying on deterrence were soon heard from. In conformity with the custom of minimizing public differences on policy they exercised restraint, but not at the cost of obscuring their position.

Small verbal clues were the first signals of what soon revealed itself as an important political debate. On New Year's Day, 1954, in a written reply to questions put by an American correspondent, Malenkov said that he knew of "no objective impediments to the improvement in the relations between the Soviet Union and the United States of America." On the same day, Voroshilov, the occupant of the honorary post of Chairman of the Presidium of the Supreme Soviet, said that the power of the Soviet Union had grown, "despite the designs of the external and internal enemies of socialism." Thus one major Soviet political figure denied that there were barriers to continuing peace with the United States, while another stressed the hostility of the capitalist enemies.

In March, 1954, a number of important Soviet figures in

unison contested the view that the Soviet acquisition of nuclear weapons had made the United States more pacific. On March 6, Khrushchev accused the reactionary capitalist forces of seeking a way out of their difficulties "by the preparation of a new war."[11] Voroshilov, speaking on March 10, said that despite Soviet economic and diplomatic successes "we live in encirclement all the same."[12] The phrase "capitalist encirclement," so often used by Stalin to justify domestic sacrifices, had become rare in the Soviet Union since Stalin's death. Kaganovich argued that the collapse of the colonial system made the imperialists seek a solution in war.[13] Bulganin also rejected the notion that Soviet strength forced peaceful ways on the United States when he dismissed as reckless the assumption that the imperialists "spend enormous material and financial resources on armaments only to frighten us. We cannot depend on the humanitarianism of the imperialists who, as life has shown, are capable of using any weapon of mass destruction."[14] Molotov and Khrushchev, in speeches on March 11, again stressed the aggressive intentions of the imperialist camp.[15]

These statements might have passed unnoticed but for the fact that only a few weeks later Malenkov retracted his optimistic views about the prospects for peace. The opposition to Malenkov was implicit rather than explicit. The latter possessed enough political power in the early part of 1954 to confine his opponents to oblique criticism. None took the obvious course of quoting Malenkov against himself by recalling that at the Nineteenth Party Congress in 1952 Malenkov had said that a new war would mean the collapse of capitalism. More recently he had spoken of the collapse of civilization, indicating a mutual compelling interest in the preservation of peace.

Malenkov's opponents apparently were able to prevent the public repetition of the phrase "destruction of world civilization." A careful search has uncovered only one instance to the contrary: on March 27, 1954, a Soviet domestic radio commentator said that a war in which atomic and hydrogen bombs were used meant colossal destruction: "More than that it threatens the very existence of human civilization."[16]

There were no more references to the destruction of world

civilization. Indeed the major party organ, *Kommunist,* pointedly rejected the Malenkov view without mentioning his name. The journal said that if the imperialists unleashed a third world war it would lead to "the complete destruction of that whole [capitalist] system."[17] A week later, on April 26, Malenkov reversed his March position by saying that a third world war "would inevitably lead to the collapse of the capitalist social system." This went beyond his statement of October, 1952, at the Nineteenth Party Congress, where he did not use the word "inevitably." Nevertheless the retraction of his recently adopted views seemed to contain a certain reservation. Malenkov did not specifically repudiate his words of a month before, and used the term "collapse," rather than "destruction of," to describe what would happen to capitalism. In doing so he avoided the exact words of the *Kommunist* editorial of the week before. Malenkov's description of how such a war could come about was also so phrased as to suggest reservations:

> If, however, the aggressive circles, relying on atomic weapons, should decide on madness and seek to test the strength and might of the Soviet Union, then it cannot be doubted that the aggressor would be crushed by that very weapon and that such an adventure would inevitably lead to the collapse of the capitalist social system.[18]

This was something less than a total abandonment of his earlier position. True, he no longer said that an American war against the Soviet Union would be deterred. Should Soviet deterrence fail, however, war would come because the enemy had decided on madness. This is a strange phrase; people rarely decide to be mad.

Malenkov had implied very strongly that peace was assured because all would lose by the destruction of civilization. Defeatism is the only epithet a good Bolshevik could apply to such an analysis. To suggest that the Bolsheviks could do nothing to win a war initiated by the capitalists was defeatist. To suggest that such a war was ruled out because the capitalists did not want it was complacency. In the years that followed, Soviet statements expressed increasing confidence that Soviet

THE SOVIET VIEW OF DETERRENCE

military strength would deter the United States from making war, but never again did any Soviet statement even imply that increasing military strength guaranteed peace to the Soviet Union. Rather, the tone adopted was that aggression had been restrained. Mikoian, speaking on the day of Malenkov's retraction, typified the dominant Soviet position when he argued that

> ... the newest weapons—the atomic and hydrogen bombs —which are the means for unleashing wars in the hands of the aggressors, in our hands are the best means for safeguarding the peace because they tie the hands of those who would like to fight. ... The aggressive forces are preparing a new world holocaust for the sake of profit, for the sake of the unlimited increase of their profits.[19]

Malenkov's revised formulation, to the effect that capitalism would collapse in a new war, was widely repeated. On May 3, for instance, a Soviet marshal in command of troops in the Ukraine used the formula.[20] Marshal Vasilevskii repeated the same phrases.[21] On June 12, Khrushchev in a speech in Prague used the very words of Malenkov.[22] Three days later Khrushchev apparently spoke extemporaneously when he slipped the following sentences into a speech at Prague:

> Comrades, I think that Hitler's last war should teach some people sense. Hitler also thought that the Soviet Union stood on feet of clay. But you and I, comrades, are alive while Hitler has already rotted. [Applause] If we remain strong, all those enemies who raise their hand against us will follow Hitler's example and that of Mussolini. Only the latter was hanged by his feet, and the former just killed himself.[23]

Although in the latter half of 1954 most important public figures continued to insist that a future war would mean the collapse of capitalism, the opposition had not been finally demolished. No one said as yet that Malenkov had been mistaken in declaring that the whole of civilization would be destroyed by a future war. The rejection of Malenkov's views continued to be indirect: it took the form of a flat statement

that only capitalism would collapse, and did not refer to Malenkov. Furthermore, Gus's radical statement on the possibility of
paralyzing laws continued to be attacked. For example, in a
book on military theory that went to press in October, 1954,
Colonel Piatkin attacked certain comrades who still talked
about destroying objective laws and paralyzing the action of
these laws. As an example he gave the attempt to show that the
law of the irregular economic development of capitalist countries could be paralyzed.[24] It will be recalled that this theory of
the irregular economic development of capitalist countries is
the basis of Lenin's proposition on the inevitability of war in
the imperialist stage of history.

It was not until the beginning of 1955, when it became
clear that Malenkov was about to be demoted, that the theory
of the possible permanent deterrence of the United States
was subjected to direct attack and officially designated as incorrect. The likelihood of war and the amount of Soviet defense
expenditures was an important issue in Malenkov's political
defeat, as the next chapter will demonstrate. It was not until
his dismissal from the premiership that the party magazine
Kommunist made a direct attack on his thesis concerning "the
destruction of world civilization." The magazine described the
thesis as essentially a capitalist trick to induce a false sense
of security. By saying that the existence of atomic weapons had
liquidated the danger of a new war, the capitalists were trying
to pose as saviors of peace while actually pursuing aggressive
purposes. In propagating this thesis of the destruction of world
civilization the capitalists were exploiting the sincere desire of
the peoples to maintain peace and prevent an atomic war:

> This circumstance explains to a considerable extent the
> fact that the thesis of "the destruction of world civiliza-
> tion" has been accepted on faith and disseminated to some
> extent even among those who are opposed to war and its
> imperialist instigators. A few, it turns out, have been in-
> clined to believe in the "absolute power" of contemporary
> weapons of mass destruction and have exaggerated the
> strength of the instigators of a new war. . . . These people
> were unable to discern promptly the real sense and purpose

of the fable about the "destruction of world civilization"
. . . and began to repeat it uncritically in their oral and
written statements.

However grievous the consequences of atomic war might
be, it must not be identified with "the destruction of world
civilization." Such an identification willynilly brings grist
to the American imperialist mill; it can create the incorrect concept among the partisans of peace that, as they say,
the atomic threat is such that the instigators of war will not
dare to use their own bombs, since they will not decide to
commit suicide. Such a concept blunts the vigilance of the
people toward those who in the preparation of atomic war
would like to take the peoples by surprise.

The article went on to explain that capitalism, not world
civilization, would be destroyed in a future atomic war. The
capitalists disseminated the slogan of the destruction of world
civilization, according to *Kommunist,* in order to spread fatalistic and pessimistic ideas among the masses so that they would
feel: "Why struggle? Nothing will change anyhow! The end
of the world is coming."[25]

As soon as Malenkov was deposed, then, his thesis of a
peace based on mutual deterrence was characterized as a capitalist slogan whose purpose was to lull vigilance and spread defeatism.

After Khrushchev and Bulganin installed themselves as
the leaders of the new government, they never altered their
basic position that war was always possible, although they
estimated the likelihood of war as circumstances required. From
February, 1955, when Malenkov fell, to the summit meeting
in July, the new leaders avoided stressing the likelihood of war;
they seemed compelled to represent themselves to their own
people as peacemakers. Yet immediately after Khrushchev's
acquisition of control in the Presidium of the Central Committee of the CPSU, it became official policy to acquire and
maintain the ability to deliver a pre-emptive attack against
the United States. The fantastically expensive preparations to
get in a first blow should an American attack appear probable
were only justifiable on the theory that war was possible. The

decision to be ready to make a pre-emptive attack if necessary was mentioned discreetly in several public statements by generals in April, 1955, but these were drowned out by the strident optimism that heralded the Geneva Summit Conference of July, 1955. Although before this conference the Soviet leaders expressed hopes for the further improvement of international relations and an abatement of the cold war, they never said that a complete mutual understanding was possible or that there was no more danger of war. Nor have they done so since that time.

At the end of 1955, during their trip to India and Burma, Khrushchev and Bulganin went further than ever before in describing the horrors of a nuclear war. They continued to eschew the theme of mutual destruction, although they came closer to it than they had done in the past. The Soviet version of the joint statement issued by the Russians and Indians at the end of the tour referred to "conditions leading to a devastating and ruinous world war." The Indian rendering of the same phrase referred to "conditions leading to the inconceivable disaster of another world war."[26] The Russian version of the text seems deliberately to stop short of Malenkov's phrase, "the destruction of world civilization." "Devastating" is the term ordinarily employed in Russian to describe the destruction of World War II; "inconceivable," the word employed by the Indians, suggests an unprecedented disaster such as the destruction of world civilization.

Bulganin seems to have made a slip and overstepped the agreed limit when he endorsed one of Nehru's statements:

> The Prime Minister of India . . . was absolutely right to demonstrate that coexistence was the only sensible possibility for all governments because in the opposite case there would be only one alternative—mutual destruction.[27]

The phrase "mutual destruction" is even closer to the idea of mutual deterrence than "the destruction of world civilization," and it is significant that the Soviet press made little mention of Bulganin's words.

Perhaps to correct any misapprehension, Bulganin stated

flatly on New Year's Day, 1956, that it was incorrect to say: "As long as East and West possess hydrogen bombs the possibility of thermonuclear war is automatically excluded." Such assertions, he said, only lull the vigilance of the fighters for peace, but "naturally the fact that in present conditions atomic and hydrogen weapons cannot be employed with impunity exerts a certain deterrent influence on those circles who want to unleash war employing the means of mass destruction."[28]

Since 1956 official Soviet spokesmen have continued to increase their estimates of how grievous the consequences of a nuclear war would be for the whole world. In a speech made on March 14, 1958, Khrushchev came very close to approving the hitherto proscribed formula that a nuclear war would mean the end of world civilization:

> A future war, if it breaks out despite the will of the peoples, threatens to be the most destructive of wars—a nuclear war. In addition to immediate destruction, the employment of nuclear weapons will poison the atmosphere with radioactive fall-out and this could lead to the annihilation of almost all life, especially in countries of small territory and high population density. There all will be literally wiped off the face of the earth.[29]

The difference between the phrases, "annihilation of almost all life" and "destruction of world civilization," seems trivial at first glance. The latter phrase, however, implies that a nuclear war is not worth fighting because victory would be meaningless; the former phrase, Khrushchev's, implies that enough could be saved to assure the ultimate victory of communism. One Soviet leader's failure to maintain this distinction was immediately corrected by the press. On April 26, 1958, Voroshilov referred, in a talk over the Moscow radio, to two wars of bloodshed unleashed by German militarism. "Today it would not be [merely a matter of] bloodshed," he continued, "but simple annihilation of all life on earth. We know what nuclear weapons are." These two sentences did not appear in the account published by *Pravda* on the following day.

A corollary of the growing admission that a new war would

be terribly destructive to all was the growing conviction that such a war would not occur. At the Party congress of February, 1956, Khrushchev significantly modified the Party doctrine concerning war in a world where "imperialism" still existed.

Khrushchev's report to the Twentieth Party Congress devoted several paragraphs to the possibility of preventing war. He recalled the Marxist-Leninist proposition that war was inevitable as long as imperialism existed, but unlike standard Soviet textual exegesis he put the formula into the perspective of time. The theory of the inevitability of war had been developed when imperialism controlled the whole world and when the political and social forces opposed to war were weak and poorly organized and could not make imperialism refrain from wars. These conditions had changed: imperialism had become weaker and socialism stronger. Although this proposition had been absolutely right in its time, the present position was radically different. Nevertheless, while the camp of socialism had become stronger, the basis for the outbreak of war continued to exist because imperialism still existed. The greatest vigilance was necessary, for as long as capitalism existed the reactionary forces would seek the course of military adventures and aggression and might try to unleash war. "But," he added in very non-Leninist fashion, "there is no fatal inevitability of wars."

There were many well-armed forces in the world, continued Khrushchev, which would not permit the imperialists to start a war, or would spoil their plans if they managed to start one. All these antiwar forces ought to be strong and ready. They should not weaken their efforts for the preservation of peace.[30]

The phrase "no fatal inevitability of wars" seems awkward. Khrushchev could simply have said that, while war always remained possible, the prospects for peace were better, but he and the Party had to tread warily. On the one hand the new regime needed peace and wanted the credit for making a virtue of necessity. If they continued to insist that war was inevitable as long as imperialistic capitalism existed, no one would believe that they meant what they said about "peaceful coexistence." On the other hand, since they actually believed that war was possible and became more likely as the Soviet Union relaxed its guard, they could not afford to imply that imperialism had changed its nature and no longer threatened war. Hence Khrushchev's somewhat equivocal optimism, as it appeared in the phrase "no fatal inevitability of wars."

Other major speakers at the Twentieth Party Congress more or less elaborated Khrushchev's ideas. Only Molotov and Kaganovich departed noticeably from them. Molotov, in expanding Khrushchev's new formula, avoided implying that Lenin's theory of the inevitability of war in the imperialist stage of history was outdated and needed qualification. He described the Leninist theory in terms of a conflict between the forces that wanted war and those that wanted peace. Now that the forces for peace had grown greatly, a real possibility of preventing war existed. Molotov stressed, however, that there could be no reliance on the ability of these forces to deter capitalism from initiating war:

> We should not minimize the danger of war nor surrender to the illusion that peace and a quiet life are assured in all circumstances. We must always be vigilant and watchfully follow the aggressive plans of the imperialists. We should not surrender to complacency as if it were possible to convince the imperialists with nice speeches and pacific plans.[31]

Like Molotov, Kaganovich avoided saying that Lenin's formula about the inevitability of war had become dated. In the increased strength of the forces opposing the imperialist pressure toward war he found the reason for "the contemporary balance of forces," which led to the conclusion "that there is no fatal inevitability of war. . . ." The prevention of war was possible, but only if several conditions were met. These were the exposure of imperialism's aggressive schemes, a fruitful struggle for disarmament, the strengthening of the defensive might of the Soviet Union, and the perfecting of her armed forces.[32]

During 1956 Soviet publicists pushed two themes: one, that nuclear weapons were equally dangerous to all, and two, that the West might still employ nuclear weapons in an aggressive surprise attack against the Soviet Union. For example, in a letter to Eisenhower in January, 1956, Bulganin wrote: "Everyone knows that the newest means for the conduct of war . . . place the people of all countries in an equally dangerous position. . . ."[33] The theme was repeated a week later. An article in *Pravda* talked of the reliance of the Americans, especially Generals White and Twining, on nuclear weapons whose destructive force was "equally dangerous for all." Generals should know this better than anybody else.[34]

In a reply to a letter by Bertrand Russell that had been published in *Pravda,* the Soviet academician Skobel'tsyn took issue with Russell's statement that the mutual possession of nuclear weapons created a balance of forces and therefore promised peace. Even Russell, wrote Skobel'tsyn, recognized that such a balance was precarious and therefore could readily be disturbed.[35]

General Pokrovskii, who was already prominent in his own country and who was soon to become well known abroad through some of his statements on the ballistic missile, made clear why Soviet official opinion regarded the nuclear balance as precarious. His explanation was so vivid and so unusual in its specificity that it merits quotation in full:

> No one can guarantee that there will not emerge in some country a reactionary military dictatorship similar to that of Nazi Germany which would recklessly disregard all considerations of the peoples' peace and security. In that event sudden atomic attack would become a by no means unlikely prospect. Of course it would not be left without retaliation. But there can be no doubt that technically nuclear weapons make it easier to unleash war than conventional weapons.

> Thus, if the development of conventional armaments in no way prevents the outbreak of war, there is still less reason to believe that nuclear weapons can play the role of peace preservers. Experts know only too well that the stockpiling of atomic weapons does not diminish but greatly aggravates the danger of another war.[36]

Throughout the first half of 1957 the general tone of the Soviet press conveyed the opinion that, although Soviet strength had greatly increased, the danger of war was still very real. A Soviet officer writing in *Red Star* pointed with obvious pleasure to the difference between General LeMay's present opinions and those of five years earlier. Five years ago General LeMay had said "that the United States could win a war against the Soviet Union without suffering serious losses." Now, however, LeMay was afraid to make such predictions because he understood that "Soviet atomic bombers could deal serious destruction" to America itself. Despite the greater realism of LeMay's present attitude, many important political and military figures in America still did not share this view and continued to seek means to destroy others while themselves remaining unharmed.[37]

In February, 1957, Foreign Minister Shepilov made a major foreign-policy speech in which he painted a more optimistic picture of the likelihood of peace, a picture which, as we shall seek to demonstrate later, was connected with his dismissal a few days afterwards. This speech was an aberration: the press in general and the military press in particular re-emphasized that there was no assurance of peace through deterrence. A writer in a philosophical journal, for example, explained that nuclear weapons had the double-edged effect of sobering the capitalists and simultaneously arousing in them baseless hopes for a new blitzkrieg. Therefore the danger of war would continue to exist.[38]

A military writer in *Red Star* pointed out forcefully that the absence of "absolute inevitability" did not imply the improbability of war. He seems to have been the first to draw public attention to the fact that recent Soviet propaganda had drawn too optimistic conclusions from Khrushchev's somewhat vague words at the Twentieth Party Congress:

It is necessary, if even briefly, to note that some of our propagandists give a one-sided interpretation of the question of wars in the contemporary epoch. In explaining this proposition of the XXth Congress of the Communist Party of the Soviet Union they often concentrate chief attention on the question of the possibility of *preventing* wars in

contemporary historical conditions. And insofar as the possibility of the *outbreak* of new wars prepared by the imperialists is concerned—of this they speak in passing as if
it were something secondary and insignificant. Such an approach to the question of wars in the contemporary epoch
contradicts the very spirit of Soviet military ideology. What
is basic for Soviet military ideology is the proposition of
the XXth Congress of the Communist Party of the Soviet
Union . . . that even now the economic basis for war exists
and that the imperialists will seek to unleash war. Our
chief attention should be devoted to that aspect of the
question.[39]

The theme of the increasing likelihood of war was very
prominent in the first few months of 1957. (The reasons for
this will be explored in a subsequent chapter.) Khrushchev
himself, in two interviews with foreigners, raised the specter
of a war started by accident, a new theme. In an interview
with Turner Catledge of *The New York Times* on May 10,
1957, Khrushchev implied that the chances for war were increasing with the continued accumulation of nuclear weapons:

> In this connection it should be realized that, given the
> existence of atomic and hydrogen arms and given the ex-
> istence of rocket technology and intercontinental missiles
> it is not to be excluded that a war can be unleashed as a
> result of some kind of fatal error, which will lead to un-
> told tragedy for the peoples not only of our two countries
> but for the peoples of the whole world.

Expanding on this theme, Khrushchev asserted that some
irresponsible American statesmen were pursuing an adventuristic policy:

> It is one thing when a skilled acrobat balances on a tight-
> rope. If he loses his balance and falls off only one person
> perishes. Even that is a pity. But if a statesman who is con-
> ducting a policy of "the brink of war" falls, then his mis-
> take can lead to the death of millions of people. This must
> not be forgotten. It cannot be forgotten also that certain
> American officials themselves talk of how they conduct a

policy from "a position of strength" and conduct it "to
the brink of war."

Later in the interview, when Khrushchev was asked whether he
thought the chances for peace or the chances for the outbreak
of war were greater, he replied that it was very difficult to say
which way the scales would tip:

> The questions of war and peace depend on many circum-
> stances and depend not only upon the Soviet Union but
> upon other governments. I shall speak concretely, most of
> all on the United States of America and the Soviet Union.
> There are many generals in the United States who make
> very stupid statements that they can wipe the Soviet Union
> "from the face of the earth." But these braggarts should
> remember that the other country too can reply in kind. In
> general a hubbub on this question is a stupid hubbub.
> It is hard, I repeat, to say in which direction the scales will
> tip.[40]

Khrushchev's imagery is interesting. The role of a statesman walking a tightrope, falling, and then plunging the world
into war was clearly not one for which the speaker was casting
himself. The reference to "brinkmanship" made it obvious
enough to whom Khrushchev was referring. He pictured a
United States that was playing a dangerous game with alarms
of war, though not necessarily making a deliberate plan to attack the Soviet Union. Earlier Soviet statements had implied
unequivocally that the United States was plotting war on the
Soviet Union at an opportune moment. On May 28, 1957, in
his interview with a Japanese newspaperman, Khrushchev
again pointed to the danger of war being unleashed because of
some accident.[41]

Khrushchev's new emphasis on accident suggests that he
considered the United States to be deterred from making war
by Soviet strength. By stressing war by accident instead of a war
planned by the United States, Khrushchev implied that Soviet
military strength was already exerting a deterrent influence.
One might also argue that Khrushchev in an effort to be tactful
said war by accident when he meant war by design. But Khrush-

chev's repeated mention of the war-by-accident theme and the increasing detail in which he described the outbreak of an unwanted war suggests that he really believed in the possibility of war by accident. Whatever relative weight Khrushchev privately assigned to the possibilities of war by accident or by design, he has insisted that war continues to be possible, and that as long as this is true the Soviet Union has to prepare for war. On one occasion, when he was very anxious to make a good impression on Americans, he nevertheless stuck to this point of view. During a television interview, later widely disseminated in the United States, Khrushchev was asked how he could talk of coexistence with the United States if he really believed that the United States was planning a war against the Soviet Union. Khrushchev answered:

> But what should we do? We would like it if you are not planning war, but you are planning it. And we take this into account.[42]

In his interview with the Japanese newspaperman, Khrushchev spelled out the theme at even greater length. The Japanese suggested that if the Soviet Union unilaterally ceased testing nuclear weapons this could lead to a general cessation of tests. Khrushchev rejected the suggestion and gave as his reason the dangers of reducing Soviet strength when its deterrent effect was an essential support of peace:

> If we stop our tests then we weaken our defensive might to some extent. And it is our own power that deters the forces of war and strengthens the forces of peace. Would not some weakening of our power impel the imperialist forces to an adventuristic step? They might be heartened by such a circumstance.

Khrushchev then cited some "bellicose" statements made by General Norstad to prove that one must not forget the hotheads who talked about destroying the Soviet Union in a few hours. Khrushchev, drawing his imagery from the animal world, then drew an imaginary picture of a weak Soviet Union:

We do not want to be like the lamb defenseless before the wolf. Both the lamb and the wolf live on the same earth. But by the right of might the wolf eats the lamb. We do not want to be in the lamb's spot. We want to have fangs so that the wolf knows that an attack on the peace-loving cannot be carried out with impunity. The wolves may lose their skins and, perhaps even worse, their heads.

When Khrushchev's Japanese interviewer asked if he agreed with the American position that the mutual possession of nuclear weapons could be made to serve the interests of peace, Khrushchev replied that the Russians did not share such views. These were the views of men of war, not men of peace. Khrushchev feared that as these weapons accumulated some would be tempted to use them: "Hotheads begin to think: 'Isn't it time to begin real war?' "[43]

Since 1953, when the possibility of mutual deterrence was cautiously broached in the Soviet Union, the dominant Soviet attitude has been consistent. It was only for the brief period of a month between the middle of March and the middle of April, 1954, that Malenkov's statement about "the destruction of world civilization" was permitted to stand. That phrase implied only the possibility, not the guarantee, of a continued peace. Since even this mildly optimistic implication was not permitted to remain unmodified, one may be sure that strong feelings were aroused among Malenkov's opponents at the very hint of a trend toward complacency. They have uniformly maintained the position that, no matter how strong the Soviet Union, the possibility of war always exists. Various reasons were given for this stand. According to Bulganin, the capitalists were not accumulating all these weapons just to frighten the Soviet Union. Even if they were not planning a war at the moment, argued Khrushchev, they might be propelled into some kind of madness and unleash a world war. The forces of peace and the forces of war were in constant struggle within each capitalist country and there was always the chance that the more bellicose elements would win out. Even if it were accepted that Soviet strength sobered the feverish warmongers in capitalist countries, there was always a chance that through some accident war would break out. Thus, in the mind of the Soviet leaders, there existed the constant possibility of an outbreak of war.

NOTES

1. I. Stalin, *Ekonomicheskie problemy sotsializma v SSSR (Economic Problems of Socialism in the U.S.S.R.)*, Moscow, 1952, pp. 85, 86.
2. M. Gus, "The General Line of Soviet Foreign Policy," *Zvezda (The Star)*, Leningrad, November, 1953, p. 109.
3. V. Kruzhkov, "V. I. Lenin, the Coryphaeus of Revolutionary Science," *Kommunist*, No. 1, 1954, pp. 21, 22.
4. Colonel G. Fedorov, "Marxism-Leninism on War and the Army: 1. The Origin and Essence of Wars," *Red Star*, January 6, 1954.
5. V. Tereshkin, "The Great Mass Movement of the Present Day," *Zvezda*, Leningrad, February, 1954, pp. 139-140.
6. Colonel A. Piatkin, "Some Questions of the Marxist-Leninist Science of War," *Voennaia mysl' (Military Thought)*, No. 3, March, 1954, p. 16.
7. A General—Retired, "Where the 'Policy of Strength' Leads," *Izvestiia*, January 19, 1954.
8. "On the Thirtieth Anniversary of the Day of V. I. Lenin's Death. Comrade P. N. Pospelov's Report at the Ceremonial Memorial Meeting in Moscow," *Pravda*, January 22, 1954.
9. "The Speech of Comrade G. M. Malenkov at a Meeting of the Electors of the Leningrad District of the City of Moscow, March 12, 1954," *Pravda*, March 13, 1954.
10. "Speech of A. I. Mikoian," *Kommunist* (Erevan), March 12, 1954, full text. *Pravda*, March 12, 1954, contains the abbreviated text.
11. "Speech of Comrade N. S. Khrushchev at the Meeting of the Electors of the Kalinin Electoral District of the City of Moscow, March 6, 1954," *Pravda*, March 7, 1954.
12. "Speech of Comrade K. E. Voroshilov at the Meeting of the Electors of the Kirov Electoral District of the City of Leningrad, March 10, 1954," *Izvestiia*, March 11, 1954.
13. "Speech of Comrade L. M. Kaganovich at a Meeting of the Electors of the Tashkent-Lenin Electoral District, March 11, 1954," *Pravda*, March 13, 1954.
14. "Speech of Comrade N. A. Bulganin at a Meeting of the Electors of the Moscow City Electoral District, March 10, 1954," *Izvestiia*, March 11, 1954.
15. "Speech of Comrade V. M. Molotov at a Meeting of the Electors of the Molotov Electoral District in Moscow, March 11, 1954," *Pravda*, March 12, 1954; "Speech of Comrade N. S. Khrushchev at the Second Congress of the Polish United Workers' Party, March 11, 1954," *ibid.*
16. Viktor Shragin, Soviet Home Service, Moscow, March 27, 1954.
17. Editorial, "The Invincible Movement of Mankind toward Socialism," *Kommunist*, No. 6, April, 1954, p. 8. This issue went to press on April 20, 1954.

18. "The Speech of the Chairman of the Council of Ministers of the U.S.S.R., the Deputy G. M. Malenkov," *Izvestiia*, April 27, 1954.
19. "The Speech of the Deputy A. I. Mikoian," *Pravda*, April 27, 1954.
20. "Speech of the Commander of Troops of the Kiev Military District, Marshal of the Soviet Union V. I. Chuikov," *Pravda Ukrainy*, May 4, 1954.
21. Marshal of the Soviet Union A. Vasilevskii, "The Great Lesson of History," *Red Star*, May 7, 1954.
22. "The Speech of Comrade N. S. Khrushchev at the Xth Congress of the Communist Party of Czechoslovakia, June 12, 1954," *Izvestiia*, June 13, 1954.
23. N. S. Khrushchev, speech at a workers' rally in Prague, June 15, 1954, as broadcast by Radio Prague, June 15, 1954. This text differs quite extensively from the official text published in the Soviet newspapers.
24. Colonel A. Piatkin, "Some Questions of the Marxist-Leninist Theory of War" in *Marksizm-Leninizm o voine armii i voennoi nauke (Marxism-Leninism on War, the Army, and Military Science)*, Moscow, 1955, pp. 70, 71.
25. "The Peoples Decide the Fate of the World and Civilization," *Kommunist*, No. 4, March, 1955, pp. 12-23, particularly p. 16.
26. The official Soviet version of the text in English appears in *Documents Supplementary to "New Times,"* No. 51, December 15, 1955; for the Indian version I have used the text of the Joint Soviet-Indian Statement, *The New York Times*, December 14, 1955.
27. *Pravda*, November 24, 1955. *Missiia druzhby (Mission of Friendship)*, Vol. 1, Moscow, 1956, p. 62, has the same text.
28. "The Answer of the Chairman of the Council of Ministers of the U.S.S.R., N. A. Bulganin, to Questions of the Chief of the Washington Bureau of the Telenews Television and Chronicle Company, C. Schott," *Pravda*, January 1, 1956.
29. "The Speech of Comrade N. S. Khrushchev," *Pravda*, March 15, 1958.
30. *XX S"ezd Kommunisticheskoi partii Sovetskogo Soiuza 14-25 Fevralia, 1956 goda Stenograficheskii otchet (XXth Congress of the Communist Party of the Soviet Union, February 14-25, 1956, Stenographic Report)*, Vol. 1, Moscow, 1956, pp. 37, 38 (hereinafter cited as *XXth Congress Report*).
31. *Ibid.*, pp. 457, 459.
32. *Ibid.*, p. 512.
33. "Message of the Chairman of the Council of Ministers of the U.S.S.R., N. A. Bulganin, to the President of the United States of America, Dwight D. Eisenhower, January 23, 1956," *Pravda*, January 26, 1956.
34. V. Borovskii, "Atomic Weapons Should Be Prohibited," *Pravda*, February 3, 1956.
35. Active member of the Academy of Sciences of the U.S.S.R., D. Skobel'tsyn, "The Problem of Disarmament Should be Solved," *Pravda*, March 29, 1956.
36. Professor Georgi Pokrovskii, "Atomic Deadlock?" *News*, Moscow, No. 6, 1956, pp. 13-14.
37. A. Turov, "The U.S.A. Brandishes Atomic Weapons," *Red Star*, January 25, 1957.

38. E. G. Panfilov, "Has War Ceased To Be the Continuation of Politics?" *Voprosy filosofii (Questions of Philosophy)*, No. 1, 1957, p. 246.
39. Colonel G. Fedorov, Candidate in the Philosophical Sciences, "On the Content of Soviet Military Ideology," *Red Star*, March 22, 1957.
40. "N. S. Khrushchev's Interview with the Chief Editor of the American Newspaper, *The New York Times*, Turner Catledge, May 10, 1957," *Izvestiia*, May 14, 1957.
41. "Interview of N. S. Khrushchev with the Chief Editor of the Japanese Newspaper, *Asahi Shimbun*, Mr. Tomo Hirooka, Transcript of Proceedings," *Pravda*, June 30, 1957. The interview took place on June 18.
42. "Interview of N. S. Khrushchev with Correspondents of the American Radio Television Company, Columbia Broadcasting System, May 28, 1957," *Pravda*, June 4, 1957.
43. Khrushchev interview with Hirooka, *Pravda*, June 30, 1957.

CHAPTER FOUR

THE LIKELIHOOD OF WAR AND SOVIET DOMESTIC POLITICS: 1953-1954

The last chapter sought to demonstrate that the Soviet leadership, despite some tentative detours, has adhered to the policy of preparing for the worst contingency. However likely that contingency, the same thorough preparations were required. Thus one would suppose that budgetary discussions were unaffected by the question of the likelihood of war. Indeed this question was irrelevant to the true Bolshevik, who prided himself in furthering the trend of history no matter what the cost.

The ascetic bent of Bolshevism sees peril in self-indulgence; the Bolshevik is psychologically conditioned to regard self-sacrifice as the necessary concomitant of a sound policy. He has no difficulty in accepting the axiom that the Soviet Union must always be ready for war as long as war is possible. In the period after Stalin's death, however, the desire to relax tugged hard. If peace were indeed 95 per cent assured, as the Malenkov school of thought seemed to believe, could not military expenditures be somewhat reduced and life become easier? This mood was familiar enough in democratic countries; its appearance in the Soviet Union demonstrated the strength of the reaction against conditions of life under Stalin.

The Soviet debates over the likelihood of war are not easy to analyze, because public discussion in the Soviet Union does not necessarily reflect the basic problems confronting the leaders. The debate on the likelihood of war was the public manifestation of different points of view among the leaders on several varied issues. First and foremost was the question of the distribution of military strength in the world. If some political leaders feared that Soviet military strength was inadequate, or growing too slowly in comparison with Western military strength, they did not think of referring publicly to this weakness. Instead of arguing openly for what they really wanted, namely that military expenditures be expanded to make good an existing deficiency, they called attention to some such external danger as "increasing international tension." The principle embodied in this style of debate applies, with modifications, to other countries. A democratic government that has held office long enough to be responsible for the current state of the military establishment is not likely to be able to increase it except on the ground that the international situation has changed for the worse. To ask for more funds because the military forces are too weak to perform what may be required of them is to admit a past error in judgment. The opposition to the government in power is usually willing to make political capital out of poor military preparedness. It is at this point that Soviet practice diverges from democratic experience. There is no organized opposition, and if there were, the Bolsheviks would see something close to treachery in a public airing of the weakness of the Soviet Union. Thus any public debate on the adequacy of the military establishment must necessarily be carried on in terms of changes in the international situation.

A public Soviet discussion on the likelihood of war may be a front for fears, not only of current weakness, but also of future dangers. Statesmen of any country rarely describe a situation in terms of a threat that will materialize in the future. It is more usual to say "The wall is cracking and the building is about to collapse," than "If the crack in the wall is not repaired now, the building will become unsound in five years." The Soviet leaders conform to this pattern. A Soviet appraisal of the ratification of EDC, which promised the eventual rearming of Germany, presented it as an immediate threat to the Soviet Union.

Public Soviet discussions of the likelihood of war serve to conceal issues of basic domestic importance. The question "What is to be done?" is still as urgent as when Chernyshevskii posed it in 1863 and Lenin posed it again in 1901. Now that Stalin's death has proved to mark an epoch in Soviet history, the new political leaders cannot agree among themselves how far to modify existing institutions and practices. Differences over the allocation of resources to investment and to military strength have become public. If the satisfaction of consumer demands is still to be postponed, the Party, whose task it is to exhort and drive, still has a major function; if on the other hand consumer needs are to be met, the Party will be overshadowed by the executive. In the past, priority for heavy industry and Party pre-eminence were always associated with the slogans "We live in capitalist encirclement" and "The backward are beaten." The people must make sacrifices in a time of national danger. Thus the likelihood of war is closely linked to the fundamentals of Soviet domestic policy. The answers to such questions as "What is to be done?" and "Whither Russia?" depend on the official estimate of the safety of the state.

Alarms of war may offer political advantage to the alarmist in a factional fight. To the factionary, of course, his attaining office, or continuing in it, is a matter of major ideological import. The opponent's faction, he believes, will take the country to the dogs by perverting true Bolshevism or by failing to adjust it to the changing situation. When, in the early months of 1957, Khrushchev raised a wholly contrived danger of war, he himself and those who supported him probably believed that his displacement would be accompanied by dangerous political changes. The alarm of war was raised to keep one faction in office, and this suggests that a lower probability was assigned in fact to the likelihood of war. It is difficult to resist the conclusion that in the Soviet Union the employment of such alarms for minor purposes betokens a low estimate of the likelihood of war. The one element seemingly never present in a public Soviet debate on the likelihood of war is a real danger of war. If such a danger were believed to exist it would be considered much too important for public discussion.

A particular controversy may encompass several or all of the strands described above. It is the variety of latent motives behind any public Soviet discussion of the likelihood of war that makes it at once instructive and difficult to untangle.

In the Soviet Union when a man publicly makes a far-reaching prediction, it can only mean that he has reached a high level of political importance. In short, he speaks for the Party. If such a man retracts his prediction under duress, he thereby demonstrates that he has lost some of his political importance. The power to make or unmake important predictions is an attribute of political predominance within the Soviet leadership. From the Soviet leader's point of view, to make predictions is to enjoy the feel of power. If he is a leader, others expect him to make predictions. But prediction is much more than a mere symbol of authority. Today's prevalent prediction is the basis of today's policies.

As we have seen, the difference of opinion about the likelihood of war that arose within the top Soviet leadership provided one of the criteria for identifying the winners in the factional struggle between Malenkov and Khrushchev. The outcome of that debate became the basis for determining the internal policies of the Soviet Union. Evidence will now be presented to demonstrate the contention that it was Khrushchev and his group who always inclined in moments of crisis to stress the likelihood of war, while Malenkov and his group tended to belittle it.

There were two periods in which this sharp difference of emphasis became important: the early part of 1954 and the first few months of 1957. In 1954, just before and just after Mr. Dulles announced his policy of massive retaliation, the likelihood of war was the subject of a public debate, which concealed differences among the leaders on other basic issues, of which the most apparent concerned the allocation of resources to heavy industry and light industry and, to a lesser extent, to Soviet satellites and allies. In April Khrushchev's faction succeeded in imposing on its opponents a public recog-

nition of the need to increase the armed forces, but the victory
was not complete until the beginning of 1955 when Malenkov
was forced out of the premiership.

In the conflict between Khrushchev and Malenkov it became abundantly clear from public statements that the Soviet
military leaders, possibly excepting those in the air force, were
ranged on Khrushchev's side.

With the accession of Khrushchev and Bulganin to power
in February, 1955, a paradoxical development took place:
military preparations were accelerated but the alarms of war
dropped off. In *Military Thought* the military stated the official
requirement for a pre-emptive capability, arguing that surprise
attack had assumed major importance in modern warfare. Since
it was now thought possible for a successful surprise attack to
shape the outcome of a war, the Soviet Union had to be prepared to slip in a paralyzing blow before the enemy could
do so. The military posture required for such a state of readiness was much more expensive than one designed primarily
to deter enemy attack. It necessitated great expenditures not
only on weapons of offense but also on measures for active and
civil defense.

Nevertheless the public statements of the top leaders about
the dangers of war became much calmer and more reassuring.
Almost from the moment that Khrushchev and Bulganin acquired full power the prospects for peace seemed to improve.
Starting with the reconciliation with Yugoslavia and the sign-
ing of the Austrian Peace Treaty, Khrushchev and Bulganin
seemed intent on proving to the Soviet Union and to the world
that they could preserve peace more effectively than their predecessors. The summit meetings at Geneva climaxed their
program for easing world tensions. The "spirit of Geneva"
brightened the international scene for a short time, only to be
dimmed, though not extinguished, by later events. In 1956 predictions of war with the West were avoided. Only after the
Hungarian and Egyptian crises were safely resolved did the
Soviet leaders again talk of the imminence of war. In the first
months of 1957 the top leadership was divided once again over

the likelihood of war. Shepilov publicly took a more optimistic view than Khrushchev, thus breaking with him. Shepilov's subsequent dismissal from the post of Foreign Minister was the penalty for changing sides.

Conflict continued among the Soviet leaders. Apparently the persons dismissed from their high posts in June, 1957, were opposed to Khrushchev's formula for governmental reorganization. Their failure to speak for Khrushchev's plan signalled their opposition. In his struggle with this group, Khrushchev again employed the argument that war was much more likely than his opponents thought. As soon as he had secured the approval of his reorganization plan, he dropped the alarms of war and reverted to a more temperate appraisal of the future. In the crisis of June, 1957, Khrushchev enjoyed the support of the military leaders who, in the aftermath of the crisis, seemed eager in their published writings to hold Khrushchev to promises of continued emphasis on heavy industry.

This interpretation of Soviet views on the likelihood of war is based on rather imperfect evidence. Soviet information policy leaves one very much in the dark as to what is going on in Soviet governing circles. From the materials presented in the rest of this chapter, and in the following one, the reader can judge for himself the validity of the conclusions reached.

*   *   *

One of the first hints of a high-level Soviet debate on how to adjust Soviet policies to the realities of the nuclear age was contained in the Soviet reaction to President Eisenhower's speech of December 8, 1953, which sharply presented the opportunities and dangers arising from the mutual possession of nuclear weapons.

Eisenhower stated that at least one Soviet test up to that time had involved thermonuclear reactions and frankly recognized that the American monopoly of atomic weapons had "ceased to exist some years ago." He expressed horror at the prospect of the two great powers remaining permanently armed to the teeth and threatening "the probability of civilization destroyed."* He made a direct appeal to the Soviet leaders to begin to negotiate in a modest way on the problems of nuclear disarmament.

The President's speech must have meant a great deal to the Soviet leaders. Even today we cannot be sure of the exact nuclear strength possessed by the Soviet Union at the end of 1953, but it does seem clear that the numbers of her weapons and her delivery capability were then far behind those of the United States. The tone and content of Eisenhower's speech, therefore, left ample leeway for future developments and applied to the present only in a limited sense. The Soviet leaders, however, could readily interpret the President's words to mean that the United States recognized the existence of something like nuclear parity at that time or in the near future. Those Soviet leaders who were not irrevocably set against any form of *détente* with the United States could argue that here was their chance to negotiate from strength. Those who felt that Eisenhower's offer was only a trick to induce the Soviet Union to relax its guard were likely to see only danger in negotiation. Arguing a priori, then, we may say that Eisenhower's speech was likely to be a divisive influence among the Soviet leaders. The available evidence confirms this speculation.

On December 9, the day immediately following Eisenhower's speech, the Soviet press made no reference to it. This was to be expected, for the Soviet press rarely reacts immediately to major foreign events. On December 10, *Pravda* was the only newspaper that appeared on the Moscow streets; *Izvestiia, Trud* (*Labor*), and *Komsomolskaia Pravda* failed to appear. In this unique occurrence the Yugoslavs detected evidence of a dispute between two factions in the Presidium, one favoring some kind of accommodation with the West on an international basis and the other opposing it. The Yugoslav press speculated that the suppressed editions of *Izvestiia, Trud,* and *Komsomolskaia Pravda* had carried a blast against Eisenhower's speech.[1] With the advantage of hindsight, however, one may wonder whether *Izvestiia* did not plan to report Eisenhower's speech

* The TASS rendering of "destroyed" was *unichtozhen,* which means literally "annihilated."

too extensively or too favorably. This interpretation is consistent with the paper's attitude a year after these events. Whatever the details of the case, the suspending of three newspapers strongly suggests a divergence of opinion at the top.

The official Soviet reply to the President's address was dated December 22, 1953, and it is consistent with the hypothesis of a high-level debate. The Soviet declaration carried water on both shoulders. It was pessimistic about any large results from token transfers of nuclear material from warlike to peaceful uses; it insisted that the abolition of nuclear weapons was the only solution. At the same time it agreed to accept Eisenhower's invitation to negotiate. Interestingly, the reply did not comment on Eisenhower's statement that both societies would suffer mutual destruction in a nuclear war.

Public statements of the Soviet leaders gave hints of disagreement. In his New Year's statement Voroshilov spoke of the enemies of the Soviet Union, while Malenkov, on the same day, insisted that there were no objective impediments to the improvement of relations between the Soviet Union and the United States. At a lower level, Gus's views on the possibility of lasting peace evoked, among other things, Colonel Fedorov's extreme statement that wars were *absolutely* inevitable as long as capitalism existed. From the side of the optimists, apparently, came an extremely mild Lenin anniversary speech delivered by Pospelov on January 21, 1954.[2]

The clearest signs of a dispute concerning the likelihood of war and the Soviet military posture appeared during the elections to the Supreme Soviet .We sometimes forget that there are elections in the Soviet Union and that the custom of delivering election speeches has been retained there. The election addresses of 1954 are useful to the analyst because the two factions within the leadership favored different policies that a single party formula failed to conceal. The party line was in effect bifurcated.

Before the elections for deputies to the Supreme Soviet, the Communist Party normally publishes an appeal to all the electors. It is essentially a collection of generalizations about the domestic and international situation and embodies the

Party's official line. In the 1954 election the appeal had a few paragraphs on the international situation and its implications for military posture. These attempted to smooth over certain inconsistencies, but did not quite manage to conceal them. Two paragraphs in particular seem to reflect divergent outlooks about military preparedness. The first of these reminds one strongly of Malenkov's point of view:

> In the postwar years our county has become still more strong and powerful. *It possesses everything necessary* to guard the peaceful toil of our people and to bring to his senses any one who dares encroach upon our freedom and independence. We do not fear threats on the part of any aggressors and we stand firmly and consistently for peace and the interests of our people and the people of the whole globe. We are certain that there are no disputed questions in the present international situation which cannot be resolved in a peaceful way [author's italics].[3]

"*It possesses everything necessary. . . .*" This was to be the refrain of the Malenkov forces until almost the end of the year 1954.

Another paragraph addressed itself to the dangers to peace and the possible need to fight a war:

> Vigilantly standing guard over the interests of the people and their peaceful toil, the Communist Party cannot help but consider that there are reactionary imperialistic forces abroad who strive to sharpen and strengthen international tension and to unleash a new war. Therefore, while conducting a firm and consistent policy of peace and defending and guarding with all its might the cause of peace, which is great and holy for all the people of the world, *the party considers it necessary steadily to perfect and strengthen the armed forces of the Soviet government in order to assure the security of our motherland* [author's italics].[4]

These two paragraphs were different in emphasis but not incompatible in logic. The Soviet Union might well be satisfied with her current military posture while planning to increase her strength to meet future developments. This interpretation would be acceptable were it not for the way each faction pressed its own policy by emphasizing one or the other paragraph. *Pravda, Izvestiia, Sel'skoe khoziaistvo (Agriculture)*, the organ of the Ministry of Agriculture, and *Red Star* in the first issues following the election appeal, set the pattern for the majority of the Soviet press by paraphrasing both paragraphs. In contrast, *Trud,* the newspaper of industry, and *Red Star* in its later issues, quoted editorially only the second paragraph, which referred to the need to strengthen the armed forces, and omitted any reference to the paragraph saying that the Soviet Union possessed everything necessary to guard the country.[5]

The military, taking advantage of the anniversary of the Red Army when generals traditionally publish articles in the Soviet newspapers, made it abundantly clear on which side of the argument they stood. Lieutenant General Kozlov wrote for *Red Star* and omitted any reference to the first of the two paragraphs quoted above.[6] General Zheltov did not raise the question of the adequacy of current Soviet defenses, but called for strengthening the defensive capacity of the whole motherland, together with the armed forces, as the best means to curb aggression.[7] Marshals Sokolovskii and Vasilevskii cited only the paragraph from the appeal that stressed the need to increase the strength of the armed forces.[8]

The faction advocating expansion of the military forces was to prevail. The relatively complacent views of Malenkov, Pospelov, Pervukhin, and Saburov were heard through March, but Khrushchev, Bulganin, Molotov, Kaganovich, and Voroshilov expressed the views of what was to become the dominant faction. The trade-marks of the Malenkov group were, first, their concentration on the message contained in the phrase, "It possesses everything necessary . . .," and second, their failure to call for a strengthening of the armed forces. The Khrushchev trade-marks were the citation of the second paragraph quoted above and a summons to increase military power.

Pospelov restricted himself to repeating almost verbatim the Malenkov paragraph from the appeal to the voters and he failed to call for an increase in military strength.[9] Pervukhin,

who spoke in Tbilisi, Georgia, repeated almost without change
the Malenkov paragraph, and this part of his speech was omitted
in the Moscow reports. Pervukhin also failed to call for an
increase in the armed forces.[10] Saburov's speech was clearly on
Malenkov's side, since it failed to call for expansion of the
armed forces.[11]

Mikoian seemed to take a somewhat special position in the
debate over military policy. He had been more unequivocal
than anyone else about his belief that Soviet nuclear strength
was sufficient to deter the United States from making war. At
Erevan in Armenia, he argued that great destruction would be
visited on both sides in the event of a nuclear war and gave
this as the main reason for the recession of the danger of war.
This part of the speech was not printed anywhere in the Soviet
Union except at Erevan. Unlike other members of the Malenkov
group, however, he called for strengthening the armed forces,
just as did those who were minimizing the prospects of peace.
This part of Mikoian's speech was picked out for emphasis in
all the generally available newspaper versions. These versions
included everything but the paragraphs about the receding
danger of war.

It is a measure of the strength of the Khrushchev group
that it was able to keep out of the central press Mikoian's
trenchant arguments against its position. The speeches of lesser
figures in the provincial cities were reprinted in condensed
versions in the Moscow press without any indication that they
had been abbreviated so as to favor the arguments of the
Khrushchev-Bulganin group.

It was Malenkov himself who made the most radical statements concerning the imperative need for peace in the nuclear
age. He even seemed to imply that it might be possible to
eliminate the cold war:

> Every thinking person cannot but reflect on the question
> of how to take a further step forward, how to find a real
> basis for the firm foundation of peace and the security of
> the peoples. It is not true that mankind faces a choice be-
> tween just two possibilities: either a new world holocaust
> or the so-called cold war. The peoples [of the world] are

vitally interested in a firm consolidation of peace. The Soviet government stands for further relaxation of international tension, for a firm and lasting peace and resolutely opposes the policy of cold war for this policy is a policy of preparation for a new world holocaust, which, with the present means of warfare, means the destruction of world civilization.[12]

This declaration ran counter to the orthodox Bolshevik analysis of international politics, which allowed of only two alternatives: war brought about by the imperialist powers or a period of uneasy peace during which the communist forces of peace would restrain the capitalist aggressors. Malenkov did not give a very elaborate description of his third alternative, but the rejection of "the policy of cold war" seemed to look toward a permanent accommodation between capitalism and communism, some lasting agreement to live and let live. Here is what he said:

It is thus understood that as long as aggressive circles which still hopelessly dream of devastating our socialist country exist in the world, the Soviet Union is obligated to maintain its armed forces in such a situation that they can make short shrift of any adventures of the aggressors.[13]

A careful reading of this paragraph reveals that the barrier to the third alternative was the existence of "aggressive circles," not simply the existence of capitalism and imperialism. Aggressive circles might become less aggressive, especially as it was clearly in their interest to do so. The issue of the inevitability of war in a world divided between capitalists and socialists had been sidestepped. Malenkov's most belligerent phrases were not incompatible with an ultimate reduction of the Soviet armed forces, for "aggressive circles" might fade into the background. The opposition emphasized that capitalism might always fight.

The plausibility of this analysis is heightened by the fact that Malenkov never again mentioned the possibility of a third alternative, just as he never again repeated his statement about the destruction of world civilization. It can be deduced that the majority faction among the leaders linked these views with complacency about military preparedness.

Malenkov's opponents presented a very different picture in their election speeches. On March 6 Khrushchev said that "the Communist Party and the Soviet government cannot but realize that there are reactionary forces in the capitalist countries which seek to find a solution to their economic difficulties and the exacerbated contradictions of the imperialist camp by the preparation of a new war."[14] Five days later in Poland, Khrushchev said that "the reactionary forces of the capitalist countries impede in every way the weakening of tension in international relations."[15] Sharper even than the party chief, Molotov found it "impossible not to take into account that before everyone's eyes the policy of the preparation of a new war is being carried out by the reactionary forces. . . . It is impossible, of course, to ignore the circumstance that the aggressive forces continue to proceed in the same direction as always. The arms race continues."[16] Kaganovich referred to Lenin's 1921 thesis that the collapse of the colonial system meant the ultimate collapse of capitalism and concluded: "Thence their nervousness, their desire—however they can—to change the developing international situation by force and to find an 'escape' through war. That is why they create tension in the international situation and develop the arms race."[17] Voroshilov talked of an imminent economic crisis in the United States that would be accompanied by a reduction in the standard of living and a consequent increase in unemployment: "This explains the attempt of the reactionary circles to avoid economic crises by inspiring a war psychosis and creating an international atmosphere of even more tension and by continuing the arms race."[18]

All the election speeches of the Khrushchev group argued that the war plans of the capitalist countries were a natural feature of capitalism. Sweet reasonableness, even a full understanding of the great evils to be suffered by all from a nuclear war, could have no effect on their warlike course, which was predetermined by the laws of history. Bulganin had this to say:

We would commit an irreparable error if we did not strengthen our armed forces. Very many facts indicate that the imperialist forces headed by the U.S. are openly conducting a policy of the preparation of a new war against us. . . . The intensified arms race, which has developed in the countries of the Anglo-American bloc, and the construction of military bases in Europe and on other territories, and the policy of the revival of German militarism all show quite clearly the direction in which the imperialist circles are trying to go.

In these conditions we do not have the right to waste time, and even less right to sink into complacency and to reassure ourselves because we emerged victorious in the war and because our army is the strongest in the world. It is well known that he who does not go forward falls behind; and the backward are beaten. . . .

The most important thing in military affairs is the uninterrupted perfection of the armed forces. This is especially true of aviation, where technological progress is very rapid. All these years we have sought to develop our air technology and not to fall behind the demands of the present; and we have succeeded. . . .

We cannot assume that the imperialists expend enormous material and financial resources on armaments only to frighten us.

We cannot depend either on the humanitarianism of the imperialists who, as life has shown, are capable of using any weapon of mass destruction.

We must always be ready to give a crushing rebuff to any enemy no matter what weapons he possesses.[19]

Bulganin's statement was the most direct rebuttal of Malenkov's views. Over the years, indeed, Bulganin had always been sharpest in condemnation of the Malenkov line. After Malenkov was dismissed from the chairmanship of the Council of Ministers in February, 1955, Bulganin delivered slashing attacks on the former Premier's policies.

In his election speech Bulganin did not content himself

with a routine statement that the Soviet armed forces must be increased; he declared that it would be an irreparable error not to strengthen them. Furthermore, instead of making trite remarks about eternal vigilance, Bulganin called attention to the specific dangers of wasting time, of sinking into complacency, and of trying to live on past successes. The implication was quite clear that some people were guilty of these mistakes. Bulganin heightened the effect of his admonitions by repeating the phrase that Stalin had employed to justify his heavy industry program, namely, "the backward are beaten." He suggested very strongly that the imperialists were planning to attack the Soviet Union and would not be satisfied with maintaining a balance of power and mutual deterrence. This seems to be the only possible interpretation of Bulganin's statement that it could not be assumed that the imperialists were expending enormous resources only to frighten the Soviet Union and of his statement that it was impossible to depend on the humanitarianism of the imperialists, who were known to be capable of anything.

An important element in Soviet appraisals of the danger of war was the current estimate of American intentions. In 1954, first Mr. Dulles's speech on massive retaliation, and then the culmination of the Indochina crisis in the spring furnished the data for a Soviet assessment of American intentions. Early Soviet fears, soon to be modified, apparently forced Malenkov to retract his more optimistic opinions.

On January 12, 1954, Secretary of State Dulles analyzed Soviet policy as one aimed to divide and weaken the free nations by forcing them to overextend their strength and bring themselves to "practical bankruptcy."[20] That would be the "moment for the decisive blow," said Dulles, quoting Stalin. The Soviet Union with its extensive land borders could impose a series of Koreas upon the free world. Although the free world intended always to challenge local aggressions as they arose, it would be better advised to seek a policy more suited to the long run. Dulles argued for local defenses all over the world, "but there is no local defense which alone will contain the mighty land power of the Communist world." Local defenses must be reinforced by the further deterrent of massive retaliatory power. A potential aggressor must know that he cannot always prescribe battle conditions that suit him: "Otherwise, for example, a potential aggressor who is glutted with manpower might be tempted to attack in confidence that resistance would be confined to manpower. He might be tempted to attack in places where his superiority was decisive."

"The way to deter aggression is for the free community to be willing and able to respond vigorously at places and with means of its own choosing." Dulles made it quite clear that this departure from the old policy of meeting each emergency as it arose had been decided by "the President and his advisors, as represented by the National Security Council." The Secretary's announcement was no mere trial balloon: "The basic decision was to depend primarily upon a great capacity to retaliate, instantly, by means and at places of our own choosing. Now the Department of Defense and the Joint Chiefs of Staff can shape our military establishment to fit what is *our* policy instead of having to try to be ready to meet the enemy's many choices. That permits of a selection of military means instead of a multiplication of means. As a result, it is now possible to get, and share more basic security at less cost."[21]

A reasonably careful reading of Dulles's statement made it clear to Western observers that it was not the American intention to retaliate with a nuclear strike to every and any local emergency. But in the American as well as in the European press it was interpreted to mean simply that henceforward the United States would be more likely than before to retaliate to local aggression with a massive nuclear attack. The world press, and especially the Western European press, was agitated about the implications of Dulles's speech, fearing that the new policy might miscarry.

From the first the Russians obviously took Dulles's speech on massive retaliation very seriously. The speech was delivered on January 12, 1954, and reported in the Soviet press on January 14, after the standard time lag. The press reports were brief and the most noteworthy feature of Dulles's speech, his reference to massive retaliation, was not even mentioned. Evidently more time was required to develop an agreed official interpretation of this important policy statement. When Soviet propagandists do not react immediately and in a routine way to a major foreign statement, the matter is probably undergoing review at the highest level. Not until March 17 was the Dulles speech again mentioned in the Soviet press and then only in passing. The first evaluation of it came as late as March 26.

On March 17, an editorialized news account of foreign events pointed out that the Americans intended to expand the war in Indochina. Eisenhower had stated at a press conference that, if American technicians and instructors sent to Indochina were killed, the United States could not be drawn into the war without a declaration by Congress. The Soviet writer interpreted Eisenhower's reply to a journalist's question about the technicians to mean that the United States was considering how to enter the war. According to this writer the American press could not make out whether or not the President's answer contradicted "Dulles's recent statement about the so-called 'instantaneous retaliatory (?) actions'."* According to the Soviet analysis, as published in *Pravda*:

> The essence of the matter is that such a statement by the Chief of State of the United States of America can be explained only by the desire not to be limited in the future to the provision of materiel, arms, and equipment for the war in Indochina but to pass to even further intervention directed toward the expansion of the war in this area of Asia. . . .

> Furthermore, the President did not find it necessary to deny the view expressed by the American Senator Stennis and by the correspondents at the press conference that the fact of the loss of American soldiers on the field of battle in Indochina might be the occasion for the official entrance of the USA into a war against the people of Indochina.[22]

On the day these words appeared in *Pravda*, *The New York Times* printed an article written by Dulles for the April Issue

* The question mark is in the original.

of *Foreign Affairs* making it clear that the policy of massive retaliation depended on the co-operation, and implicitly on the agreement, of America's allies. In some cases an attack by a communist power would mean a general war, but the United States meant to have the means for response on a selective basis. In some areas, however, the main reliance would have to be on retaliation with great force in places of America's own choice, but this did not mean that every local war would become a world war. Naturally the United States would not announce in advance what it would do in a specific situation. Here Mr. Dulles recalled his earlier warnings that if there were open Chinese aggression in Indochina there "would be grave consequences which might not be confined to Indochina."[23]

The first full Soviet treatment of Dulles's "massive retaliation" speech appeared in a *Pravda* editorial on March 26, 1954. Quite unusually, it was on the right-hand side of the page, while in the normal editors' space on the left was a routine piece on the necessity of improving navigational techniques. Perhaps for this reason, the editorial was not picked up and reported by American correspondents in Moscow. According to *Pravda*, Dulles had delivered his speech of January 12 in "a bellicose fever, losing all sense of reality." The editorial interpreted him to have said that "the United States intended in case of any local conflict, wherever it happened, to begin military operations where they pleased and against whom they pleased using all kinds of weapons including atomic bombs." To Dulles was attributed the implication that America's allies in the NATO and the Rio Pact would automatically participate in this warfare and that their consent did not even have to be requested. The result, said the Soviet editorial, was widespread domestic and foreign criticism. More balanced Americans, like Adlai Stevenson, pointed out that the execution of such a policy "could lead to the destruction of our cities."

The foreign allies of the United States were alarmed at the thought that their countries could be drawn into a new world war by "a handful of American politicians who were capriciously trying to seize the right of deciding the fate of other governments as they thought fit." *Pravda* provided facts to support the argument. The Canadian Minister of Foreign Affairs, Lester B. Pearson, when in Washington on March 15, had expressed dissatisfaction that the fate of Canada "could be decided not by us ourselves but on the other side of the border." The English press had pointed out that the United States could draw England into a world war not of her own choosing.

In his appearance before the Senate Foreign Relations Committee (March 20) Dulles had tried to smooth over the bad impression made by his January 12 statement on massive retaliation, but in essence American policy remained unchanged.[24] *Pravda* did not trust Dulles's second thoughts.

It seems quite obvious from the long delay between Dulles's speech and the Soviet commentary on it that the analysts were both puzzled and shaken. The tone of the editorial just quoted seems to be one of relief that things were not quite as bad as they had thought. It also seems very likely that the editorial was written with the purpose of smoking out some further American reaction which would give the Russians some clues as to what was meant. Writing a few days later, one of the important foreign editors of *Pravda,* Yuri Zhukov, complained that no American correspondents accredited to Moscow had written a line on the March 26 editorial. Zhukov attributed this silence to the embarrassment of the warmongers after they became "convinced that their maneuvers had suffered defeat." He summarized an Acheson statement in *The New York Times* arguing that the massive blow advocated by Dulles would only bring destruction to the United States in the form of a counter-blow. According to Zhukov, Acheson had emphasized that the administration's policy would destroy the American alliance system, because the allies would consider that their very existence had been thoughtlessly subjected to a needless risk. Acheson had pointed out that the United States could not count on the allies' permission to use bases on their territory. American newspapers, said Zhukov, had ignored the Soviet exposure of the emptiness of Dulles's threat because they did not want to make matters worse for themselves.[25]

The Russians interpreted the Dulles speech to mean that

the United States would refuse to settle local conflicts, in order to use them as a springboard to larger conflicts. They implied very strongly in their press treatment that America intended to extend the Indochina fighting to China and possibly beyond but did not suggest the possibility of an American surprise attack on the Soviet Union. The Soviet appraisal of events in Indochina is important as a clue to the Soviet estimate of the world political situation at the time when Malenkov was forced to revise his optimistic estimates of the future.

The Russian analysts had a knotty problem in judging American intentions in Indochina. In 1950 Secretary of State Acheson had clearly indicated that the United States did not consider South Korea a vital area; the Russians could not have received stronger assurance that the Americans were unwilling to defend South Korea. The almost instantaneous reaction of the Americans to the North Korean attack in 1950 came as a surprise to the Russians. The Russians must surely have concluded either that the United States had laid a trap for them, which would have been explaining American behavior in Soviet terms, or that Americans were quite unpredictable. Since the Americans had intervened in Korea after they had indicated that they probably would not, how could one be sure that they would not intervene in Indochina when they had already threatened to do so? Even a shrewd American analyst could not have been confident in March or April, 1954, that there would be no American intervention in Indochina. Indochina was more important strategically to the United States than Korea and communist domination of it would have been a setback to the whole policy of containment. Numerous American statements, one by the Vice-President, urged intervention in Indochina. In March and April, 1954, the Russian analysts could not reasonably have excluded the possibility of American intervention in Indochina.

The Soviet press reports seemed to demonstrate the American intention to participate in the Indochina war and to expand its scope. On March 22, 1954, they announced that a communications and transport squadron of American planes had been sent to Indochina from Japan. This squadron included B-26's. The dispatch quoted Stassen as saying that the United States would continue to supply Indochina up to and during the Geneva talks on peace in Indochina.[26] On March 24, *Pravda* quoted an American article "Will American Soldiers Fight in Indochina?" as saying that the Americans had to intervene in the war because the French were not prepared to fight.[27]

On the following day *Pravda* quoted James Reston in *The New York Times* to the effect that the Pentagon had discussed the possibility of recruiting an international corps of aviators to aid either the French or the Bao Dai Government. *Pravda* stressed the importance of the second alternative, because it implied American readiness to carry on the war in disregard of, or counter to, French interests.[28]

The Soviet press' reporting of events fitted into the arguments of Malenkov's opponents. Malenkov suggested that the United States was seeking an amelioration of international tension because it feared the future nuclear strength of the Soviet Union, and that the latter could seize this opportunity to arrive at an accommodation with the United States and to make an end of the cold war. Malenkov, if challenged to explain Dulles's talk of "massive retaliation" and the American plans for intervention in Indochina, could have said only that Dulles's views were those of a minority and that the dominant group in the United States administration had effectively repudiated the policy of massive retaliation. The dominant group of Soviet leaders rejected such a reassuring explanation. To them the apparent dangers seemed real enough to be taken at face value. America, they recognized, was far ahead of the Soviet Union in nuclear strength and in delivery capability. Why should Eisenhower want to drag the Soviet Union into some sort of international agreement whereby each power would deliver stocks of nuclear material to those countries which wanted to operate reactors for peaceful purposes? It could only be because he hoped to gain something at the expense of the Soviet Union. The more cautious Russians would enter no agreement that might involve an open confirmation of American superiority in nuclear weapons. For this reason alone they could not allow disarmament talks to progress. The impediments placed by the United States in the way of the liquidation of the Indochina war obviously meant that the American strategy was to expand the war in Asia and then, perhaps, to make war against the Soviet Union.

For Malenkov's opponents to overcome him and make his policy appear reckless it was not necessary to prove the imminence of war. So serious were the implications of their analysis that it was enough to demonstrate the mere possibility that it was correct. The Soviet Union had to be prepared to meet the worst eventualities, even if no more than a possibility of their occurrence could be demonstrated.

Under the pressure of events at home and abroad, therefore, Malenkov was forced on April 26, to retract his optimistic prognosis of March 2 and to adopt the more pessimistic view of the future of peace. Malenkov's retraction has already been described in part. It will be recalled that he withdrew his prediction of the destruction of world civilization in the event of nuclear war. He was also forced to modify his low estimate of the likelihood of war, but was able to maintain the position that international tension had been recently relaxed in an important way, an index of his residual power. Even here, however, he had to qualify his opinion with a warning against the dangers of overestimating the significance and extent of the relaxation. Malenkov himself ascribed this counsel of caution to others:

> A sober approach to the evaluation of the international situation has always characterized the Soviet people and today they warn against overestimating the significance of the relaxation of international tension already achieved, because the opponents of peace have not abandoned their aggressive aspirations. . . .

Malenkov's April speech differed from his March speech in another important particular. Whereas in March he conspicuously failed to call for an increase in military strength, while his opponents were calling for one, in April he not only made good that failure but also promised that "in the future" the armed forces would have everything they needed.[29] The phrase, "in the future" was almost unprecedented in Soviet statements about increasing military appropriations. Soviet statements usually called for increases in the armed forces without committing themselves to continued expansion in the future. In April Malenkov did so commit himself.

The policy of not increasing, or of decreasing, military appropriations was finished. The reduction of emphasis in Malenkov's April speech on the consumer goods program, long associated with Malenkov's name, was the corollary of his retreat on the military issue. Speaking on the same day, Pervukhin, then a supporter of Malenkov, also called for the further strengthening of the defensive capability of the country, something he had signally failed to do in March.[30]

Malenkov's opponents revealed in their subsequent speeches that although he had made major concessions he had not abandoned his basic position. Differences on the assessment of the international situation and the likelihood of war continued. In April, as we have seen, Malenkov was still insisting that international tension had decreased. Meanwhile Kaganovich repeated his March statement that the Soviet Union was encircled—the old Stalinist formula that had fallen into disuse—and Khrushchev insisted that the imperialists "were increasing tension . . . and were not sparing in threats to the Soviet Union."[31] Where Malenkov had only mentioned American irrationality as a bare possibility, Khrushchev, in a long tirade against Dulles, went so far as to cast doubts on the latter's mental balance:

> Mr. Dulles acts as if he had become sick with some sort of rage. We know that a person in a rage is mad. But is it fitting for a statesman to announce the foreign policy of his country when he is drunk with fury and malice toward other people?[32]

From that point onward Malenkov's opponents continued to stress publicly that war might come at almost any time, and that surprise had become important in determining the outcome of wars. The statement about military surprise had appeared hitherto only in the military press.

Malenkov's opponents did not attack him on his own ground. Instead of denying his contention that the terrible consequences of nuclear war would effectively deter one power from attacking another and so open the way for a decline of international tension, they contented themselves with reiterating that anything could happen and that the Soviet Union must be prepared for all eventualities. In the spring, summer, and fall of 1954 the possibility of a surprise attack against the Soviet Union was not a major theme of Soviet propaganda. But since prominent figures such as Bulganin warned against surprise, the new theme apparently had political importance.

Bulganin, as we noted above, warned against complacency and stressed the impossibility of counting on American humanitarianism when the United States was investing billions in weapons. The next statement along these lines was made by Marshal Vasilevskii in an article in *Red Star* for May 7, 1954. Particular interest attaches to Vasilevskii's arguing the danger from surprise, for he had been one of the most conservative champions of the validity of the permanently-operating-factors formula. This formula minimized surprise so that it was noteworthy that Vasilevskii now insisted that the Soviet Union must constantly be on guard "so that nothing unexpected can catch us unawares. Whoever forgets vigilance and is slack about it commits the greatest crime against the government and against the people." The possibility of surprise attack was a new and still uncommon theme in Soviet public speeches. Perhaps Vasilevskii was willing to shift a bit on the subject of surprise in order to attack Malenkov. In a rare reference to "the head of the Soviet Government, Malenkov," Vasilevskii quoted, against Malenkov's early position, his retraction that talked about capitalists deciding on madness, making war, and suffering the destruction of their system.[33]

Following this line, the Soviet press started to pay more attention to items stressing American unpredictability and the possibility of anything's happening. For example, in June, 1954,

General Gruenther had made a speech in which he said that atomic weapons would be required for infantry support in Europe in the event of war. The Soviet commentator explained this attempt to make nuclear weapons compensate for small armies as a realization of the difficulty of getting cannon fodder. Furthermore, said the Soviet writer, "General Gruenther and those who stand behind him are apparently possessed by the mania of world conquest which possessed Hitler too."[34]

When Malenkov suggested that the capitalists would have to be mad to unleash war, his opponents countered by trying to show that they were indeed mad. In April Khrushchev hinted that Dulles was of unsound mind. In May Vasilevskii drew special attention to Malenkov's phrase about capitalist insanity. In June a Soviet writer said that General Gruenther and the people behind him were just as crazy as Hitler.

Some Soviet leaders may have had sincere doubts about American rationality and may have been genuinely concerned about the international situation, but it seems more likely that the cry, "the Americans are mad," was only a dramatic justification of the warning, "anything can happen." That talk of American insanity was deliberately fostered to justify a program of the expansion of the military forces is further suggested by Khrushchev's speech at a workers' rally in Prague on June 15, 1954. The speech was broadcast by Prague radio and was printed next day in the Soviet press in a severely edited version, with the poor sequences eliminated, the incorrect grammar improved, and much of the content changed. Unusually blunt, Khrushchev spoke not just of "aggressive circles," but of "enemies." He came very close to saying that the much excoriated policy of "the position of strength" was sensible. In describing the reluctance of the West to negotiate when they had a monopoly of the atomic bomb, he asked:

> And what does it indicate? It indicates that which Churchill has said so well from, one might say, the point of view of his class. He said: "with the Bolsheviks one should talk from a position of strength because they are our class enemy."

Khrushchev implied that the stronger side would not negotiate because it aimed to dictate. After an awkward, halting detour around the politically impossible statement that the Soviet Union must operate from a "position of strength," Khrushchev quoted Krylov's couplet: "To live with the enemy one must be strong." Then he described how the Soviet Union had made herself strong by creating the atom bomb and outstripping the capitalists in the construction of the H-bomb.

Although Khrushchev spoke unrestrainedly of capitalist stupidity and lack of judgment, he did not suggest that capitalist leaders were insane. This suggests that the theme of "American insanity" was polemical and did not represent a true Soviet concern. He warned that the capitalists might share Hitler's fate if they, too, underestimated the strength of the Soviet Union. Soviet strength was required first as a military safeguard and second to improve the Soviet bargaining position in international negotiations. Failure to increase her military strength might deprive the Soviet Union of security in the event of war and of political advantage in time of peace.

Malenkov moved more and more into the shade partly because he failed to get a summit meeting which might have given substance to his assertion that there was a way out of the grim choice between hot war and cold war. Only two months after Malenkov had become Chairman of the Council of Ministers, Churchill had publicly revealed his hopes for success in dealing with the post-Stalin government:

> It would, I think, be a mistake to assume that nothing can be settled with the Soviet Union until all has been settled. . . . I think that a conference of the highest level should take place between the leading powers without long delay.[35]

Churchill's speech offered the Soviet leaders some grounds for believing that it was possible for the Soviet Union to deal with the West on equal terms. As the months passed, however, it became clear that Churchill's willingness to negotiate at the highest level was not matched in the United States. All the facts have not yet been made public, but it seems that Churchill was eager and Eisenhower cool. The President never ruled out the possibility of a top-level, four-power conference, but he repeatedly stated that such a conference would have to wait upon a Soviet demonstration of good intentions.

On July 4, 1954, Churchill wrote privately to Molotov that the United States would not participate in a high-level conference at that time, though Eisenhower had become more favorable to the idea. Instead of a four-power meeting Churchill suggested an Anglo-Russian meeting. Molotov approved, but Churchill then asked for a postponement and, after a Russian counterproposal for a general European conference with the participation of the United States, the negotiations died.[36] The Churchill-Molotov correspondence appeared in the London *Soviet News* in March, 1955. The British government has never denied its authenticity. It affords only a glimpse into the matter, and we do not know whether the United States was asking only for a small down payment of Soviet reasonableness in return for her willingness to negotiate, or whether Malenkov's opponents sabotaged the negotiations to undermine his prestige. What is important to our argument is that Malenkov's failure weakened his political position within the Soviet Union. Had Malenkov succeeded in a summit conference he might have imposed on his colleagues the view that nuclear weapons made war unlikely and he might have fared better. Public approval of his success in reducing international tension would have been a political asset. The genuine popular desire for peace, of little weight in affairs under Stalin, is now a factor in the power struggle at the top in the Soviet Union.

Through the summer and early fall of 1954 Malenkov's opponents emphasized the possibility of war and the need for Soviet vigilance. Bulganin said it was self-evident that, until the United States agreed to renounce nuclear weapons, "the Soviet Union will need to have these weapons so that, in the event of the unexpected happening, we shall not be disarmed."[37] At the end of July a *Pravda* article discussed the danger of war. After charging American diplomacy with opposition to collective security, the author contended:

However, having said "a," one must says "b," i.e., that United States diplomacy is not out to ease international tension and consolidate peace but to prepare a new war. . . . It is also impossible to ignore the openly provocative speeches made by the military leaders of the Atlantic bloc. The Supreme Commander of the North Atlantic armed forces, United States General Gruenther, in an interview in *Newsweek* stubbornly pursued the idea that the alleged present superiority at the disposal of the bloc will decline noticeably in the next few years. Is this not an instigation for a so-called preventive war?[38]

A *Red Star* article was able to list a goodly number of American statements to support the thesis of American aggressiveness:

On March 29, Secretary of State Dulles spoke of the possibility of armed intervention in Indochina. Then the Chairman of the Joint Chiefs of Staff, Admiral Radford, demanded the extension of the war from the territory of Indochina to the territory of the Chinese National Republic. Following him on May 27, Admiral Carney proposed beginning "a preventive war" against the socialist camp. On June 8, at a dinner given by the Union of English Speaking Peoples, the Commander-in-Chief of the North Atlantic bloc in Europe, General Gruenther, threatened the Soviet Union with the employment of atomic weapons. A list of similar speeches by the warmongers could be extended.[39]

William Bullitt, the Soviet writer continued, was proposing an aerial and naval war against China.

At the end of September, in China, Khrushchev said that the Soviet Union did not want war, "but if the imperialists, losing control of themselves, dare to initiate war against us, then imperialism will suffer total defeat." Khrushchev also charged that the imperialists, who had not yet abandoned hopes of reimposing the yoke of imperialism on the liberated peoples, sought to ignite the flame of war in Asia.[40]

Before suffering dismissal, Malenkov made one last sally. Since the spring the Soviet press had devoted less and less attention to him, yet he was not completely beaten. His man, Saburov, was chosen to deliver the major speech on the anniversary of the Russian Revolution. (The speech was actually given on November 6.) Saburov effectively reneged on the concessions made by Malenkov and Pervukhin during the previous April and reiterated Malenkov's optimistic views about the prospects for peace. Saburov was breaking the pattern set by Beria, Pervukhin, and Voroshilov in the three previous major speeches of November 7, when he failed to call for an increase in military might. Moreover, his speech was imbued with a sober optimism about the prospect of an international settlement, although he did mention the difficulties in the way.[41] Malenkov's opponents seem to have had prior knowledge of Saburov's address. Immediately before and immediately after it, the press directly challenged Saburov's failure to call for an increase in the armed forces and questioned his optimism about the prospects for a relaxation of tension. This concerted attack indicates that Saburov's omission of a call for an increase in armaments was due to the survival, as late as November, of policy differences at the highest level.

On November 5, the day before the Saburov speech, *Red Star,* the newspaper of the Ministry of Defense then under Bulganin, called for an increase in the fighting power of the Soviet armed forces.[42] This had been the usual way of countering the past statements of the Malenkov group. On the same day, General Kolesnichenko also called for a further strengthening of the defensive capacity of the Soviet Union. Although he gave the Soviet Union credit for having successfully prevented war so far, he called attention to the continued imperialist policy of initiating war.[43]

In his Order of the Day to soldiers participating in the Red Square parade, an order that was published simultaneously with Saburov's speech, Bulganin said that it would be necessary to continue strengthening the might of the armed forces because the capitalists were continuing the policy of the preparation of a new war.[44] In his speech on Red Square Bulganin took issue with Saburov's optimism when he pointed out that "so far no changes have taken place in the international situation which would give us grounds for reducing our attention in any degree to the question of strengthening our defensive capability."[45] In Minsk, Marshal Timoshenko also called for strengthening the armed forces, on the grounds that "the easing of tension should not be overestimated."[46]

On November 12 *Red Star* went even further in opposing Saburov's position than before the speech. Repeating Bulganin's call for strengthening the armed forces, the editorial added: "The Communist Party considers that there is no sphere, including military affairs, where it is possible to stop at what has been attained."[47]

Foreign policy and military posture, although of great importance, did not exhaust the areas of disagreement among the Soviet leaders. The proportionate effort to be devoted to heavy industry and to light industry, an issue in its own right, was directly affected by the debate on military preparedness. The relative roles assigned to the Party and to the governmental organs were a subject of dispute and of shifting emphasis. The breaking in of new lands was being advanced as an alternative to a more intensive agriculture, with greater incentives to the peasantry. The great variety of issues and the imperfection of our information make it impossible to say whether foreign policy and military posture were the only major areas of policy on which differences of opinion existed, or whether Saburov's failure to call for an increase in armaments had a wider significance.

Saburov's speech makes one wonder whether world events between April and November worked in Malenkov's favor. Had they emboldened him to one more attempt to promote his views? The Soviet press had been making a great fuss about Western plans for a European Defense Community (EDC), which would have facilitated the rearming of Germany. For all we know, Malenkov may have used the French rejection of EDC at the end of August to argue among his colleagues that America was impotent to impose her will on Europe. The French rejection of EDC induced a tone of optimism in the Soviet press that reached a climax in November. This is a puzzling circumstance because on October 3 events had taken a turn that strengthened the position of the Western allies. That day Great Britain made a solemn pledge to keep four divisions on the continent. Anyone reasonably familiar with Western European politics must have known that such a pledge was unprecedented in British history and also that the chief French objection to some kind of Western defense community was the previous British reluctance to bear burdens that France was expected to assume. Therefore some explanation is required for Saburov's optimistic assessment of the international situation after the British commitment. The British move practically guaranteed German rearmament.

Either the Russians misunderstood the Western European political situation (which is not at all impossible) or Malenkov had improved his position in the factional struggle to the point where he could once more press his optimistic views about the international situation. The second explanation is particularly attractive because the issue of *Kommunist* for November, 1954, presented a sanguine view of events. Since *Kommunist* was the most authoritative Party organ, Malenkov's views were for the moment being put forward as the official line. The editorial in this issue connected the failure to ratify EDC with a reduction of the war danger:

> Favorable conditions for the regulation of other unresolved international problems [other than Korea and Indochina] have been created. . . . The Soviet people are convinced that at the present time there are no questions which cannot be justly resolved in the interests of all people given good will on both sides. . . . The characteristic feature of the present political and strategic situation is that the forces which strengthen the cause of peace are growing but at the very same time the subversive activities of those who are trying to push mankind into a new world war are being intensified. . . . However, the present relationship of forces on the international scene proves the hopelessness of any such attempt by the imperialists. . . . The USA only in the most recent years has spent about fifty billion dollars in creating aggressive blocs. . . . And yet right now American imperialism is just as far from accomplishing its plans of world mastery as at the mo-

ment that it entered upon this hopeless task. The brand-
ishing of atomic weapons, military hysteria, and the ad-
venturous policy of provocations lead to the isolation of
the USA on the international scene. Subversive activities in
Asia raise up the Asiatic peoples against the USA. *Despite the USA and as a result of opposition to it, a certain
diminution of international tension has been attained*
[author's italics].

The foreign policy of American monopoly capital has suffered failure after failure but it has not yet suffered final
defeat and dreams madly, is ready to rush into any adventure and to take up any provocation.[48]

This editorial passage in the most authoritative of journals,
Kommunist, breathes a confidence not to be found in the analyses of the preceding months. Conditions for an improvement
in the diplomatic situation are said to be favorable. In the
present state of international forces imperialism cannot hope
to accomplish its aims. The billions that the United States has
spent on its alliance system and on its bases have been wasted.
American militarism has served only to isolate the United
States: it has not prevented a weakening of international tension. The Soviet editor expressly related his optimistic tone to
the French failure to ratify EDC: "Not a single modern war
has begun without the prior hammering together of aggressive
blocs," nor has a single modern war begun without being
started by militaristic Germany. The French failure to ratify
EDC means no consolidation of the Western alliance system
and no German rearmament.

The optimism of the editorial extended to the internal politics of the Western nations. Not a single aggressive war has
started without the imperialists' first stupefying a significant
part of their own population and stifling all opposition to
their aggressive plans. But the American progressives (the Communists and fellow travelers are meant) and even the liberals
are infused with the peace spirit and have spoken out for it.
Even the "right-wing leaders of the social democratic parties"
(much hated by Soviet officialdom) dare not oppose the wishes

of the masses for peace and, in Germany and France, they have opposed German rearmament.

Had this editorial appeared a month previously, its hopes for Western disunity would have been more understandable. The Soviet press reported these events in a way that suggested lack of understanding of European politics. Its argument was about as follows: the French Parliament rejected EDC at the end of August because the forces of peace triumphed within France. The fear of revived German militarism effected the rejection of this plan. At the end of October the London and Paris meetings worked out a substitute for EDC, which would permit German rearmament, and dropped some of the supranational features of EDC. The Soviet press described the great opposition to these arrangements in terms that made it seem unlikely that the agreements would be ratified. The Soviet press hardly noticed the unprecedented British commitment, and concentrated on the hubbub raised by the plan's opponents.

Such a misreading of the situation accords with the doctrinaire Soviet outlook on foreign policy. The conviction that England runs the Continent and that the United States runs England caused the Russians to interpret the British concession as a staged gesture, for the Bolsheviks assume that all is prearranged in the capitalist world. Moreover, Soviet hopes were bolstered by Mendès-France, who then seemed to be the most influential statesman in France, and who made his misgivings about German rearmament quite clear.

Some such reconstruction of the Russian analysis helps to explain Soviet optimism one month after the British commitment, and eight or nine days after the Paris Agreements on West European Union had been signed by the French, British, German, and other governments. Ten days later, on November 13, a Soviet official protest described the Paris Agreements as a threat to stability and made a counterproposal for an all-European security pact.[49] The tone was more hostile than alarmed.

Another *Kommunist* editorial, written about this time, took a sober and calm view of the situation. The ratification of the Paris Agreements, said the Soviet commentator, would make it very difficult to solve urgent European problems, especially the German problem, yet the partisans of peace were still a force to be reckoned with.[50]

An article in the December issue of *Kommunist,* although retaining the line that the defeat of EDC had decreased international tension, was perhaps as alarmist about the danger of war as anything since Stalin's death. The defeat of EDC, it was argued, impels the enemies of peace to so frantic an activity that it has "created a real danger to peace." The situation is serious, the editorial said, because "the aggressive forces of imperialism who suffered such a failure with EDC are trying, but now under a different banner, to carry out their criminal schemes and to put into the hands of the German militarists— yesterday the hangmen of Europe—the weapons which were dashed from the hands of their soldiers by the anti-Hitlerite coalition." The Paris Agreements of October 23, 1954, envisaged a military alliance "whose purpose it is to speed up preparation for a new war." The West German revenge seekers do not hide the fact that twelve divisions are only a beginning and that they hope soon to have thirty and then sixty divisions.

In typical communist style the previous month's estimate was not merely modified but reversed. Now readers were told that Churchill, in October, 1942, had prepared a plan for making Germany a member of an anti-Soviet alliance. Whereas the month before even the American liberals were said to be "infused with the peace spirit" and to be speaking up against war, now *Kommunist* insisted on the connection between "the preparation of a new war and the accelerated process of making the United States of America fascist." There was no support for the idea, so recently expressed, that international tension had decreased. "The most recent events," said *Kommunist,* "especially the program of the Western powers for the ratification of the Paris Agreements . . . increase the danger of war. There must be no illusions on that score."

Having stated the awful prospects facing Europe and the Soviet Union, the writer concluded, not surprisingly: "The nations of the camp of peace, democracy, and socialism, in the full realization that the war is designed primarily against them, will not permit themselves to be taken by surprise. They are doing everything necessary to guard their peaceful toil, to guarantee the inviolability of the frontiers and territory of their governments and to assure defense against any possible aggression."[51]

Less than a month after *Kommunist's* reversal of judgment about the danger of war, *Pravda* launched a campaign against Malenkov. The approaching remilitarization of Germany made it possible for Malenkov's opponents to repudiate him, since his policies assumed the possibility of agreement with the West.

Malenkov had hoped for a summit meeting to dramatize Western willingness to make such an agreement. He had seemed to argue, as we shall see shortly, that Western European nations retained enough sovereignty and independence not to be classed as American puppets. Although a four-power summit conference had failed to materialize, the French Government had demonstrated its independence by refusing to ratify EDC. Up to this point events had supported Malenkov's cause. The Western European nations, however, had been able to overcome the strong opposition to the rearming of Germany and were now on the point of making legal arrangements to that end. According to the Russian concept of war as described in Chapters 2 and 7, German militarization was a necessary preliminary to a Western war plot.

In a future war, the Russians expected the United States to rely greatly on the effect of a surprise aerial attack, but also to assign a large role to tactical atomic weapons. In the Russian view the United States could not deploy the tactical weapons and advance overland without German troops. The Russians had scant regard for the French, but respected the Germans who had beaten them badly and had withdrawn from Russia only when greatly inferior in strength.

The Russians at that time had to reckon with the fact that West European political-military power was potentially equal to Russia's. From the viewpoint of each single Western European nation the Soviet Union seemed overwhelmingly stronger, but from the Soviet viewpoint the West European industrial complex and population resources were comparable to those of the Soviet Union. Germany had recently dealt a nearly fatal blow to the Soviet Union with little help from others. A union of Germany, France, Britain, and Italy—not to speak of the United States—could represent a serious threat.

Since the communists assumed that capitalism would make a desperate effort to prolong its existence before its inevitable demise, German rearmament seemed to them the harbinger of the final conflict between the two world systems. The growing danger to the Soviet Union happened also to furnish ammunition against the Malenkov faction. With a sense of righteous self-assurance Malenkov's opponents went over to the attack in December, 1954.

It would certainly be an error of oversimplification to assert, in the absence of detailed knowledge, that Malenkov's foreign policy was diametrically opposed to that of Khrushchev. One would have to suppose that Malenkov had been a secret non-communist all his life. Such a notion is absurd. The truth seems to be that Malenkov believed Western unity to be a mere façade. A combination of war weariness, fear of the great destructiveness of nuclear weapons, and the Soviet possession of those weapons, seemed to create a situation favorable for dividing the Western alliance.

As soon as he took office in March, 1953, and again on August 8, Malenkov held out the hope of the disintegration of NATO if international tension were reduced. Malenkov was suggesting that the Western alliance system was so fragile that a change in the international atmosphere could cause its collapse.[52]

We do not know what tactics, if any, Malenkov had in mind to bring about the collapse of the NATO system. But an article written by Gus in November, 1953, suggests that Malenkov did have a plan and offers some clues as to what it was. The previous chapter described Gus's suggestion that the law of the inevitability of war could be paralyzed. The condemnation of his idea by military writers and especially by Khruzhkov, the chief ideological opponent of Malenkov, suggests that Gus was putting up a trial balloon for Malenkov. Gus's article contains the only known argument in Marxian terms for Malenkov's ideas. Whether or not Malenkov approved every item in Gus's article, the fact is that its arguments went much further in support of the Premier's thesis than he himself had done in his public statements.

Gus contended that all Western schemes for a united Europe were reactionary. The Americans talked of "the obsolete principle of the sovereignty of nations" and of the necessity for "world government." They were dreaming of the American Twentieth Century. But Soviet policy was for the independent existence of sovereign nations.[53]

Developing the theme of dissension within the Western camp, Gus pointed out that American insistence that their allies curtail normal economic relations with communist nations was inspired by economic competition between the United States and Western Europe. Pressure for the restoration of the China trade had grown sharply, especially in Britain, since the conclusion of the Korean armistice.[54] Here Gus was demonstrating the validity of Malenkov's prophecy of August that the relaxation of international tension would open more widely the fissures in the Western alliance system.

A limited accommodation with capitalism was made possible by the divisions within the capitalist camp. The limit was "Collaboration cannot lead to the transformation of one system into the other."[55] Within this limit Gus argued for major Soviet policy changes:

> Every agreement between the two systems should be the fruit of a reasoned, mutually advantageous, voluntary deal [sdelka] and not the result of the imposition of one country's dictate upon the other. . . . This was the case even in the first years of the existence of the Soviet government. And now when the international position of the U.S.S.R. is firm as never before there is not the slightest chance for the success of a diplomacy of threats and blackmail or the imposition of any conditions whatsoever upon the Soviet people.
>
> Therefore our agreements with the capitalist world always have been and always will be the fruit of mutual agreement and the result of mutual concessions [ustupki]. . . .

In other words, we always remember that our bourgeois
opposite number, whether it be a trading, economic, or
political bargain, will not enter upon it if he does not receive "a just profit," and in certain cases we are ready even
to go as far as giving him an "increased gain" but in order
that we too receive a proper benefit.[56]

Later in the article Gus warned, as did Malenkov in his speech
of August, 1953, that the capitalists misinterpreted "expedient
and necessary concessions" as a sign of the weakness of the
Soviet government.[57]

If we supplement Malenkov's speeches with this article of
Gus's we get a clearer view of the former's intentions. The
advantages the Soviet Union might derive from the disintegration of the NATO alliance were so great that a few concessions
from the Soviet side would be amply rewarded if they led to
dissension among the Western allies. Against this argument we
can set a speech by Khrushchev in June, 1954, in which he declared that Soviet concessions would only provoke further
demands. Since this was the opposition's line, we can more
readily understand the Malenkov group's almost pathetic insistence that the capitalists must not misinterpret the Soviet
desire for peace as a sign of weakness.

Since his retraction in April, 1954, Malenkov seems to have
been on the defensive, with only intermittent bursts of offensive
activity. During December, 1954, and January, 1955, the political forces gathered that were to bring about his resignation
from the premiership in February.

NOTES

1. Novosad, Vojvodina Regional Service in Hungarian, December 12,
   1953. I am indebted to Melville J. Ruggles for calling this Yugoslav
   reaction to my attention.
2. See Chapter 3.
3. "Appeal of the Central Committee of the Communist Party of the
   Soviet Union to All Electors, to the Workers, Peasants and Soviet
   Intelligentsia and to the Fighting Men of the Soviet Army and Navy,"
   Red Star, February 11, 1954.
4. *Ibid.*

5. "The Inspiring Appeal of the Communist Party," *Pravda*, February 13, 1954; "Toward New Victories in the Struggle for Communism," *Izvestiia*, February 13, 1954; "For the Victory of the Bloc of Communists and Non-Party Members," *Sel'skoe khoziaistvo (Agriculture)*, February 13, 1954; "The Great Unity of the Party Government and People," *Trud (Labor)*, February 13, 1954; "The Communist Party, the Organizer of the Victory of the Soviet Armed Forces," *Red Star*, February 21, 1954.
6. Lieutenant General Kozlov, "The Communist Party—The Organizer and Leader of the Soviet Armed Forces," *Red Star*, February 16, 1954.
7. A. Zheltov, "The Armed Forces of the Soviet Government," *Pravda*, February 23, 1954.
8. Marshal of the Soviet Union V. Sokolovskii, "Guard the Peace and Security of the Motherland," *Izvestiia*, February 23, 1954; Marshal of the Soviet Union A. Vasilevskii, "On Guard over the Security of Our Soviet Motherland," *Red Star*, February 23, 1954.
9. "The Speech of Comrade P. N. Pospelov at the Meeting of Electors of the Kursk Election District, March 10, 1954," *Red Star*, March 11, 1954.
10. "Speech of Comrade M. G. Pervukhin at the Meeting of Electors of the Tbilisi Kalinin Electoral District, March 11, 1954," *Zaria Vostoka (Dawn of the East)*, March 12, 1954. The reduced text is in *Pravda*, March 12, 1954.
11. "The Speech of N. Z. Saburov," *Sovetskaia Belorussiia (Soviet Belorussia)*, March 13, 1954.
12. "The Speech of Comrade G. M. Malenkov at a Meeting of the Electors of the Leningrad District of the City of Moscow, March 12, 1954," *Pravda*, March 13, 1954.
13. *Ibid.*
14. "Speech of Comrade N. S. Khrushchev at the Meeting of Electors of the Kalinin Electoral District of the City of Moscow, March 6, 1954," *Pravda*, March 7, 1954.
15. "Speech of N. S. Khrushchev at the Second Congress of the Polish United Workers' Party, March 11, 1954," *Pravda*, March 12, 1954.
16. "Speech of V. M. Molotov at the Meeting of the Electors of the Molotov Electoral District in Moscow, March 11, 1954," *Pravda*, March 12, 1954.
17. "Speech of Comrade L. M. Kaganovich at a Meeting of the Electors of the Tashkent-Lenin Electoral District, March 11, 1954," *Pravda*, March 13, 1954.
18. "Speech of Comrade K. E. Voroshilov at the Meeting of the Electors of Kirov Electoral District of the City of Leningrad, March 10, 1954," *Izvestiia*, March 11, 1954.
19. "Speech of Comrade N. A. Bulganin at the Meeting of the Electors of the Moscow City Electoral District, March 10, 1954," *Izvestiia*, March 11, 1954.
20. "Outlines of Strategy: Address by the Secretary of State before the Council of Foreign Relations, January 12, 1954," *Documents on American Foreign Relations, 1954*, New York, 1955, pp. 9-10.
21. *Ibid.*

22. Observer, "Peaceful Regulation or the Expansion of the War," *Pravda*, March 17, 1954. Italics, which are in the original, mark specially important passages.
23. "Text of Magazine Article by Dulles on Present Defense Policy," *The New York Times*, March 17, 1954; "Text of Statement by Dulles before Senate Foreign Relations Committee," *The New York Times*, March 20, 1954.
24. Editorial, "The Sowers of Fear and the Instigators of War Hysteria," *Pravda*, March 26, 1954.
25. Iu. Zhukov, "International Review," *Pravda*, March 31, 1954.
26. A. Kozhin, "The Schemes of the Enemies of Peace in Asia. The Chinese Press Reveals the Intrigues of the Imperialist Aggressors," *Pravda*, March 22, 1954.
27. Anonymous, "Plans Directed Toward the Expansion of the War in Indochina," *Pravda*, March 24, 1954.
28. M. Afonin, "How the Pentagon 'Prepares' for the Geneva Meeting," *Pravda*, March 25, 1954.
29. "The Speech of the Chairman of the Council of Ministers of the U.S.S.R., the Deputy G. M. Malenkov," *Izvestiia*, April 27, 1954.
30. "Speech of the Deputy M. G. Pervukhin," *Pravda*, April 27, 1954.
31. "Speech of the Deputy L. M. Kaganovich," *Pravda*, April 27, 1954; "Speech of the Deputy N. S. Khrushchev," *Izvestiia*, April 27, 1954.
32. "Speech of the Deputy N. S. Khrushchev," *Izvestiia*, April 27, 1954.
33. Marshal of the Soviet Union A. Vasilevskii, "The Great Lesson of History," *Red Star*, May 7, 1954.
34. A. Belskaia, "General Gruenther Makes It Clear . . .," *Literaturnaia gazeta (Literary Gazette)*, June 12, 1954.
35. "Churchill's Statement on Foreign Policy," *The New York Times*, May 12, 1953.
36. "Correspondence between Sir Winston Churchill and V. M. Molotov on a Meeting between the Heads of the Governments of Britain and the U.S.S.R.," *Soviet News* (London), March 22, 1955.
37. "Speech of Comrade N. A. Bulganin at the Celebration of the Tenth Anniversary of the Polish Peoples' Republic in Warsaw, July 21, 1954," *Izvestiia*, July 22, 1954.
38. Iu. Pavlov, "The Policy of Setting Up Aggressive Blocs Endangers the Security of the Peoples," *Pravda*, July 31, 1954.
39. Colonel P. Vasil'ev, "On Bullitt's Provocative Article," *Red Star*, August 10, 1954.
40. "Speech by Comrade N. S. Khrushchev at the Great Meeting in Peking Honoring the Fifth Anniversary of the Founding of The Chinese Peoples' Republic, September 30, 1954," *Pravda*, October 1, 1954.
41. "The Thirty-seventh Anniversary of the Great October Revolution. A Report by M. Z. Saburov . . . on November 6, 1954," *Pravda*, November 7, 1954.
42. "The Soviet Army—A Real Peoples' Army," *Red Star*, November 5, 1954.
43. Major General I. Kolesnichenko, "The Socialist System Is the Basis

of the Power of the Soviet Government and Its Armed Forces," *Red Star,* November 5, 1954.

44. "Order of the Minister of Defense of the U.S.S.R.," *Pravda,* November 7, 1954.

45. "The Speech of Marshal of the Soviet Union N. A. Bulganin," *Pravda,* November 8, 1954.

46. Speech by Marshal Timoshenko at Minsk as broadcast on November 8, 1954.

47. "Persistently Strengthen the Might of the Soviet Armed Forces," *Red Star,* November 12, 1954.

48. Editorial, "Socialism and Peace," *Kommunist,* No. 16, November, 1954, pp. 3-12. This issue went to the printer on November 4, 1954.

49. "The Note of the Soviet Government to the Governments of the European Countries and the USA," *Pravda,* November 14, 1954.

50. V. Zagladin, "The Paris Agreements Are Incompatible with the Interests of Assuring Security in Europe," *Kommunist,* No. 17, November, 1954, pp. 112-122.

51. Editorial, "The Peoples Will Not Reconcile Themselves to the Policy of the Preparation of a New War," *Kommunist,* No. 18, December, 1954, pp. 3-13.

52. "Speech by Comrade G. M. Malenkov, Chairman of the U.S.S.R. Council of Ministers," *Pravda,* August 9, 1953.

53. M. Gus, "The General Line of Soviet Foreign Policy," *Zvezda (The Star),* Leningrad, November, 1953, p. 110.

54. *Ibid.,* pp. 113-114.

55. *Ibid.,* p. 113.

56. *Ibid.,* p. 114.

57. *Ibid.,* p. 115.

CHAPTER FIVE

THE LIKELIHOOD OF WAR AND SOVIET DOMESTIC POLITICS: 1955-1957

On February 8, 1955, Malenkov resigned his post as Chairman of the Council of Ministers of the U.S.S.R. Malenkov's career and downfall were, as the previous chapter pointed out, closely connected with the development of Soviet military policies. In tracing this connection to February, 1955, we have made certain general assumptions about the manner in which Soviet policy differences are resolved. It is now time to examine these assumptions more closely, so that the reader may himself judge the validity of the reasoning based on them. The first step will be to review briefly the history of the Malenkov era.

Immediately after Stalin died in March, 1953, Malenkov became both Chairman of the Council of Ministers and Secretary of the Communist Party. He held the second post for only a few days before he resigned it to Khrushchev. Beria held high posts and received considerable press prominence until he was arrested as a traitor in July, 1953. Malenkov's eminence was progressively reduced until, in February, 1955, he was demoted to the office of Minister of Electric Power Stations. Two years later he was removed from this post and assigned to an obscure managerial position in Soviet Asia.

This brief recapitulation of well-known events serves to illustrate the absence of constitutional provisions for the transmission of the powers of state in the Soviet Union. Despite intermittent efforts to assert that ultimate power lies with the Central Committee of the Communist Party, it remains a fact that each shift of power has come about through an alteration in the balance of forces at the highest political level. Exactly how these forces are brought into balance we do not know. The reasons for the shifts in power, however, are less obscure.

Stalin had ruled by virtue of the awe and fear he inspired in the whole Soviet Union. Continual arbitrary arrests and imprisonments maintained his hold of terror. When Stalin died his successors feared an explosion of forces they could not control. In what was practically their first announcement the leaders warned of the dangers of panic and disorder. Later they asserted that some capitalists had wanted to take advantage of Stalin's death to attack the Soviet Union.

The very fact of Stalin's death worked an organic change in Soviet society. His successors, in adjusting to that fact, made changes that in turn created the necessity for further changes. No constitutional framework existed to circumscribe the form and extent of these changes. For example, when the top members of the ruling clique found it necessary to expel Beria from their number and to reduce the activity and the influence of the secret police, the only method considered effective was drastic: the arrest of Beria, his secret trial, and his execution as a traitor. The course of the political crisis of June, 1957, showed that policy changes are made as a result of *ad hoc* shifts in the balance of political power and not through established channels. While these shifts of power do not occur according to law and are not susceptible to any kind of judicial review, it would be a mistake to imagine that custom does not govern them to some extent. There are in the Soviet Union, as in any other settled society, certain permanent social groups with relatively unchanging interests and outlooks. Through these an element of uniformity is imposed on top-level political changes.

Two types of groups influence national policy. Among the first type are the police, the army, and the Party—groups that can make their weight felt directly since they are official institutions. Among the second type are the peasantry, the youth, and the intellectuals—social groups whose influence is indirect.

The importance of the secret police is obvious. With their intimate knowledge of the personal history of important persons, and with their unlimited powers, they occupied a unique position as an instrument of Stalin's dictatorship. Almost immediately upon his death the chief symbol of that instrument, Beria, was liquidated. Such a step was probably considered an urgent necessity by representatives of several interest groups. A police of tremendous powers held firmly in the hands of a single dictator made sense, but in a collective dictatorship, in which Beria occupied what seemed to be the second position, who could guarantee that the instrument of power would not seek to become the wielder of power? The elimination of the police as a major power in the state was bound to be popular since almost all had suffered at their hands in the past, and all feared them in the future.

Among the interest groups that acquiesced in, or actively supported, the elimination of the police, the armed forces occupied a special place as the only armed group besides the police. The professional army cadres had suffered humiliation and decimation at the hands of the secret police in 1937 and 1938. The ubiquity within the armed forces of secret police officers who reported up through an independent chain of command was a constant reminder that another purge could be instituted.

Stalin's death breathed political life into the inert Army. Once active support had been solicited from the Army by the new civilian leaders, the Army could not be debarred permanently from participation in internal politics. The demotion of Zhukov in 1957 demonstrated that the Army already had a political role and that the Party had been successful in reducing it. There is a general tendency in the Soviet Union for the once-dependent instrument of power to seek an independent political role. It is this that makes the political importance of particular institutions at any given time so difficult to assess.

The Communist Party of the Soviet Union has also changed

its role considerably since the death of Stalin. Stalin had converted the Party, which had originally been the holy vessel of communist doctrine, into a mere instrument for the execution of his personal will. Its more than six million members, whether acting of their own volition or at Stalin's instance, provided the mechanism that moved the countless levers of Soviet society. In the months following Stalin's death the Party's area of competence seemed to shrink, while governmental institutions expanded their authority. This shift of weight favored Malenkov's policy of greater emphasis on consumer goods. Sacrifice of present comforts for the sake of the future has always been the Party's credo. The improvement of the standard of living demanded the talents of the industrial manager rather than those of the party boss.

Khrushchev's displacement of Malenkov in February, 1955, marked a revival of the Party's influence. Yet Khrushchev himself, by his scathing denunciation of Stalin in the "secret speech" at the Twentieth Party Congress in February, 1956, by implication rejected much of the Party's past. He brusquely told the party leaders to learn the business that they presumed to direct in the name of the Party. Since then Stalin's reputation has been partly restored, the Party's prestige has been somewhat elevated, and its members have been assigned by Khrushchev to new and important positions in the decentralization of industry. Furthermore the constant repetition since 1953 of the fiction that the Central Committee of the Party is the ultimate authority in the Soviet Union may have enhanced the committee's position.

The industrial managers have always played a vital economic role. Under Stalin the industrial manager lived well when most fared badly, but at any moment he might be capriciously imprisoned. He had to concentrate on fulfilling the state plans, without resistance to what was absurd or impracticable and without the possibility of independent action. The industrial managers of today do not seem to have become an independent political force. But the state prefers to elicit their initiative and enthusiasm rather than the automatic obedience that characterized the Stalin era.

The army, the police, the Party, and to a lesser extent the industrial managers, are clearly marked groups. Less highly organized groups must be taken into account, though their disaffection would not present an immediate political crisis. Of these, the Soviet peasants are the largest, if not the most important. In their public speeches the Soviet leaders, especially Khrushchev, have emphasized the past mismanagement of agriculture and have admitted that past governmental policies forced the peasants to act against their own and the common interest. The post-Stalin regime, by fits and starts has sought active co-operation and improved efficiency from the peasants by large-scale investment in agriculture. Unless food and labor shortages are mastered, the consumer goods program cannot progress. In a sense, therefore, the government must woo the peasantry, but the latter, scattered over the country, have no means of bringing direct pressure on the leadership in order to promote their own interests.

Another potentially powerful but presently impotent group comprises the students. The political inconsequence of students in the Stalin period represented a break in the Russian tradition. Today numerous travelers to the Soviet Union report the agitation of the student body, which finds expression in pointed questions about the internal and external policies of the regime. Some believe that the student body is merely letting off surplus steam and that the regime is wise to permit this. Others assert that student pressures can lead to consequences even more serious than the riots of 1956 in Poland and Soviet Georgia. No one, not even the Soviet leaders, can foresee the future role of the students.

These considerations apply, of course, to other social groups. If each group formulated its demands and secured their acceptance, the present regime could not survive. On the other hand, the regime must go some distance in meeting these demands if only to prevent them from growing too insistent. Meeting one demand reduces the resources available for meeting others. The present regime's freedom of action is severely limited by the need to satisfy the economic, political, and psychological demands of so many groups without any firm knowledge of what groups can be slighted without danger of an explosion. The inevitable tendency is to play safe and give each group something. The list of fixed requirements is long.

The general standard of living must continue to rise; it cannot safely turn downward for any length of time. The wages of the industrial class, including the managers and the shock workers, must be increased to improve morale. The curtailment of the sources of new urban labor, the increased mechanization of industry, and the greater demands for industrial output make the improvement of labor efficiency a requisite. At this stage forced labor is less economical than in the past and apathetic workmen are as undesirable as ever. Agricultural production must increase through greater investments in equipment and labor. Common prudence would recommend a steady expansion of basic industry; the Bolshevik faith demands great efforts to that end. Nuclear war can be avoided, or survived, only if a most expensive military establishment is maintained.

These vast requirements, formidable as they are, do not exhaust the constraints on the freedom of action of the present Soviet regime. Ideological taboos flourish in all their vigor. It is an article of faith that Soviet socialism is the best system of political economy and government. The one party system, the dead-end *kolkhoz* system, cannot be changed without tempting the wrath of the god of history. In the Bolshevik view only extreme emergencies justify temporary retreats in the advance toward their historical goals.

To adjudicate the claims of conflicting interests in society is the function of any government. This task is especially difficult in the Soviet Union where there are no commonly accepted procedures for making such decisions. Each crisis has been worked out somehow, although we do not know exactly how. Take the protracted crisis we have been discussing. Until January, 1955, Malenkov headed the preponderant faction in the Soviet leadership. His military and economic policies had been under fire from an opposing faction that was free to offer discreet public criticism and to achieve preponderance by detaching some of Malenkov's support. This procedure is at once similar to, and profoundly different from, that by which majorities are achieved in parliamentary governments. Realignments, pooling of interests, and sacrifice of principles are common to both systems, but in the parliamentary system the fate of the loser is known beforehand. Since Stalin, it is true, only Beria has paid with his head for losing, but who can guarantee that the next loser will not suffer the same fate? It testifies to the essential unity of aim and solidarity of Stalin's successors that they have managed to frame and execute policy with some success in this most uncertain atmosphere without physically liquidating more than one major figure.

Khrushchev owes his retention of office and his extension of power to his knack for choosing the winning side—and for helping it to win. A master of equivocation, he seems to promise all things to all men, to pursue incompatible courses, to juggle many balls in the air. His policy seems inconsistent and improvised. If some of his associates, unknown to us, have accused him of sacrificing principles to expediency, others must have observed that by his very flexibility he is carrying the entire communist system through a period of most delicate readjustment.

The above analysis of top-level Soviet politics puts into perspective the events of December, 1954, and January, 1955. The available press evidence shows that the anti-Malenkov forces first threw down the gauntlet. In a *Pravda* article written on the seventy-fifth anniversary of Stalin's birth, December 19, 1954, heavy industry was described as the cornerstone of the socialist economy and the source of the wealth, might, and defensive capability of the Soviet government. Malenkov had indicated that heavy industry and military strength had already achieved a satisfactory level and that now consumer goods could be sharply increased. The *Pravda* article contradicted this point of view, arguing that "in the conditions of the present international situation, the further strengthening of the defensive might of the Soviet government, the elevation of vigilance, and the strengthening of the Soviet armed forces acquire special significance. . . ." The Communist Party always had devoted, and was now devoting, primary attention to the com-

prehensive development of heavy industry, the cornerstone of
the might of the Soviet Union: "And now while carrying out
the program of the further improvement of all branches of the
socialist economy and the program of the systematic improvement of the material welfare of the people, the party will push
heavy industry forward above everything else and unswerv-
ingly."[1] Here was a clear indication that Malenkov's program
for giving priority to light industry was considered dangerous
to the security of the Soviet state. Two days later both sides of
the argument were stated in unequivocal terms, one in *Pravda*
and the other in *Izvestiia*.

V. Kruzhkov, the same who had dismissed as contrary to
Marxism the possibility of paralyzing the laws of the development of capitalism, wrote an article on Stalin for the *Pravda*
issue of December 21. Kruzhkov quoted Lenin on the need to
build up heavy industry in order to maintain the independence
of the Soviet Union, as if nothing had changed since Lenin's
day. (Malenkov had described Lenin's dictum as the correct
basis for policy in Lenin's time.) Over and over again Kruzhkov
described heavy industry as the cornerstone of Soviet power.
He quoted Stalin as having said the backward were beaten.
Heavy industry had been decisive for the victory in the last
war. Kruzhkov pointed out that, in conditions where the aggressive imperialist forces were aggravating the international
situation, the armed forces should be strengthened: "The Party
calls upon the Soviet people to direct its primary attention . . .
to the growth of heavy industry."[2] Here gathered in one place
are all the familiar themes of the anti-Malenkov group.

In an editorial in the same issue of *Pravda,* the same points
were made, if anything more sharply: "The growth of heavy
industry is the basis for the further development of the whole
economy and the guarantee of the inviolability of the borders
of our motherland. . . ." The need to strengthen the defensive
might of the Soviet Union was directly linked with imperialist
plans for a new war and the revival of the German army, which
was to serve as the shock force against the Soviet state.[3]

Izvestiia took the opposite side in the debate. Konstantinov,
in an article on the date of Stalin's birth, devoted paragraph

after paragraph to the importance of the masses and to the
great role the Party had played in victory in the Great Fatherland War, but he failed to make the familiar connection between heavy industry and Soviet victory. In the following statement he differed flatly with *Pravda:*

> The chief concern of the Communist Party in the sphere
> of internal policy is for the further rise in the productive
> forces of the country so that the material welfare and cul-
> tural level of the popular masses should grow without
> interruption and that the life of millions of toilers should
> become even better from year to year.[4]

The editorial in the same day's *Izvestiia* was not quite as
uncompromising as Konstantinov's article, but its divergence
from *Pravda* was clear enough:

> The chief concern of the Party and the government is the
> maximum satisfaction of the constantly growing material
> and cultural demands of all members of the society.[5]

Never before had the two conceptions of state policy been
contrasted more clearly: "The Party calls [for] primary attention . . . to heavy industry," and "The chief concern of the
Party . . . is the maximum satisfaction of the constantly growing material . . . demands of all. . . ." During the month of
December Khrushchev twice put himself on the heavy industry
side of the argument. In a speech on improving building methods, he said that heavy industry was the basis of the whole
economy and the source of the country's defensive capability.
The further development of heavy industry was necessary to
assure the inviolability of the Soviet borders and to achieve
success in raising the standard of living.[6] The only possible
counterargument was that the Soviet borders were quite
secure. As early as September, 1954, Khrushchev had told a
visiting English scientist, John Bernal, that the development
of all branches of Soviet industry would proceed according to
an existing plan that devoted the main attention to heavy
industry.[7] The interview was printed late in December. It
seems unlikely that the publication of an interview three

months after it took place was a mere coincidence. The decision to do so must therefore be placed in the context of the Khrushchev group's struggle against Malenkov and his policies. The publication of this interview only three days after *Pravda* and *Izvestiia* had taken directly contrary views served two purposes. First, it reminded people of Khrushchev's great importance, for his tone in addressing Professor Bernal was that of a confident spokesman for the whole regime. Second, it made clear that Khrushchev was then, as he had earlier been, a proponent of continued emphasis on heavy industry.

The Khrushchev faction, having re-emphasized the long-established connection between heavy industry and the security of the Soviet Union, proceeded to drum up support for its policies by pointing to the danger of war. Major General Talenskii, in an article written for wide circulation, said that "at any moment . . . mankind might be faced with the accomplished fact of the beginning of a destructive atomic war."[8] This was the sharpest public statement about the likelihood of war made by a Soviet official in the entire period under review. A few days later General Gritchin recalled that American aircraft had penetrated Soviet air space and sarcastically referred to the Forty-ninth Air Division's "tactical" capability, implying that its true mission was a strategic attack against the Soviet Union.[9]

On January 8, 1955, Khrushchev told an audience of young people, about to go out to the new virgin lands, that the industrialization of the country was the Party's general line. That policy had brought victory in the last war. Now the Soviet Union was in capitalist encirclement and Soviet industrial triumphs made the enemies of the Soviet Union fearful.[10]

Khrushchev's opponents gave the impression of fighting a rear-guard action against superior forces, but they had not yet surrendered. In a lecture passed for the press on January 10, an economist, discussing the proportion of resources to be allocated to capital formation and to the production of consumer goods, admitted that heavy industry had to continue to expand, but stated flatly that "a certain backwardness in the production of goods in popular demand had not yet been mastered." At the present time it was possible to develop heavy industry and light industry simultaneously. Here was an echo of the basic theme of Malenkov's speech in August, 1953, namely, that the period of forcing forward heavy industry was past and that a new stage had been reached.[11]

The basic tone of Khrushchev's remarks on January 8 had been that the requirements for heavy industry were exactly the same as they had always been in the past. The editor of *Pravda,* Dmitri Shepilov, elaborated Khrushchev's terse statement in a signed article. Shepilov took direct issue with the dangerous counsels of the Malenkovites to whom he ascribed the belief that the primacy of heavy industry had only been necessary when the country was backward. Now that a mighty industry had been created the situation had altered radically and therefore, said the "pseudo-economists," *since 1953* the Soviet land had entered a new stage of economic development. (The phrase here put in italics clearly intimated that Malenkov was the leading "pseudo-economist.") These pseudo-economists, continued Shepilov, wanted equal rates of development for heavy industry and light industry and even advocated preferential treatment for light industry. Such a program could only injure the country: "Stalin showed more than once that in the face of capitalist encirclement we cannot halt the tempo of the forward movement of heavy industry. . . . To hold it back means to fall back. And the backward are beaten." Shepilov went on to quote some highly technical language from the writings of the economists whom he was attacking, and concluded:

> In generally understandable language this means: we surrender the advantage of forcing forward the development of heavy industry, machine construction, energy, chemical industry, electronics, jet technology, guidance systems, and so forth, to the imperialist world. . . . It is hard to imagine a more anti-scientific, rotten theory, which could disarm our people more.[12]

Shepilov's catalogue proceeded from the general to the particular, from "heavy industry" to "guidance systems." He implied that the Malenkov faction was not only guilty of a general negligence to push heavy industry but also of a specific failure to develop guidance systems, an essential component of both long-range missile systems and active air-defense systems.

It is not surprising to find that three days later an editorial in the official organ of the Ministry of Defense repeated Shepilov's remarks about the dangerous errors of the pseudo-economists, which would lead to the weakening of the defensive capacities of the Soviet Union "in conditions where the imperialist countries are openly conducting a policy for the preparation of a new war."[13] It does come as something of a surprise, however, to read in the same editorial that certain economists on the teaching staffs of higher military institutes shared these "anti-Marxist" views. Colonel Kuznetsov was singled out for his zealous defense of these terrible views at the Zhukovskii Air Academy. This revelation that the whole military establishment did not speak with one voice is indeed rare in Soviet official publications. The hapless Colonel Kuznetsov was almost certainly expressing more than his personal views when, at the most important institute of air force research and higher education, he advocated more emphasis on light industry. Perhaps the air force, heretofore the least politically important of the Soviet armed services, had decided that its interests lay in the support of Malenkov and his views. One may surmise that Malenkov, who relied so heavily on deterrence, was willing to maintain the rate of growth of the air force or even to increase it, while making his economies at the expense of the ground forces. No other explanation offers itself for *Red Star*'s deliberate linking of the air force with Malenkov's ideas. There is nothing intrinsically unreasonable, of course, in the three services competing for position and funds during a period of major revision of strategic concepts, or in their appealing to different factions within a divided top leadership. Unfortunately, almost nothing more is afforded us than this single glimpse into the effects of the political conflict on the military. The successful elimination of the Malenkov heresy from the air force school was referred to twice later, and that is all we know.[14]

The speeches and printed interviews of early February carried forward the theme of the optimists' unforgivable recklessness in the shadow of war clouds. Most critical of all was Bulganin, who succeeded to Malenkov's vacated post. He had been among the first to call attention to the danger of surprise attack and was the sharpest in attacking Malenkov. He echoed many others in his remarks about the importance of heavy industry for defense, but was the only one to suggest that Malenkov had depleted the state reserves in his efforts to economize: "It would be an unforgivable mistake to slacken our attention to this very important matter [of the state reserves] or to yield to the temptation to solve individual current problems at the expense of state reserves. . . . To increase the state reserves . . . is our most important task."[15]

Marshal Zhukov, who gained greatly by Malenkov's dismissal, warned that the very existence of atomic weapons made it necessary to reckon with the possibility of their employment because "certain madmen might go to the length of using them in spite of everything."[16]

At the very meetings of the Supreme Soviet where Malenkov's resignation was formally accepted, however, it became apparent that war alarms had been raised mainly as a pretext for deposing Malenkov. The cries of "imperialist aggression" and "capitalist encirclement" were hyperboles meant to convey that Malenkov's satisfaction with the current military posture was unsound. In Soviet political disputation it is insufficient to charge that the opponent has a policy that may ultimately bring great dangers. The policy under attack is always described as having already created a critical situation.

On the very day of Malenkov's resignation Molotov made a speech analyzing the international situation that indicated the trumped up nature of the war warnings. As a matter of routine he condemned American aggressiveness, but he went on to offer evidence of the weakness of the American cause. In an unusually realistic analysis of the American political scene, Molotov argued that the Democratic Party's involvement in the Korean war caused it to lose the 1952 election. The Republicans won the Presidency, said Molotov, not because they had announced an aggressive foreign policy, but because they then seemed to favor the conclusion of the war in Korea. All this goes to show, argued Molotov, that the situation is characterized by numerous contradictions within the capitalist camp and that the public opinion of wide circles of voters plays a role in the formulation of policy in the imperialist camp. These differences within the imperialist camp afford an opportunity for the execution of the Soviet foreign policy which is, of course, in the interests of the strengthening of peace.[17] The attribution of political power to "voters," instead of to "capitalists" and "the forces of peace," was quite unusual. The implication that the danger of war could not be so great if the Republicans had won on a peace platform had been avoided by spokesmen of the Khrushchev school while Malenkov was under attack. Now that Malenkov was out, his successor promised peace through military preparedness. A continuation of the cries of capitalist encirclement and the danger of war would have detracted from the promises of peace. From this time until the summit conference the incidence of statements on the likelihood of war fell sharply.

A long *Kommunist* article, already referred to, had interpreted the theory of the destruction of world civilization in a nuclear war as a propaganda tool of capitalist aggressors, who hoped thereby to spread defeatism among their enemies. Konstantinov, who had argued the Malenkov case in *Izvestiia* on December 21, 1954, now recanted and lumped the theory of the destruction of world civilization with the discredited policy of emphasizing light industry. Now the argument was complete. The capitalists promoted the theory of the destruction of world civilization in order to foster complacency. Emphasis on light industry was a consequence of that theory.[18]

In the months that followed Malenkov's downfall Khrushchev trumpeted the relaxation of international tension. After Soviet overtures to Austria and what really amounted to a bilateral arrangement with her, a four-power agreement to withdraw from Austria was promulgated on May 15, 1955. Simultaneously a rapprochement with Yugoslavia was achieved, and by the end of May the Big Four Summit Conference was settled. Against all these visible signs of the relaxation of tension, it would have been inappropriate to insist on the likelihood of war. In the early part of 1955, therefore, the Soviet press took the line that tension had been reduced, though it was pointed out on several occasions by military people that peace could not be counted on. Marshal Rotmistrov pointed out in an article that had appeared somewhat earlier in *Voennaia mysl'* (*Military Thought*), and now appeared in slightly different form in *Red Star,* that surprise was more likely than before because of the developments in weapons and the preference of Americans for this tactic. Essentially, Rotmistrov was arguing that nuclear weapons made surprise attack a possible winning strategy and therefore that to count on deterrence was ridiculous.[19]

Shepilov, in a speech on the eighty-fifth anniversary of Lenin's birth, pointed to the continuing intrigues of the enemies of peace and said that the Soviet Union was taking the necessary steps to increase the strength of the armed forces. The Soviet Union, he promised, would not be caught unawares by the imperialists if they unleashed a new world war.[20] This indirect reference to military surprise was far more moderate than Talenskii's statement a few months before that destructive atomic war might break out at any moment. Shepilov's tone implied that the imperialists had not given up their war plans, but that the Soviet Union was strong and the imperialists would rue the day if they made war.

Marshal Zhukov, speaking on the tenth anniversary of Germany's surrender, struck a balance between the deterrent strength of the Soviet Union and the continuing danger of war. While he emphasized the destructiveness of hydrogen weapons in densely populated countries—a theme to become increasingly prominent in Soviet propaganda—he insisted that the ratification of the Paris Agreements and the arrangements for rearming Germany had increased international tension.[21]

In May the Soviet military press made numerous statements about the nature of surprise.* These emphasized the changes wrought in warfare by the new weapons. They did not suggest, as Talenskii had done, that war might be imminent. Public

* Examined in Chap. 6.

statements about imminent war would not have contributed to
the success of the forthcoming Geneva meetings. Success at
Geneva would yield domestic political advantages to the leadership. Malenkov had offered the prospect of peace through
amicable negotiations; Khrushchev now offered peace through
military strength. Moreover, he stole Malenkov's thunder by
negotiating as well.

Today we know that Khrushchev's position was not as
secure in 1955, or even in 1956, as it became subsequently. Had
the victory of his policies brought an increase of international
tension his opponents might well have tried to unseat him.
Khrushchev's policy of carrying the big stick had prevailed;
to maintain his position he had to speak softly, at least for a
while. Domestic and international policy were both served
by an almost total absence of statements on the war danger
during the rest of 1955 and 1956. The official Soviet line, as
reported by Bulganin to the Supreme Soviet when he and
Khrushchev returned from a much-publicized trip to India and
Burma, was that the prospects of peace had greatly improved:

> The past year will go down in history as the year of a
> definite turning point in the tense international situation
> which has existed in recent times.[22]

An editorial in *Kommunist,* the main party organ, quoted
Bulganin's report and described the events of 1955 as representing a gradual improvement in the international situation. The
Geneva Conference had been forced on the West by public
opinion. The Bandung Conference of Asiatic countries also
had been a great contribution to peace. Events that earlier
would have been treated as evidence of the imperialists' ap-
petite for armed aggression were now interpreted merely as
part of an effort to spread the cold war. Thus the formation
of SEATO was said to evince a desire to spread the cold war to
the Asian continent. *Kommunist* referred to Dulles's article
in *Life,* which used the much-discussed phrase "brink of war,"
as "playing with fire" and emphasized that even the Western
proponents of the policy of strength had criticized Dulles for
his tactlessness. That the forces of peace were growing daily

was borne out by the events in French Indochina and by communist electoral victories in France.[23]

The relatively moderate tone of this editorial is not difficult to explain. When Khrushchev at the Twentieth Party Congress introduced the formula that wars were not "fatalistically inevitable," he suggested that the prospects for peace had improved. A simultaneous press campaign to the opposite effect would have hurt Khrushchev politically by calling in question his powers as a prophet. It would have been inappropriate, at the very least, for the Soviet press to say after Khrushchev returned from his visit to England that the prospects for peace had diminished. A *Kommunist* editorial, dealing with the possibility of preventing war, declared that Bulganin and Khrushchev's London conversations had taken place in an atmosphere of frankness and realism and had "made an important contribution to the improvement of relations between the U.S.S.R. and Great Britain and to the extension of the general peace and the security of the peoples."[24]

In mid-1956 political developments in the satellites took a turn that threatened the Soviet position in Eastern Europe and Soviet prestige throughout the whole world. A crisis arose for which the blame could be placed at Khrushchev's door. By choosing the party leaders in the satellite countries he had assumed responsibility for what happened there. His "secret" speech to the Twentieth Party Congress, made public in June, 1956, brought matters to a head. By the fall of 1956 revolutions in Hungary and Poland were brewing and the possibility of Western intervention could not be excluded. If Khrushchev's opponents could make the point that the international situation had deteriorated so far that war with the West was possible, the Party chief's position would be as weak as it possibly could be. On the other hand, if Khrushchev could maintain that international tensions were abating, the crisis in Eastern Europe could be represented as a serious but surmountable problem. This explains why he chose the second alternative, to belittle the danger of war.

The situation in the satellite countries was extraordinarily complex. During the war some of them had been allied with

the Germans. Others had been occupied and brutally mis-
treated. Some of these countries had been transferred from
German rule to Russian rule by action of the Russian armies
alone. Others, most notably Yugoslavia, had played a role in
their own liberation from the Germans. Immediately after
the war the Russians installed in each of these countries (except
Yugoslavia) a regime that permitted an amount of opposition
that was harmless from the Russian point of view.

By comparison with the situation only a few years later
Russian rule in the satellites was then moderate and restrained.
The American government interpreted Russian wartime promises to mean that the Russians would introduce parliamentary
democracy to these areas after the war. To the Americans the
political regimes in Eastern Europe even in the early postwar
years were far from satisfactory. Moreover, the West under-
standably viewed Chinese communist territorial gains, Ho Chih
Min's successes in Indochina, and the Greek communists' threat
to the Greek government, as part of a Soviet grand design for
expansion. If these troubles were instigated by local communists against Soviet wishes, as some evidence suggests, it
remains a fact that the Soviet Union never denounced their
actions. In 1947, therefore, the United States set forth the
Truman Doctrine and declared her intention to stem the tide
of communism by force if necessary.

A radical change followed in the satellite countries. Soviet
control became direct in one country after another, culmin-
ating with Czechoslovakia, and noncommunist parties were
either suppressed or denied any real power in the satellite
governments. Even in Yugoslavia, the one country where a
native communist party had established a measure of control
before the arrival of Russian troops, the Russians sought to
tighten their controls, with the result that the most forceful
of the satellite leaders, Tito, rebelled and was branded a heretic.
Tito's defection was the signal for redoubled witch-hunting
in the satellite countries, the imposition on them of programs
of forced industrialization and compulsory collectivization of
agriculture, and the creation of large armies presumably intended for disciplining Yugoslavia.

This program caused profound dislocation in the satellites. Stalin, with a lack of historical sense that accorded ill with his professsed historical materialism, precipitately sought to force countries with the most varied histories and social composition through a process of development that had taken a quarter of a century in the Soviet Union. In the Soviet Union the civil war had been followed by a period of consolidation that lasted from 1921 until 1928 or 1929. During this period much of the communist economic program was held in abeyance. The old classes with specialized skills were partially liquidated by emigration, intimidation, or execution and supplanted by new cadres. Not until all this had happened was the assault on the peasants undertaken and collectivization carried out. Only in 1934, when the industrialization program was under way, did Stalin make his assault on the older party cadres and inaugurate the reign of terror that did not subside until 1938.

In the satellites everything was done at once: collectivization, industrialization, elimination of the former governing classes, the purge of the older generation of party members, and establishment of the terror. When Stalin died none of these processes was yet complete, although it seemed as if this cruel and rapid surgery might have been completed had Stalin lived. Suddenly the pressure relaxed. The changes introduced into the Soviet Union after 1953 were automatically applied to the satellites. The reduction in the role of the police and in the tempo of industrialization were imitated in the satellites. Renewed hope in the satellite countries brought open signs of discontent of which the East German uprising was the most serious, but order was reimposed.

Into this situation Khrushchev injected himself. If Stalin had increased international tension without benefit to the Soviet Union, Khrushchev would decrease it with corresponding benefit to the Soviet Union. If Stalin had lost the most stalwart of the satellite leaders, Tito, to the capitalists who supplied him with weapons and money, Khrushchev would win him back to communism. But Tito's position in 1955 differed greatly from his position in 1948. A mere promise from the Russians to refrain from pressing the kind of claims that Stalin

had insisted on in 1948 was no longer sufficient to restore good
relations. In 1955 Tito required that the verdict of heresy
against him be reversed, without any formal commitment on
his part to be bound in ideological matters by the Communist
Party of the Soviet Union or by any international communist
organization. Khrushchev had to accept these demands as a
start, whatever his hopes for the future may have been. The
initial concessions to Tito opened up a Pandora's box. Polish
and Hungarian jails had to disgorge communists who had been
subjected to painful and humiliating treatment on the grounds
that they had been infected by the Titoist heresy. These communists were restored to membership in the Party with their
former persecutors. Amidst the resulting uncertainty and con-
fusion came Khrushchev's "secret speech" against Stalin. The
chief crimes that he ascribed to Stalin were crimes against the
personnel of the Party. The restored members of the Polish
and Hungarian parties had good cause to look at their former
jailors and wonder who were really the criminals. The police,
who were now being purged for what they had been ordered to
do, naturally became inactive.[25]

These were the basic causes of unrest that culminated in
an armed uprising in Hungary and in the accretion of a certain independence to the Polish Communist Party. During the
fall and early winter of 1956, no one in the Soviet Union
could predict the end of all these troubles that had mush-
roomed so suddenly. Would the map of Eastern Europe be
rolled to the Soviet border of 1939? Would the Soviet student
body go beyond sympathetically watching the events abroad
and reading the Polish and Yugoslav newspapers? Would the
Western powers enjoy greater success in their subversive activities in Eastern Europe? Might they go over to overt military
support of the dissident communists? These questions must
have been put many times in Moscow in those anxious months.
Many must have laid these calamities at Khrushchev's door, for
it was he who had pushed the rapprochement with Tito and
had excoriated Stalin for his crimes against Party personnel.
This was not the time to talk of the danger of war. There was
trouble enough without inventing more. Alarms of war might

serve to unite the Soviet people and to divert their minds
from domestic problems, but they had no power to unite peoples who aspired to national independence.

From the summer of 1956 to the end of the year the Soviet
press soft-pedaled the likelihood of war. In July, for example,
Kommunist charged that the enemies of socialism were taking
advantage of temporary difficulties within socialist countries
and of some socialist mistakes to deceive the people. The recent
Poznan riots provided an example of how international reactionaries seized their opportunities. In all this there was not a
single war alarm of the kind so common in 1954.[26]

In September a *Kommunist* editor discussed a doctrinal
innovation of the Twentieth Party Congress, namely, that a
parliamentary transition to socialism was possible. He emphasized that the whole world situation had changed markedly
in favor of the communists. The communists parties were
larger, the Soviet Union was stronger, the colonial system was
disintegrating. All this had combined to change the relationship of world political forces and to create new opportunities
for a peaceful transition from capitalism to socialism. In former
days the conclusion of such an argument was often that the
imperialists, maddened by the prospect of destruction, would
strike out like a wounded beast. NATO and SEATO, once
described as alliances for the preparation of war against the
Soviet Union, were now said to have as their primary object the
suppression of revolutionary activity within the member countries. By this interpretation NATO was directed against the
French communists rather than the Soviet Union.[27]

A month later the strongest accusation that *Kommunist*
could make against the imperialists was that the cold war, their
creation, was not in the interests of the people. The bourgeoisie
were accused, not of preparing a war, but of seeking to drive a
wedge between the communist parties of the peoples' democracies and those of the capitalist countries.[28] In the same issue,
an article on American military preparations in the Pacific
accused the United States of seeking to create a war psychosis
in an international situation otherwise characterized by the
reduction of tension. The American naval program, said the

article, aimed at ejecting the smaller British navy from the Pacific. Popular opposition in Asia had seriously hampered American military plans. The writer made no mention of the danger of war.[29]

In January, 1957, *Kommunist,* reviewing the events of 1956, said a great deal about the bankruptcy of imperialism but not a word about the desire of the imperialists to make war.[30]

For almost two years there had been no warnings in the press about the danger of war. At this moment Khrushchev chose to launch a new campaign stressing the likehood of general war. The international situation did not justify such alarms. American disapproval of the British, French, and Israeli invasion of Egypt had displayed for all to see a difference within the Western alliance, rather than a consolidation of that alliance for war. The Egyptian adventure had been liquidated and the Hungarian uprising suppressed without even a hint of Western intervention, so that if anything the prospects for peace were better. Why, then, did Khrushchev start to beat the war drums again? As before, we must look for an explanation within the Soviet Union, rather than outside it.

Lacking direct evidence, we can nevertheless be fairly certain that Khrushchev's position was badly shaken by the Hungarian events. It was easy to explain all the disturbances in Eastern Europe as the result of the Party chief's rapprochement with Tito and denunciation of Stalin. When the Plenum of the Party's Central Committee met on December 20-24, 1956, for the first time since February when they had convened for a day, Khrushchev's name was not even mentioned. The newspapers said that Bulganin reported on the improvement of leadership in the Soviet economy, and Saburov and Baibakov on the economic plans for 1957. After these reports the Central Committee resolved to present to the Supreme Soviet (which was to meet at the beginning of 1957) several economic proposals described as putting a greater emphasis on meeting the requirements for raising the standard of living, and as designed to secure "a reduction in the scale of capital investments."[31] This sounded more than a little like the old Malenkov line.

The Plenum, in which Khrushchev apparently played either

a small role or none at all, viewed the international situation calmly. There was no word about any increased danger of general war. The conferees emphasized the competition within the capitalist camp and thought that the standard of living was falling in capitalist countries. The imperialist attempts to expand aroused popular opposition and strengthened the movements for national liberation. This led to the further militarization of the capitalist economy, which in turn aggravated its internal contradictions.[32] In other words, the capitalist camp was in rather a mess and, by implication, not unduly dangerous to the Soviet Union.

Khrushchev was obviously slighted by the December Plenum. Major party decisions were taken, according to the press, without the participation of the man whose name had overshadowed all others for almost two years. Perhaps this circumstance explains the reconvocation of the Plenum in February, remarkably soon after its last meeting. At the second meeting Khrushchev dominated the proceedings. He proposed a reorganization of the economy that differed in many essentials from the plan of December. The most prominent party members did not speak up in favor of Khrushchev's plan and only after several months of politicking did Khrushchev obtain its acceptance.

Khrushchev's recovery of the spotlight and the initiative in February lends interest to the statements on the likelihood of war that he began to make almost immediately after the conclusion of the December Plenum. In written answers to question presented by the editor of a Czech newspaper, Khrushchev took the line that peace would be strengthened in 1957, although the events in Egypt and the fascist plot against Hungary had "sharply increased the threat of a new world war."[33] At a New Year's party in the Kremlin, Khrushchev said that the Soviet people were thirsting for peace, but added: "We should not forget that a feverish arms race is being conducted in a number of capitalist countries, and therefore we must not for a second forget about our Army. We should provide it with first class equipment and supplies. We have done this, are doing it, and will do it in order to secure and extend peace, because we should defend the conquests of the Great October [Revolution], the Soviet Power."[34]

During January others, probably following Khrushchev's cue, began to take a stronger tone on military preparedness. Bulganin, in the middle of the month, spoke of the necessity of being able to protect socialism "from enemy blows from wherever they may be dealt."[35] A joint Chinese-Soviet declaration, summarizing the results of conversations held during January, observed that "the development of international events took a tortuous course. All the peace loving nations of the globe should be constantly vigilant and prepared for a persistent and prolonged struggle with the camp headed by the United States." America was pursuing a "policy of aggression and preparation for war."[36] Here, for the first time since 1955, the Soviet press accused the United States of preparing for war.

Molotov made a speech at this time in which he said that the Soviet Union, while seeking a reduction in international tension, "could not but reckon with the fact that the imperialists would not be imperialists if they were not making plans for new aggressive wars and were not continuing the arms race." A lesser figure, speaking in Siberia, stated that the threat of war and of new military adventures was far from removed. Now the task was to give a stunning rebuff to the enemy's schemes and to strengthen the Soviet armed forces.[37] Kaganovich, instead of drawing attention, like *Kommunist* early in January, to the slackening of international tension, declared that "the aggravation of relationships and the strengthening of tension is characteristic of the contemporary international situation." The reason was that the reactionaries were seeking military adventures.[38]

Red Star, in a signed article reviving a long-discarded theme, charged the American imperialists with seeking to initiate a new war in order to establish world domination. Despite the fact, recognized by General LeMay himself, that the Soviet Union had grown so much stronger, the Americans still sought ways to destroy others and to remain unharmed themselves.

The general American idea was to deflect retaliatory blows on their allies.[39]

A joint Soviet-Czechoslovak declaration of January 29 said that the imperialists were increasing international tension by undertaking new and dangerous adventures that seriously threatened the peace of the world.[40]

The old Stalinist bogey of espionage by foreigners was revived. On February 7 more than a page of *Pravda* was devoted to a press conference called by the Soviet Ministry of Foreign Affairs to demonstrate continued American subversive activities. The report alleged that some spies had entered the Soviet Union in December and January, but most of its espionage stories were more dated. The intention was obvious: to instill a sense of danger.[41]

The most authoritative statement on the war danger was made by the Minister of Foreign Affairs, Shepilov, in his speech to the Supreme Soviet on February 12. Since less than three days later Shepilov was no longer Foreign Minister, his speech merits particular attention. Amidst a mounting crescendo of warnings that war was imminent, Shepilov struck a quieter note. He seemed to be carrying water on both shoulders. The main argument of his very long speech was that there were two political tendencies in the West: the more sober one leaned toward a relaxation of tension; the other, more dangerous one had come to the fore in the latter half of 1956. The second policy had inspired the counterrevolutionary uprising in Hungary and the aggression in Egypt, but the defeat of both showed that the capitalist system was growing weaker. These events demonstrated, said Shepilov, that under modern conditions war is not fatalistically inevitable and can be prevented. The imperialists had learned that the forces opposing war were stronger, but nevertheless went on intensifying their preparations for war.

It cannot be said that Shepilov ignored the theme of growing international tension. In the first two minutes of his speech he indicated that tension had both risen and fallen in recent months. This, of course, was a more equivocal view than those recently expressed by Khrushchev, Kaganovich, Molotov, and others, who had flatly postulated an increase of international tension. Moreover, Shepilov's remarks about the possibility of an accommodation with the United States had a tone of optimism that departed even further from the Khrushchev position than the noncommittal statement that tension had had its ups and downs:

> To return again to the question whose importance is obvious to all, namely the question of the future development of relations between the U.S.S.R. and the United States of America: a myth exists, disseminated abroad by certain circles, that the normalization of Soviet-American relations is impossible because both sides are divided by insoluble problems. As a matter of fact, it is well known that our governments have lived in peace and friendship for decades. With the exception of the period of foreign intervention against the young Soviet Republic, the U.S.A. and the U.S.S.R. have never made war against each other. The deceased President of the U.S.A., Franklin Roosevelt, emphasized that between our peoples "for more than a century there has existed the happy tradition of friendship, beneficial to both sides." This tradition began to be destroyed when American ruling circles began to expand the tendency toward world dominion and to exclude international co-operation on an equal basis.

> The Soviet government believes, as it did before, that no matter how different the American and Soviet social systems there are not a few important problems in which the interests of our people go together. Both the American and the Soviet people are equally interested in the preservation of peace and in the development of peaceful co-operation. On this basis we propose to the U.S.A. the conclusion of a treaty of friendship with the Soviet Union. More than a year has passed since this proposal was made by us, however, we have not yet received an answer and this naturally is no accident. In the United States there are influential circles interested in inflaming hatred between countries. However, we do not confuse these circles and the American people and we are certain that sooner or later the good common sense characteristic of the Ameri-

can nation and sober understanding will conquer over the
egotistical conceptions of those who seek to intensify tension in American-Soviet relations.[42]

The evidence seems fairly strong that this speech, with its
overtones of optimism about the future, was not well received
by those who found it useful to insist on the likelihood of war.
The Central Committee of the Communist Party met suddenly
on February 13-14 and immediately thereafter Shepilov retired
from his ministerial position.

On February 14 the Central Committee adopted a resolution on a report by Khrushchev on the reorganization of the
management of the Soviet economy. Everybody who read the
resolution must have been struck by the contrast between it
and the resolutions of the December Plenum, where Khrushchev had been so inconspicuous. Although it is difficult to
point to any particular phrase, the whole tone of the resolution
tended to emphasize heavy industry. There was no hint of the
December resolution to reduce the scope of investment.[43]
Clearly the February Plenum of the Central Committee had
eaten out of Khrushchev's hand.

A few days later Major General Kozhedub of the air force,
writing in the organ of the Soviet air arm, presented a picture
of the prospects of foreign policy that lacked the optimism
of the retired Shepilov. The aggressive circles in the capitalist
countries, above all, in the United States, were said to oppose
peaceful coexistence and to be spinning plans for the initiation
of a new war. The United States was spending as many billions
as during the Second World War and was behind the Hungarian counterrevolution. The Twentieth Party Congress, wrote
the General, had emphasized the need for the greatest vigilance,
because as long as capitalism existed the reactionary forces
representing the interests of capitalism and monopoly would
continue to seek military adventures and aggression. Major
General Kozhedub, perhaps significantly, failed to add the
formula, devised by Khrushchev, to the effect that wars are no
longer fatalistically inevitable.[44]

At a reception in the Bulgarian Embassy on February 18,

Khrushchev made a speech marked by two novelties. First, he talked about his capitalist opponents as "enemies," something that he had not done in any published speech heretofore; second, he hinted for the first time at the danger of surprise attack. (Others, of course, had mentioned it before him.) The most significant passage was as follows:

> The capitalists . . . are assigning hundreds of millions of dollars to subversive espionage and diversionary activity against the Soviet Union and other socialist countries. They spend many billions of dollars on arms, on the building of military bases on foreign territory. Should we smile and make believe that we do not notice it? No. We see what all the enemy schemes are and adopt the necessary measures in order that the enemy should not take us unawares. . . . We do not want to fight and we are not preparing to attack anyone. But if we are attacked then we will defend ourselves and when we defend ourselves it will be difficult for the attacker to defend himself.[45]

On March 18 a *Pravda* writer once more raised the whole question of the inevitability of war. The dictum of the Twentieth Party Congress that there was no fatal inevitability of war, he wrote, certainly did not mean that a new peaceful phase in the development of capitalism had arrived: "Capitalism has been, remains, and in the future will be the source of threats of aggression and war." The very fact that the sphere of capitalist rule was being restricted intensified the capitalist desire to start a new war, through which they hoped to recover their lost positions. These formerly standard Marxian arguments had been almost absent from the Soviet press during 1956. In the early part of 1957, when it suited Khrushchev's purpose, the analysis once more went beyond the conclusion that capitalism was declining. It now went on to say that the continuing losses of capitalism would drive the imperialists to desperate measures, including war.[46]

In an interview given to a small American newspaper, Khrushchev continued to support the theme that the international situation had become worse. He dodged a question as to when in the preceding eleven years the war danger had been greatest, but made it clear that he believed the present danger to be great. All danger of war came from the American policy of working from "a position of strength." The dangers of war spreading from Korea and Indochina had been liquidated by negotiation. The Geneva meeting of 1955 did cause a certain dispersion of international tension. "Unfortunately this period didn't last long. The attack on Egypt and the subsequent attempts of some powers to fill in the 'vacuum' invented by themselves in the Arab east has again significantly aggravated the international situation and created a serious threat to peace in this region." Thus Khrushchev contended that the present danger of general war was more serious than at any time since the settlement of the Indochina question in the spring of 1954.[47]

As might be expected, *Red Star,* the newspaper of the Ministry of Defense, reinforced this line, emphasizing the need to recognize the possibility of an outbreak of a war. The writer accused Soviet propagandists of perverting the true balance, established at the Twentieth Party Congress, between the possibility of preventing wars and the possibility of the outbreak of wars. The propagandists, said *Red Star* with a good deal of truth, had been concentrating their chief attention on the possibility of preventing war and had slighted the possibility of its outbreak.[48]

The diplomatic correspondence of the Soviet Union, obviously intended for publication, reflected the Soviet estimate that the danger of war was closer. Bulganin, for example, in a message to the Norwegian Prime Minister published on March 27, noted: "The international situation has recently seriously deteriorated. Dangerous attempts have been undertaken to undermine the relaxation of international tension already achieved and to place the peoples at the brink of war. Indeed it is a secret to no one that in November of last year there were days when we stood before a serious danger of war." Bulganin went on to say that the rebuff received by the aggressors in Egypt and the liquidation of the fascist uprising in Hungary had prevented this terrible danger from materializing, but that the situation remained tense. The arms race continued and the United States did not conceal her intention to employ her armed forces in the Near East. The anounced plans of the United States to locate special atomic units in new places spoke neither for the policy of peaceful coexistence nor for the desire to reduce international tension.[49] In a similar message to the Danish Prime Minister, Bulganin spoke of American international policy as "leading to the increased threat of a new war."[50]

At practically the same moment the Central Committee of the Communist Party was assembling to hear Khrushchev report on his scheme for reorganizing the economy of the country. In concluding his long speech, Khrushchev made it clear that his plans would further the policy of priority for heavy industry. The Party, he warned, had always condemned "surrendering to the false concept of directing basic resources to the development of light industry," which might yield the temporary appearance of success, but would undercut the basis for future economic development. Eight months later Khrushchev told a foreign newspaper man that the reorganization plan, by decentralizing management, had "improved our strategic position."[51]

As might be expected, Khrushchev also emphasized that armaments were necessary for the maintenance of the defensive capability of the U.S.S.R.: "That is why the enemies of the Soviet Union always have directed and are directing their efforts to the discrediting of this great Leninist idea [of priority for heavy industry] which is the general line of the Communist Party of the Soviet Union."[52]

In conformity with his political style of promising everybody everything, Khrushchev went on to pledge a sharp increase in the production of meat and dairy products in the near future. He did not explain how priority for investment in heavy industry could be reconciled with such a startling increase in the production of consumer goods.[53]

It is not quite clear just how far Khrushchev's reorganization plan differed from the one proposed without his participation. Both plans were extremely complicated, and a detailed comparison of them would be inappropriate here. It is suf-

ficient for present purposes to establish that it was a political
necessity for Khrushchev to ensure that the plan adopted was
his.

It is suggested that Khrushchev revived talk of the imminence of war in order to overcome, at the least, reluctance to
support him and his plan, and more probably, active opposition. The speed with which he reversed his position on the
danger of war once he had had his way with his opponents
cannot be explained by any notable change in the international
situation, for there was none. It can be understood only against
the background of Soviet domestic politics. Only two weeks
later Khrushchev was saying that life had again become normal:

> International events became even more strained in con-
> nection with the imperialist aggression in Egypt. As is
> known, here too, the imperialists miscalculated and met
> with a deserved rebuff. Now the passions, if they have not
> subsided altogether, have quieted down noticeably and
> life flows in its normal course. We should direct all efforts
> to reduce international tension and attain an improvement
> in the relations between all countries. . . .[54]

In a joint Soviet-Albanian communiqué, published the following day, it was laid down as a general statement that, "as a
result of the joint efforts of the socialist governments and the
peace loving forces of the whole world, a relaxation of tension
in international relations had been attained."

On April 23 Madame Furtseva, whose rapid advance in the
Soviet hierarchy had coincided with Khrushchev's, continued
the theme of the relaxation of tension. She argued that the
healthy nationalist groups in Western Europe and in the
United States, who realized the disastrous nature of their
governments' policies, were indubitably capable of changing
them to conform with the true national interests of their
countries. Most optimistically, considering the alarms of war in
January and February, Madame Furtseva said:

> It is possible to count both on common sense prevailing
> and on the triumph in international affairs of the policy
> of peaceful co-existence between different governments.

> We believed and continue to believe that a stable peace
> can be assured in and for our time. . . . We are convinced
> that the present somewhat sharpened international situa-
> tion is a temporary phenomenon. . . . If the peoples will
> be vigilant and not permit themselves to be involved in a
> struggle against each other and if in the future they con-
> tinue to be guided by the defense of peace which is of com-
> mon interest to them, no plots and sallies of the imperi-
> alists will menace the solid camp of the progressive forces.[55]

All the evidence presented in this and the preceding chapters seems to point to the conclusion that public Soviet statements about the imminence of war are often employed for
domestic political purposes, whether or not they happen, at
the same time, to represent a genuine fear of war. In some
cases, as in 1957, alarms of war clearly have no relation to the
international situation and are employed only as a weapon in
domestic arguments. As we have seen, Khrushchev was dis-
inclined to use such a weapon when there seemed to be a
real danger of general conflict—in the Suez affair, for example.
It may be, therefore, that the private and the public Soviet
estimates of the likelihood of war seldom if ever coincide.
When the danger is great, there is little disposition to cry wolf.
When the danger recedes, there is a temptation to make domestic political capital out of the fear of war. Soviet leaders who
succumb to this temptation do not worry that their war alarms
will precipitate the very disaster they warn against. One of
their basic beliefs is that American policy is determined, not
by Soviet statements, but by the necessities of the capitalist
system. Moreover, they have been convinced for some time that
Soviet power effectively deters the United States from making
war.

The seemingly mercurial Russian views about the likelihood of war, then, have little to do with Soviet long-term plans
to be fully prepared for any military emergency. They have still
less to do with Soviet analyses of the nature of a future war,
should one break out. The next chapter is devoted to Russian
ideas on the possible nature of a future war.

NOTES

1. Academician M. Mitin, "I. V. Stalin—The Foremost Theoretician of Marxism," *Pravda*, December 19, 1954.
2. V. Kruzhkov, "I. V. Stalin—The Great Continuator of V. I. Lenin's Work," *Pravda*, December 21, 1954.
3. Editorial, "The Great Triumph of the Idea of Marxism-Leninism," *Pravda*, December 21, 1954.
4. F. Konstantinov, "The Great Continuator of Lenin's Immortal Work," *Izvestiia*, December 21, 1954.
5. Editorial, "Under the Great Banner of Marx, Engels, Lenin, Stalin," *Izvestiia*, December 21, 1954.
6. "Speech of Comrade N. S. Khrushchev to the All-Union Conference of Builders . . .," *Trud (Labor)*, December 28, 1954. This speech had been delivered on December 7, 1954.
7. "Interview of Comrade N. S. Khrushchev with the English Scientist and Public Figure, John Bernal," *Trud*, December 24, 1954. This interview was published in the whole Soviet press.
8. Major General N. Talenskii, "On Atomic and Conventional Weapons," *Mezhdunarodnaia zhizn' (International Life)*, No. 16, 1955, p. 22.
9. Lieutenant General I. Gritchin, "What the American Atom Brandishers Should Not Forget," *Pravda*, January 7, 1955.
10. "Speech of Comrade N. S. Khrushchev," *Komsomolskaia pravda*, January 8, 1955.
11. I. D. Shirinskii, "The Law of Plans (Proportional Development of the Economy)," Moscow, 1955. A public lecture passed for the press on January 10, 1955. Date of delivery of lecture was not given.
12. D. Shepilov, "The General Line of the Party and the Vulgarizers of Marxism," *Pravda*, January 24, 1955.
13. "The Bases of the Might of the Soviet Fatherland," *Red Star*, January 27, 1955.
14. Editorial, "Ideological Work among the Troops Should Be on the Level of the New Demands," *Red Star*, June 10, 1955; editorial, "The New Academic Year in the Higher Military Schools," *Red Star*, September 1, 1955.
15. "The Speech of N. A. Bulganin," *Izvestiia*, February 10, 1955.
16. Interview with G. K. Zhukov by the American Journalist, William Randolph Hearst, Jr., . . .," *Pravda*, February 13, 1955.
17. "Report of the First Vice Chairman of the Council of Ministers and the Minister of Foreign Affairs of the U.S.S.R., Deputy V. M. Molotov," *Pravda*, February 8, 1955.
18. F. Konstantinov, "I. V. Stalin and the Question of Communist Construction," *Pravda*, March 5, 1955.
19. Tank Marshal P. Rotmistrov, "For Creative Examination of the Questions of Soviet Military Science," *Red Star*, March 24, 1955.
20. D. T. Shepilov, "The Ideas of Lenin Illuminate the Road to Communism," *Pravda*, April 23, 1955.
21. Marshal of the Soviet Union G. Zhukov, "The Tenth Anniversary of a Great Victory," *Pravda*, May 8, 1955.

22. Bulganin's Report to the Supreme Soviet as quoted in the editorial, "The Inspiring Example of Socialist Labor and the Struggle for Peace and the Friendship of the People," *Kommunist*, No. 1, 1956, p. 5.
23. *Ibid.*
24. A. Nikonov, "In the Contemporary Era War Can Be Prevented," *Kommunist*, No. 6, April, 1956, p. 44.
25. See Paul Kecskemeti, "Limits and Problems of Decompression: The Case of Hungary," *The Annals of the American Academy of Political and Social Science*, May, 1958, pp. 97-106 for a lucid and persuasive treatment.
26. Editorial, "The Unity of the International Communist Movement Is Unshakable," *Kommunist*, No. 11, July, 1956, pp. 6, 7.
27. A. Sobolev, "On the Parliamentary Form of the Transition to Socialism," *Kommunist*, No. 14, September, 1956, pp. 14-32.
28. Editorial, "October's Cause Lives and Conquers," *Kommunist*, No. 15, October, 1956, pp. 3-12.
29. M. Petrov, "American Military Preparations in the Pacific," *Kommunist*, No. 15, October, 1956, p. 90 *et passim*.
30. Editorial, "Raise High the Banner of Marxist-Leninist Ideology," *Kommunist*, No. 1, January, 1957, pp. 3-14.
31. "Resolution of the Plenum of the Central Committee of the Communist Party of the Soviet Union (Adopted on the Basis of the Reports of Comrades Baibakov, N. K., and Saburov, M. Z.),"*Pravda*, December 25, 1956.
32. *Ibid.* On the following day a *Pravda* editorial on the Plenum also failed to mention Khrushchev's name.
33. "The Answers of N. S. Khrushchev to Questions by the Editors of the Newspaper *Rude Pravo*," *Pravda*, January 1, 1957.
34. "Bringing in the New Year in the Kremlin," *Pravda*, January 2, 1957.
35. "Speech of Comrade N. A. Bulganin at the Chinese-Russian Friendship Meeting," *Pravda*, January 18, 1957.
36. "Joint Soviet-Chinese Declaration," *Pravda*, January 19, 1957.
37. "Speech by N. I. Beliaev in Barnaul," *Pravda*, January 20, 1957.
38. "Speech of Comrade L. M. Kaganovich in Krasnoiarsk," *Pravda*, January 23, 1957.
39. A. Turov, "The U.S.A. Brandishes Atomic Weapons," *Red Star*, January 25, 1957.
40. "Joint Soviet-Czechoslovak Declaration Dated January 29, 1957, Signed by the Chairman of the Council of Ministers, of the U.S.S.R., N. A. Bulganin, and by the President of the Czech Republic, William Shiroky," *Pravda*, January 30, 1957.
41. "L. F. Il'ichev's Statement," *Pravda*, February 7, 1957.
42. "Speech of D. T. Shepilov," *Pravda*, February 13, 1957.
43. "Resolution of the Plenum of the Central Committee of the Communist Party of the Soviet Union on the Report of Comrade Khrushchev, N. S., Adopted February 14, 1957," *Pravda*, February 16, 1957.
44. Deputy of the Supreme Soviet of the U.S.S.R., Thrice Hero of the Soviet Union, Major General of Aviation I. Kozhedub, "Always on Guard," *Sovetskaia aviatsiia (Soviet Aviation)*, February 17, 1957.

45. "The Speech of Comrade N. S. Khrushchev at a Reception in the Embassy of the People's Republic of Bulgaria, February 18, 1957," *Red Star*, February 20, 1957.

46. M. Marinin, "Peaceful Coexistence—The High Road of International Relations," *Pravda*, March 18, 1957.

47. "Comrade N. S. Khrushchev's Answers to the Questions of the Editors of the American Newspaper, *Grand Rapids Herald*," *Pravda*, March 19, 1957.

48. Colonel G. Fedorov, Candidate in the Philosophical Sciences, "On the Content of Soviet Military Ideology," *Red Star*, March 22, 1957.

49. "Message of the Chairman of the Council of Ministers of the U.S.S.R., N. A. Bulganin, to the Prime Minister of Norway, Einar Gerhardsen," *Pravda*, March 27, 1957.

50. "Message of the Chairman of the Council of Ministers of the U.S.S.R., N. A. Bulganin, to the Prime Minister of Denmark, H. K. Hansen," *Red Star*, March 31, 1957.

51. "N. S. Khrushchev's Interview with Henry Shapiro . . .," *Pravda*, November 17, 1957.

52. "On the Further Perfection of the Organization of the Direction of Industry and Construction, Theses of Comrade N. S. Khrushchev's Report," *Pravda*, March 30, 1957.

53. "Speech of Comrade N. S. Khrushchev at a Meeting of the Agricultural Workers of the Central Black Soil Zone Regions on March 30, 1957," *Pravda*, April 1, 1957.

54. "Comrade N. S. Khrushchev's Speech at a Reception in the Embassy of the Albanian People's Republic, April 15, 1957," *Red Star*, April 17, 1957.

55. "Report of E. A. Furtseva at the Celebration of the 87th Lenin Birth Anniversary," *Pravda*, April 23, 1957.

CHAPTER SIX

SURPRISE AND THE INITIATION OF WAR

To find a precedent for the employment of war alarms to advance particular factions within the Party it is necessary to go back as far as the late twenties. In the thirties Stalin had suppressed all the Party factions that did not render him unquestioning obedience. Public emphasis on foreign dangers, contrived or genuine, was no longer needed as a weapon in intra-Party disputes. Furthermore, in the late thirties the danger of Soviet involvement in a major war was only too real, and common prudence argued against the dangerous game of playing with war scarces. The death of Stalin and the reappearance of factions within the Party leadership have obviously provided the conditions for a revival of the war scarce as an instrument of domestic politics. This revival would scarcely have been possible, however, without a genuine change in Soviet views about the likelihood of war.

A great many factors affect Soviet estimates of the likelihood of war. Since the advent of nuclear weapons an important factor has been the growing realization in the Soviet Union that the seizure of initiative and the consequent achievement of surprise give much greater advantages in modern war than ever before. Another consideration is the Russian conviction that as the Soviet Union becomes stronger in comparison with her strongest opponent the danger of a war not of Soviet making recedes. Since 1953 these beliefs have jointly affected Soviet views on national security, but for analytical purposes it is convenient to treat them separately. Both factors, however, arise from a common source, namely the changes brought about in Soviet strategic thought by a growing appreciation of the role of nuclear weapons. These changes are the subject of the present chapter.

Since the publication of Talenskii's article in November, 1953, Soviet ideas on strategy have undergone continual modification. Before 1953 there is no evidence that Soviet leaders had done any serious thinking about strategy in the nuclear age. Even after that time, many years passed before the new ideas became operative.

Every discovery must pass through several stages before it achieves its maximum effect on society. Elaborate institutional arrangements are required to put military theories into effect. Thousands, if not millions, of people must participate. Often years of research, development, training, and indoctrination must precede the desired state of readiness. Especially under modern conditions, generals cannot execute a strategy, no matter how brilliantly conceived, until great numbers of officers and noncommissioned officers have been trained to execute their various parts in the whole plan. Even when the generals have fully realized the implications of a new weapon, much planning and training are required to exploit its potentialities in practice. To take an example in the field of logistics, the American Civil War demonstrated how important railroads were for the deployment and supply of troops; but not until the Franco-Prussian War were mobilization and the initial campaign planned in terms of rail transport. When World War I broke out, all the major powers were organized to use their railroads to maximum strategic effect.

Let us suppose that a major European power, before World War I, had regarded its railroads as primarily of commercial importance in wartime, and only ancillary in mobilization and supply. Such a power would have been at a military disadvantage, not through ignorance of the principles or lack of skill in the operation of railroads, but through a failure of doctrine: the absence of an official military policy for the employment of railroads in wartime. This hypothetical case points to the importance of doctrine in military affairs. Without a suitable policy and proper training and indoctrination throughout all ranks, the possession of the latest weapons and other materiel may be of little strategic importance.

When the muzzle-loading musket was the main weapon of armies, indoctrination and discipline were suited to its qualities. The musket, although its accuracy was poor and its range short, could stop an advancing enemy when fired en masse by a compact line of musketeers. Since reloading was slow, a second line of men was ready to fire while the first was reloading and, by the time a third line had fired, the first line of musketeers was ready to fire again. If any of the musketeers fell the ranks were closed by men from behind, for the line formation had to hold. When the infantry weapon had such a low fire power, perfection in parade-ground drill and an almost mechanical obedience to command were the primary objects of indoctrination and training. With the advent of rifles, and later machine guns, the doctrine of infantry tactics had to change, for increasing fire power made the old compact line more of a liability than an asset. In the realm of infantry tactics, as in other military spheres, the introduction of new weapons has tended to precede the evolution of doctrine that they necessitate.

The problems of developing doctrine and standard procedures for the employment of nuclear weapons have been difficult for all the nuclear powers because of the enormity of the weapon and the paucity of experience in its use. A satisfactory doctrine for the employment of a new weapon usually has to wait on the tests of war. Strategic bombing is a good example. Before the Second World War British and American officers had grasped the broad strategic possibilities of air bombing, but they were far from understanding how it could be made strategically decisive. Only actual experience in war demonstrated how great a weight of bombs was required to effect a given object and the nature of the priorities in target systems that could contribute most to victory. It was not until almost the end of World War II that the principles of aerial bombardment were properly adjusted to the capabilities of the weapons involved.

The terrible destructiveness of nuclear weapons makes it undesirable, to say the least, that the birth of a sound doctrine for their employment should depend on the test of battle. It has become imperative to develop doctrines in peacetime for using them and for defending oneself against them.

Russian military writing has always stressed the importance of doctrine and of the indoctrination of officers and men. In line with this policy, Russia has probably permitted less independence and initiative to junior officers in practice than most other great powers. The absence for several years (1945-1953) of any Soviet press discussions of the strategic and tactical implications of nuclear weapons can be interpreted to mean that the Soviet Union was backward in nuclear doctrine and indoctrination and that in the event of a war, she would not have been able to use whatever nuclear weapons she possessed to the best advantage. It will be argued below that this interpretation is correct.

Until the latter part of 1953 the Soviet press, including the military press, had almost no information about the effects of nuclear weapons. The propaganda line, repeated year after year, that the Western powers were mistaken in their exclusive reliance on nuclear weapons was a poor substitute for a Soviet doctrine governing the employment of the country's brand-new, if limited, nuclear arsenal. Not only the newspapers but the military publishing houses and academies were afraid to discuss the new military problems that had arisen since 1945. The editors of *Voennaia mysl'* (*Military Thought*), writing in March, 1955, after Malenkov had been deposed and after the publication of Rotmistrov's article on the importance of surprise, looked disapprovingly at the past:

> At a meeting of the leading staff of the armed forces, Marshals of the Soviet Union N. A. Bulganin and G. K. Zhukov gave a high evaluation to our military cadres and . . . [advocated] a thorough study of modern military technology and advanced military theory. . . . But in this regard, as speeches at the meetings noted, everything is not

in good order. Military scientific work in the armed forces still lags. For too long our military scientific cadres have confined themselves to repeating truths long and well known—to the detriment of the situation and to the detriment of the investigation of a number of urgent new problems. . . .

We have no new interesting books . . . which pose the problems of military science with adequate sharpness and which propose original methods for their resolution.

Our periodical military press still does not do everything to develop Soviet military science. The articles published in the military journals are often far removed in their theme and content from urgent military problems; they are general and unspecific, one-sided and poorly conceived. In a number of cases discussions, which are one of the effective instruments for the development of military theory, are on secondary problems, proceed sluggishly, drag out; some are still not completed. These faults characterize all our journals, including . . . *Military Thought.*

The editors of our journal in particular held back without good grounds the publication of the article by Tank Marshal P. A. Rotmistrov, "On the Role of Surprise in Modern War," thereby revealing an absence of the boldness required to pose a new, urgent question of great significance for the correct understanding of the character of modern war.

If we are talking about the reasons which cause the backwardness in the development of our military science in general, then the chief of these is the *fear* to say something new, or to say something different from what has already been said by one or another authority. It is enough to familiarize oneself with the military scientific literature issued in the postwar period to become convinced of this.

Instead of taking the statements of authorities as starting propositions for the expansion and creative elaboration of military theory, and instead of boldly presenting new questions, many research people have limited themselves to mere logic chopping, to commentary on well-known statements and to the endless production of quotations. As a result of this, views once expressed by great theoreticians or important men of affairs are converted into dogma and these research works acquire a Talmudic character and actually delay further progress in military science.

Such a pernicious style in military scientific work leads to marking time and hinders correct understanding. As historical conditions change many propositions once completely justified no longer meet the requirements of a new situation. . . .

It cannot be recognized as normal, however, that books and articles issued during and after the war, instead of being objective scientific research in military theory and in the historical facts, are in the majority of cases merely a repetition of what Stalin said at various times. This business [military theory] was bound to harbor toadies eager to employ what was already prepared and quite convenient, which they often presented as their own. It was easiest of all to copy existing statements, especially from such an authority as I. V. Stalin. Such copying, which freed one from the necessity of thinking about serious questions, held back creative thought and obviously damaged our military science. . . .

One must also point to the serious neglect of theory in some important aspects of the military art, particularly strategy. Our military scientific institutes actually do not concern themselves with the theory of strategy, considering it to be a sphere for the creative activity only of the supreme high command. Therefore they do not prepare qualified scientific cadres for that purpose.

The necessity to elaborate strategic theory thoroughly in modern conditions is perfectly obvious, since the circle of persons concerned with strategic questions and participating in wartime strategic leadership is becoming ever larger. These persons, certainly, should have a comprehensive knowledge of theory for the preparation and conduct of war. . . .

Our military academies have not yet really become the creative and organizational centers of military and scientific theory. The academies have not yet acquired the rights of full citizenship in military scientific work.

Scholasticism and Talmudism are still cultivated in the scholarly practice of the academies. There are still not a few teachers who accustom the students to answering questions with memorized quotations and formulas. . . .

One of the most serious causes retarding the development of military science is the incorrect attitude toward the selection of military scientific cadres and the absence of a well thought out training system. We have not yet put an end to the bad practice of assigning to scientific and pedagogic work people who cannot cope with their work with the troops and people who have no fighting experience. . . .

The situation in the publication of military scientific literature is poor. In the postwar years hardly a single significant work in the sphere of military theory was published. Books are lacking on the history of the Soviet Armed Forces, on the theory of military science, on military ideology; there are no books on the Soviet military art and no memoirs of the prominent Soviet and foreign military leaders. . . .

The Military Publishing House publishes military literature only if articles on the subjects have appeared in the military journals more than once or if the manuscript has already traversed a long road of editing, approval, agreements and consultation. Why such a system to pass military scientific works? Is it really necessary to have so many consultations, reviews, and opinions in order to print a book on a particular military scientific theme? Unquestionably, it is not necessary. The explanation is the fear of the Military Publishing House that something might happen. The majority of reviews, assessments, and opinions are not employed to help the author in his work on the book but as an umbrella for protection against the issuance of an unsuccessful book.

This leads to a situation where every original view and thought is levelled and adjusted to the officially promulgated position. The main . . . departments of the Ministry of Defense are thereby overburdened with the superfluous

work of reviewing and approving all sorts of books and
works, with obvious detriment to their main tasks. . . .[1]

The underlying import of these strictures seems to be as
follows. Early in 1955 the military academies were still conducting their instruction in terms of World War II; and war
planning, in the absence of an up-to-date official doctrine, could
not take proper account of such novelties as nuclear weapons.
It may be argued that the long quotation from *Military
Thought,* authoritative as it undoubtedly is, condemns dogmatic conservatism in very general terms and says nothing
specific about a lack of doctrinal provision for nuclear warfare. One may argue that the Soviet Union has developed
nuclear weapons speedily and has achieved still more remark-
able advances in ballistic missiles. How, then, can presumably
intelligent Soviet planners have lacked an adequate doctrine
for nuclear warfare as late as 1955? We have tried to demonstrate above that the mere possession of the latest weapons does
not automatically produce a military doctrine to maximize
their effectiveness. Progress in the development of nuclear
weapons and delivery vehicles does not necessarily bring the
concomitant development of an up-to-date doctrine for their
employment. That doctrine has not kept pace with weapons
development in the Soviet Union is strongly suggested by the
Soviet conception of war over the years.

In the spring of 1947 the famous Soviet historian, Eugène
Tarlé, described in a public lecture the nature of a hypothetical
war between the United States and the U.S.S.R. As soon as the
war started the Soviet Union would occupy Western Europe.
The Red army would meet little resistance, for one Frenchmen
in three was a communist. The bombing of Moscow and Leningrad, or of Russian-occupied Europe, would accomplish nothing. The two sides would never be able to come to grips and
would fall back on a war of nerves. The war would begin with
the atomic bomb but would not end with it, because American
bombs would be unable to solve the problem posed by the
Russian army, the largest and best in the world.[2]

Tarlé's picture of the war of the future is quite consistent with what we know of Soviet weapons development in 1947. In the Russian view of that time the war would be *with* the United States but *for* Europe. If the Soviet Union could eject the United States from the continent of Europe and take or neutralize Great Britain, then neither side could really get at the other. The destructiveness of nuclear weapons has so permeated our thinking that we now tend to dismiss such a view as some kind of a propaganda smokescreen. Yet, as matters were in 1947, it was not an unreasonable blueprint for a major war. An American nuclear assault on the Soviet Union would then have had two weak points: the number of bombs and the delivery vehicles.

The number of bombs in the American stockpile was very low. In 1949 the Congressional Joint Committee on Atomic Energy published reliable testimony that the American weapons position in 1947 had "verged upon the tragic" and that disclosure of the small number of American bombs would have threatened the deterrent position of the United States.[3] Without the information provided by espionage, which apparently was considerable, the Russians could have deduced from their own progress and their knowledge of physics that the United States then possessed only a limited number of nuclear bombs.

Whether each of the few American nuclear bombs would reach a target in the Soviet Union depended on the American delivery system and the Soviet defenses. In the early years after World War II the mainstay of the American bombing force was the B-29, which had been designed during the war to bomb cities from forward bases. In the event of another war it was intended to employ these bombers in the same way, so that an American bombing campaign against the Soviet Union would depend on the continued operation of overseas bases. Soon after the World War the Soviet Union manufactured many Tu-4's, essentially copies of the B-29, which if skillfully employed could harry the air bases from which the B-29's had to fly, thus reducing the damage that the American Air Force could inflict. Furthermore, the Soviet Union early began to make heavy investments in warning systems and interceptors. The warning and interception plan was essentially that of

World War II and was designed to destroy a certain percentage of the attacking force. Since single atomic weapons were so destructive, an air-defense system that would probably let some bombers through was far from satisfactory. Nevertheless, in view of all the other factors then prevailing, the situation would be far from desperate for the Soviet Union. Once she had overrun the continent and knocked out Great Britain by a submarine campaign more destructive than either of the German ones, she could reasonably hope that after some bomb damage to her territory, neither the Soviet Union nor the United States could get at each other, so that eventually the United States would have to accept the Soviet possession of Europe.

It would be a mistake, however, to suppose that the Soviet leaders actively sought a war because they could envision a favorable outcome. The hazards of war are notoriously uncertain and the Soviet leaders had to reckon with the possibility of internal disaffection in the event of war. Soviet diplomacy at that time strongly suggests the desire to avoid a large war. Nevertheless, if war should come, the Soviet Union could reasonably expect a favorable outcome. Why establish a doctrine for the employment of nuclear weapons when you have none and you can foresee attaining your ends without them?

By 1949 the Soviet Union had mastered the technique of producing nuclear weapons. One would expect the Soviet leaders to have begun to think about war in terms of nuclear weapons. The evidence suggests that they believed in the importance of the new weapons but did not consider that the nature of warfare had changed. They needed no doctrine of nuclear warfare to justify heavy investments in atomic bombs and delivery systems. It was enough that the fission reaction was the most powerful explosion yet created by man, and that the United States had harnessed this reaction to military purposes. Moreover, prestige was enormously important to the Soviet leaders. The attractiveness of keeping up with, perhaps outstripping, the West in weapons development and thereby demonstrating Soviet technical mastery should not be underestimated.

That a new military doctrine was not an ingredient in the Soviet scheme of things is suggested by the history of the development of missiles in the Soviet Union. In the Second World War the Germans had developed and employed the V-2 to good effect. This missile had caused damage to London and later had interfered with the operation of the port of Antwerp. Its effects would have been far more serious had it been used in greater numbers over a longer period. Its effective range was over 100 miles and the warhead of about one ton was adequate for its purpose, area bombing. From the Soviet point of view it seemed an excellent idea to develop the V-2 further. A 1000-mile range, a two-ton warhead, and greater accuracy would make it a very promising weapon in a war of the kind foreseen by Tarlé. It could seriously hamper the operation of ports and airfields in Great Britain and make an American landing on the continent very difficult. Thus the use of ballistic missiles could be fitted into a picture of war not essentially modified by the existence of nuclear weapons.

A program of rocket-motor development could be justified for a "defense-of-Europe" role, but the recent launching of earth satellites demonstrates that the Soviet scientists must long ago have been permitted or instructed to develop rocket motors of far greater thrust than would be required to interdict ports and airfields in Great Britain and North Africa. It is unlikely that the Soviet leaders thought as early as 1947 of using missiles to carry intercontinental nuclear weapons, for the latter were then too heavy. Although it is possible that the Russians thought of improving the atomic-weapons design for missile warheads, it seems safer to follow an account furnished by the defector Tokaev in 1950. The passage of time has confirmed both the essentials and the details of Tokaev's statement. Here we read that the Soviet leaders determined in 1947 to develop very-long-range missiles and very-long-range aircraft in order to be able to hit the United States. In the long and circumstantial account furnished by Tokaev, nuclear weapons are not even mentioned.[4] Apparently the Russians decided that if rocket motors were improved they could deliver either very heavy loads of explosives at short and medium ranges or modest loads at intercontinental range. In Peenemünde, the German scientists, some of whom the Russians had captured, had already planned a ballistic missile with a 3000-mile range. The Russians probably also expected improvements in chemical explosives and perhaps even the use of nuclear warheads, but in 1947 long-range rockets meant first and foremost the ability to hit the United States with *something*. Even if the most expensive missile could do no more than deliver a thousand pounds of TNT to New York, the political and psychological value of possessing this capability must have seemed priceless to the Russians.

The Soviet leaders, as we have seen, had many reasons for adapting new weapons to an older military philosophy. When these reasons are properly understood, the complaint in *Military Thought* in March, 1955, that doctrinal stagnation had prevailed since 1945 does not seem inconsistent with the successful weapons developments of the same period.

In 1947 Tarlé's description of a war over a helpless Western Europe, in which the Soviet Union would suffer no more than an acceptable amount of damage from American nuclear weapons, was not implausible. As time passed, however, it became much less convincing. As nuclear weapons and delivery vehicles developed, what had been a sober judgment of Soviet prospects in a war with the United States became reckless complacency. A combination of factors gradually transformed the situation. The major ones were an increase in the number of American nuclear weapons, the greater effectiveness of these weapons and their delivery systems, and changes in the Soviet ability to reduce this effectiveness.

Although the number of nuclear weapons in the American stockpile has always been a closely guarded secret, official spokesmen and Congressional and other hearings have revealed that the Russian nuclear explosion of 1949 and the outbreak of the Korean War accelerated American production of these weapons. One can surmise that each year saw an increase and that by the time Stalin died the United States probably had a formidable number of bombs. The H-bomb tests of 1952 and

1954 demonstrated how greatly the destructive effect of nuclear weapons had grown.

The improvement in American delivery systems constituted a growing threat in the eyes of the Soviet leaders. The B-36's, which became operational in the late forties, were a great improvement over the B-29's largely because of their greater range, but they obsolesced as Soviet fighter aircraft outclassed them in speed. The B-47's, introduced during 1953 and 1954, again represented a great improvement because when refueled they had adequate range and their speed made them less vulnerable than the B-36's.

Soviet defenses were far from capable of meeting the growing American threat. The Soviet warning system suffered from serious gaps in altitude coverage. In 1953 Soviet interceptors were so designed that maximum attrition of an attacking bomber force could be expected only in good daylight weather.

These statements are very general, but the point that they are intended to support is probably valid: since some indefinite time about 1953 an American strike against the Soviet Union might well have meant damage so serious that the latter could never have recovered sufficiently to redress the balance and win the war. The destruction would be maximized if the United States achieved surprise. After 1953 the picture of a future war drawn by Tarlé in 1947 was hopelessly out of date. Such views could only be supported by wishful thinking.

The changes in weapons were so far-reaching that Soviet theories and practices would probably have adapted to them even if Stalin, whose name and prestige had been closely associated with the older military theories, had lived another ten years. The death of the dictator, however, probably made the task of the innovators easier. Part of the intellectual preparation for doctrinal progress was the controversy about the nature of war, described above in Chapter 2, in which the preponderant role of Stalin's "permanently operating factors" was questioned. Between the end of 1953 and the beginning of 1958 the elements of a new grand strategy emerged. It is helpful to divide this development into two stages. In the first stage, from 1953 to the spring of 1955, the older strategic views were attacked and somewhat modified, but no official position was taken in favor of a revision of Soviet military doctrine. In the second stage, from 1955 onward, the initial nuclear strike, with all its implications, was officially recognized as being critically important; and thereafter the aim of Soviet policy was to create and maintain the ability to deliver the first blow.

Appropriately, all the early evidence of ferment in Soviet thinking about military strategy was concerned in one way or another with surprise attack. As long as the old formula about the permanently operating factors remained official dogma, surprise by definition remained a subordinate factor and could not possibly decide the outcome of a war. Until 1955 surprise could only be presented as the most important of the secondary factors contributing to victory.

An article by a Soviet colonel in the issue of *Military Thought* for October, 1953, contained what appears to be the earliest public statement on the increased importance of surprise. The new weapons were now described, for the first time, as highly dangerous instruments of attack, capable of causing untold suffering. Hitherto their destructiveness had been minimized. In conformity with the still-reigning emphasis on the permanently operating factors, the author continued:

> Surprise attack, it is understood, has been and remains a collateral factor which does not decide the fate of a war. It is known from the experience of war, however, that surprise can bring great advantages to the aggressor and great harm to the one suffering attack. It would be unforgivable, therefore, not to reckon with this factor, or to underestimate it.[5]

This statement magnified the role of surprise without contradicting the existing doctrine of the primacy of the permanently operating factors.

In the journal *Voennyi vestnik* (*Military Herald*), Major General Pukhovskii singled out surprise as the temporary factor most capable of playing a significant role, especially in the initial period of a war. Development of new military weapons, he went on, meant that the factor of surprise could be even more important in a future war than in the past.[6]

A few weeks later a much more important soldier, Marshal Vasilevskii, published an article in *Red Star* that seemed to brush away these attempts to ascribe greater significance to surprise. He repeated the old statement that Soviet military science, unlike the bourgeois variety, "did not exaggerate the significance of such transitory factors as . . . surprise."[7] Only five days later two colonels stated in the same newspaper that Soviet military science, while recognizing the decisive influence of the permanently operating factors on the course and outcome of a war, was "far from denying the influence of temporary factors, particularly surprise attack, upon the course of the war."[8]

In an article written at almost the same time for *Military Thought,* Colonel Piatkin, too, gave surprise attack more than the traditional emphasis. He said it was the most important of the temporarily acting factors, and assumed still greater importance when atomic weapons were used: "However, the temporary factors cannot give permanent successes nor decide the fate of the war as a whole."[9]

In May, speaking on the anniversary of the victory over Germany, Marshal Vasilevskii said that surprise attack had a limited significance, without adding as he had done in February that it was improper to "overestimate" the importance of surprise. He continued to insist that the outcome of the war would be determined by the permanently operating factors.[10]

These verbal evidences of an unresolved conflict over the importance of surprise attack with nuclear weapons become more impressive when viewed in conjunction with the controversy then raging over Talenskii's article on the nature of war. Moreover, in February, 1955, *Military Thought* published an article on surprise by Rotmistrov that went far beyond the compromise formulations of early 1954, and the editors confessed their error in refusing publication until that time. Thus hindsight helps us to see the verbal peculiarities of the 1954 articles as harbingers of a new doctrine that was soon to put the permanently operating factors in the shade.

The switch from tentative suggestions to outright revisionism was made almost in passing by a naval captain, Avramenko, who emphasized the decisive role of the permanently operating factors, and then fairly contradicted this orthodox view by calling it incorrect to underestimate "such a factor as surprise [which], especially if new and mighty weapons were employed, might in certain conditions even determine the outcome of the war. . . ."[11]

Colonel Kargalov, in a contribution to an anthology on military science said that the newest military technology had very greatly increased the role of the surprise factor, although in an earlier version of the same article, written for *Red Star,* he had been less definite.[12] In the same collection Major General Pukhovskii made a strong statement on the growing importance of surprise:

> Of the temporary, transitory factors Soviet military science singles out the element of surprise as the most effective and capable of playing a significant role, especially in the initial, first, period of a war. It should be said that, with the development of military technology and the employment of new means of destruction, the surprise element acquires even more significance than it had in past wars. The employment by the opponent of the element of surprise cannot impose any serious damage upon the country suffering the attack if that country and its armed forces are always ready to repulse the foe. If, however, the enemy catches that country unawares [i.e., with unready defenses] and acquires the initiative even if only for a few hours, then by employing modern powerful weapons he inflicts tremendous disaster and destruction.[13]

Later in the same article Pukhovskii explicitly assumes Soviet superiority in all the permanently operating factors, as well as in atomic fission and fusion weapons: "Soviet military science assumes that at the present time the role of surprise has increased and has become one of the factors decisive for victory. But the Soviet armed forces will not permit the enemy to employ that factor and will reply with crushing counterblows to any aggressor's attempt at attack."[14] In other words, the

SURPRISE AND THE INITIATION OF WAR   183

enemy may strike the first blow, but he will fail to reap the
advantages of surprise.

In the same anthology Colonel Vasilenko stated that some
Americans, notably Senators McCarthy and Knowland and
Admirals Radford and Carney, had proposed a preventive war
against the Soviet Union. Given Soviet vigilance, such an attack

> . . . could not bring the imperialists success because the
> fate of war is decided in the last analysis by the per-
> manently acting factors. . . . However, it is impossible to
> underestimate the very great damage of which an aggressor
> who attacks unexpectedly is capable. The role of the fac-
> tor of surprise attack in connection with the appearance
> of the atomic and hydrogen bomb has grown seriously.
> This relates not only to the moment of the outbreak of
> the war, to its beginning, but to the whole course of the
> war. It should be recalled that the best means against the
> crafty schemes of the aggressors is the constant readiness
> of our army, air force, and fleet to foil the surprise attack
> and to deal crushing counterblows immediately against
> the opponent.[15]

In 1954, then, we find Soviet military writings that insist
on the primacy of the permanently operating factors and at
the same time suggest that a surprise attack with nuclear
weapons may determine the course, and perhaps the outcome,
of the whole war. This combination of ideas is at best obscure,
at worst inconsistent. The insistence that general strength will
determine the outcome of the war in the long run does not at
first seem consistent with the suggestion that the outcome can
be determined in the initial phase by nuclear surprise attack.
The difficulty disappears, however, when we notice the further
insistence on the role of defense. Adequate defenses, say Pukhovskii and others, coupled with vigilance, can and will deny
the enemy the advantages of surprise. He will be repulsed and
counterattacked. At this stage in Soviet thinking there seems
to have been a certain acceptance of the idea that the enemy
would get in a first blow. But not for long, as we shall see.

The debate over military surprise was not settled until
early in 1955. Meanwhile the man who initiated the debate on

basic military policy, Talenskii, was relieved of his post as editor of *Military Thought* some time in 1954. As soon as Malenkov was replaced, the editors of *Military Thought* published a statement on the role of surprise in modern war going far beyond anything said in 1954. Further, the editors said, as we have seen, that they had been in error in refusing to print this article when first submitted. It is not in the least surprising that the political implications of the contending strategic concepts played such an important role. The existence of a debate about the best military strategy, involving massive allocations of money and readjustments in foreign policy, necessarily aroused strong feelings in the highest decisionmaking bodies of the state. Until these bodies resolved all differences of opinion, the formulas advanced by lesser persons had to straddle two or more views. Meanwhile further development took place in the ideas of Soviet officers about the importance of the initial nuclear strike and its place in Soviet strategy.

The most important single article arguing that surprise attack with nuclear weapons differed in essentials from surprise attack in any earlier period was the one whose publication had been held up by the editors of *Military Thought*. The author, Tank Marshal Rotmistrov, carefully demonstrated how much had changed in the last few years. In the first paragraph, Rotmistrov stated the basic thesis of the revisionists, that surprise could decide the fate of the whole war:

> The experience of history has shown that the skillful employment of surprise brings true success, not only in battles and operations, but also in war. If a war starts with a surprise attack, then as a rule it [the surprise attack] essentially determines the strategic victory in the first stage of the war and secures the conditions for the advantageous development of subsequent military activities, which [development] is obtained if the initial strategic result is correctly assessed and forces and means for the purposeful exploitation of the success are prepared while the opponent has not yet been able to localize it.[16]

Rotmistrov showed how surprise had always been important in military operations and how the Russian military heroes

Suvorov and Kutuzov had employed surprise to good effect. He analyzed some surprise attacks that had been strategically important. The Japanese assault on the Russian Far East naval squadron during the night of February 8-9, 1904, eliminated Russian sea power in the Pacific and removed any danger to the supply line between Japan and her ground forces in Manchuria. In planning for the First World War, the German General Staff expected that a surprise thrust through Belgium would assure victory. The Germans counted on superior military ability and superior artillery to bring quick success. Underestimation of their opponents' military capacities and of the length of the war, however, brought defeat. The failure of the Germans to gain victory by strategic surprise did not stop them from seeking success a second time by the same method. In the Second World War the Germans did succeed in defeating Poland, France, Holland, and Belgium by employing surprise and superiority. In the forty-five-day campaign of 1940 Hitlerite Germany completely destroyed the Anglo-French army. Not only surprise, Rotmistrov explained, but political factors, made this victory possible. As a result of surprise attack Germany not only gained "intermediate strategic goals but in a very short time obtained the capitulation of a number of European governments."

In its surprise attack against the Soviet Union, continued the Russian marshal, the German army had the advantages of two years' wartime experience and a certain superiority in the quantity of military equipment. The Germans used these advantages to gain strategic results in the first phase of the war and put the Soviet army in a very difficult position.

The surprise Japanese aerial blow against Pearl Harbor in December, 1941, caused important damage to the American navy and "predetermined its two-year passivity in the subsequent phase of the war." From these historical facts Rotmistrov concluded:

> Thus on the basis of the experience of past wars it is possible to assert that surprise, successfully accomplished, not only influences the course of battles and operations but in

certain circumstances can influence to a significant extent
the course and even the outcome of the whole war.[17]

This does not mean, cautioned Rotmistrov, that surprise is the
only condition for victory, as some imperialists say, but it does
mean that one cannot afford to underestimate the significance
of a surprise blow in the first phase of the war: "To the extent
that equipment has developed and new, powerful, and effective
weapons have appeared and have been incorporated, the significance of surprise in war grows more and more." In other
words, surprise is even more important today than it was in the
historical cases cited to demonstrate its importance.

Rotmistrov took up the theme that the past was not a reliable guide. Even if one recognized the importance of surprise
attack in earlier wars, one could "not now be limited by this
experience alone."[18] Rotmistrov went on to give what has since
remained the official Soviet appraisal of the importance of surprise attack:

> Surprise attack, employing atomic and hydrogen weapons
> and other modern means of conflict, now takes on new
> forms and is capable of leading to significantly greater re-
> sults than in the past war. It must be plainly said that
> when atomic and hydrogen weapons are employed, sur-
> prise is one of the decisive conditions for the attainment
> of success not only in battles and operations, but also in
> war as a whole. . . . Surprise attack with the massive em-
> ployment of new weapons can cause the rapid collapse of
> a government whose capacity to resist is low as a conse-
> quence of radical faults in its social and economic structure
> and also as a consequence of an unfavorable geographic
> position.[19]

Rotmistrov felt that surprise attack played an important
part in the strategy of the United States and Great Britain, and
that the American and British leaders would expect, by bombing the deep rear of the Soviet Union, to put her war facilities
and industrial centers out of commission, to paralyze transportation, and to demoralize the population. Although the Americans expected so much from surprise attack, they realized that

aerial blows alone could not decide the outcome of a future war and therefore they were also assembling mighty land forces. Rotmistrov had no better answer to this imagined threat than that German surprise did not succeed, an argument that was outdated by his own admission. Imperialist strategy, he continued, was forced to rely on the surprise attack because the capitalists could not expect to sustain the strains of a long war. Moreover the imperialist aggressors had often in the past attacked by surprise. The Soviet Union "should always be ready for pre-emptive action against the aggressor's schemes." The imperialist desire to achieve surprise and take the Soviet Union unawares made it necessary for the Soviet government to be constantly ready.

Rotmistrov brought to its logical conclusion the discussion and controversy of 1953-1954. If a surprise attack could indeed determine, or even seriously affect, the outcome of a war it was even more necessary to surprise, and avoid being surprised, than in the past. A surprise attack could be frustrated if the enemy were himself surprised as he prepared to strike:

> The duty of the Soviet armed forces is not to permit an enemy surprise attack on our country and, in the event of an attempt to accomplish one, not only to repel the attack successfully but also to deal the enemy counterblows, or even pre-emptive [*uprezhdaiushchie*] surprise blows, of terrible destructive force. For this the Soviet army and navy possess everything necessary.[20]

The pre-emptive blow, then, was one designed to forestall an enemy strike. This was a new element in Soviet thinking. The success of a pre-emptive strategy, Rotmistrov continued, required prompt detection of a concrete war danger. The Soviet armed forces must not only discover the best means to repel enemy blows but also to deal advance counterblows, completely unexpected by the enemy about to attack the Soviet Union.

After advocating a Soviet strategy of "pre-emptive" attack to forestall the known aggressive plans of an enemy, Marshal

Rotmistrov carefully distinguished it from a strategy of "preventive" war:

> The growth of the role of surprise, in combination with
> the changed character of contemporary war, indicates that
> if we are forced to take up arms we should be able to gain
> the strategic initiative by using the surprise element to
> the full. . . . The aspiration to seize and hold the strategic
> initiative should not be understood as an intention to
> begin a preventive war against the enemies of the U.S.S.R.
> who are preparing to attack us. The Soviet Union
> threatens no one nor is it preparing to attack first, even
> though some governments are conducting a provocative
> military policy, surrounding the territory of our country
> with a network of bases, and feverishly pushing their satel-
> lites to war against us. But in this connection it is neces-
> sary always to remember that historically aggressors have
> frequently used the excuse of preventive war to justify
> pure aggression. Any such attempt, however it may be
> masked, demands that the Soviet army give the aggressor
> who ventures to this extreme a fitting rebuff, according to
> all the rules of the Soviet military art.[21]

The subtle distinctions that can be made between the terms
"pre-emptive" and "preventive" will be discussed later. At
present it is more important to note that readiness to strike a
pre-emptive blow became, early in 1955, a principal aim of
official Soviet policy. This bald assertion will shortly be supported by more evidence. But first it should be emphasized
that it is *not* Soviet policy to admit the adoption of a pre-
emptive strategy.

In January, 1958, an article in *Foreign Affairs** stated the
case for the proposition that the U.S.S.R. had adopted a policy
of readiness for pre-emptive war. Soviet General Kurasov
stoutly denied the truth of this proposition. His argument was
this:

> As history shows, the Soviet Union has more than once
> suffered aggressive attacks and has been forced to conduct
> hard and bloody wars in order to defend her independence

* Written by the author of this book.

as a state. A study of the initial period of the Great Fatherland War could not but direct the attention of military
thinking to the significance of the factor of surprise in
modern wars. It became patently obvious that the surprise attack of the German fascist troops permitted them
temporarily to seize the strategic initiative at the beginning
of the war. The appearance of nuclear weapons and the
possibility for their mass employment against troops and
targets in the rear produced different opinions on the
significance of surprise attack in a future war and on the
measures for opposing such an attack. This prompted
some military authors to engage in an investigation of the
significance of the factor of surprise in modern war. Theoretical statements in the press by individual authors on
measures to frustrate an aggressor's surprise attack were
interpreted in the Western press as a summons to pre-
emptive war.[22]

This somewhat equivocal denial of the existence of an official requirement that the Soviet Union be able to strike pre-
emptively is open to question on two grounds. In the Soviet
Union high officials writing in an organ of the Ministry of
War, as Rotmistrov did, do not make "theoretical statements,"
nor can they be considered to write as "individual authors,"
unless (and this is rare) the article is characterized as being part
of a discussion. The debate opened by Talenskii in 1953 was
so characterized and all the articles pro and con were clearly
designated as parts of that discussion. Second, the editorial in
Military Thought for March, 1955, which was certainly an
official statement, criticized the magazine's former policy in
holding up Rotmistrov's article, and then made the following
unambiguous statement:

> We cannot ignore the lessons of history and we must al-
> ways be ready for pre-emptive actions against the perfidy
> of the aggressors.[23]

Is it not conceivable, one may ask, that Rotmistrov's article
in February, 1955, and its editorial endorsement in March represented merely a temporary aberration of official policy? The

subsequent wide circulation of Rotmistrov's ideas makes this explanation extremely improbable, to say the least.

Rotmistrov soon repeated a number of the conclusions of his *Military Thought* article in *Red Star,* a far more widely read organ. The new version omitted a great deal of the historical argument that appeared in the earlier one and avoided the explicit statement that the Soviet Union should be ready to strike a pre-emptive blow under the appropriate circumstances. The *Red Star* article took the form of a polemic against two writers who had written about the permanently operating factors in a tone that had been standard, if not obligatory, only a year earlier. The essential points of Rotmistrov's two formulations, however, were the same. In each he used identical phrases to say that surprise attack with nuclear weapons could be one of the decisive conditions for success not only in the initial phase but in the whole war. Instead of directly advocating a pre-emptive attack, however, he used circumlocutions about frustrating the "aggressors' schemes" and "not permitting a surprise attack." The latter soon became standard in mass-media references to the subject.

At this stage Rotmistrov did not deny the validity of the formula about the permanently operating factors, but he felt that Soviet military writers erred when they said that the capitalist nations did not take the permanently operating factors into account.[24]

An editorial in the May issue of *Military Thought* left no doubt as to the official character of the pre-emptive strike doctrine:

> The matter goes beyond the exhaustive clarification of the significance of the surprise factor and the study of cases and examples of the employment of surprise in recent wars. The task is the purposeful elaboration of all aspects of this question, especially the elaboration of ways and means to prevent an enemy surprise attack and to deal the opponent pre-emptive blows on every scale—strategic, operational, and tactical.[25]

General Kurochkin, writing in the same issue of *Military Thought,* said: "In order further to guarantee the security of our Motherland against an aggressor's surprise attack, it is necessary to be in a state of full fighting readiness and to be able to deal pre-emptive blows against an enemy who is preparing to attack."[26]

Several public statements in the same month reaffirmed the need for a pre-emptive strategy. Of these, Vasilevskii's was particularly striking because he had earlier insisted on the primacy of the permanently operating factors, probably in resistance to the growing emphasis on the importance of surprise. Vasilevskii now said that the Soviet Union had everything necessary "to deprive the aggressor, should he unleash a new war, of the advantages which long preparation and the suddenness and treachery of the attack could give him."[27] Lieutenant General Braiko of the air force, writing for an air force magazine, said that this service had the duty "to deprive the aggressor of the factor of surprise and not let ourselves be taken unawares. It is necessary for us to nip in the very bud the scheming plans of the warmongers if they dare begin to execute them."[28] The editorial in the same issue of the magazine said that it was not "enough to be prepared and capable of returning blow for blow at the instigator of war." It was also "necessary to deprive the aggressor of the factor of surprise and not let ourselves be taken unawares."[29] General Shatilov, writing a month later, was even more explicit:

> Knowing the savage character of the aggressors, we cannot ignore the plans they are hatching. The Soviet Union threatens no one and is not preparing to attack anyone. But those who think they will find us passive or unprepared to repel aggression will be bitterly disappointed. It would pay the immoderately warlike generals and admirals of the imperialist camp to remember that atomic weapons as well as surprise action are double-edged weapons and that it is hardly sensible to jest with them.[30]

The point of calling surprise a "double-edged weapon" seems unmistakable: the enemy who seeks to surprise us may himself be surprised.

A few months later Marshal Rotmistrov reviewed a book

on surprise attack, written by General Popov before the new policy had been officially adopted. He was merciless in exposing the inconsistencies and absurdities of trying to say at once that surprise was terribly important and that the permanently operating factors were still all-determining. Following the usual Soviet style, Rotmistrov ignored the circumstance that the book he was criticizing had been delivered to the printer at the end of 1954. Thus he used a recently outdated book to drive home a doctrine established since the book was written.[31]

General Popov, who made a hopeless attempt to reconcile the old view of the permanently operating factors with the new view of surprise, was an easy mark. He made the point that surprise could be successful only with superiority in the permanently operating factors. Rotmistrov argued that the side inferior in a number of the permanently operating factors could employ surprise to compensate for its relative weakness. Popov, wrote his critic, had been forced to conclude from his faulty premise that Soviet surprise attack succeeded in the last war because of superiority in the permanently operating factors and that imperialist surprise attack was only adventurism. This, Rotmistrov argued, was unscientific. If success in surprise attack depended on, and was guaranteed by, superiority in the permanently operating factors—a superiority preordained for the Soviet forces—then there was no point in discussing the matter at all. Popov's thesis demonstrated his "incorrect interpretation of the significance of the permanently operating factors as a panacea for all ills." Here Rotmistrov was taking a real step forward from his position of February and March, and from the ideas expressed by the editors of *Military Thought*. No one had said in so many words that the permanently operating factors were being employed as a panacea for all ills. Rotmistrov was approaching a point where the old permanently-operating-factors formula would have to be explicitly abandoned because it interfered with the proper appraisal of surprise.

Rotmistrov attributed more to Popov than the latter meant, in order to prove that the new pre-emptive strategy was best. Popov had said that "aggressive countries, as a rule, attack the peace loving countries when they are not mobilized."[32] Rotmistrov presented this as meaning that there was a "fatalistic inevitability that the peace loving peoples must suffer the aggressor's [opening] blows, and moreover, suddenly." Using this as a point of departure, he outlined his own idea of a strategy to prevent it:

> What is all this for? What is the use of such "theoretical" calculations? What can they offer military practice? Indeed, the problem really is: *by studying the lessons of the past to avoid in the future any kind of possibility of surprise attack on our country by a putative opponent,* which demands constant vigilance by the Soviet armed forces. And in this case the author [Popov], by his assertion expressed on page 9 of the impossibility of foreseeing "the moment of surprise" and of the inevitability of its appearance, unwittingly does a disservice to the cause of inculcating vigilance and battle readiness in our troops.
>
> Naturally it is impossible to foresee every trifle in all cases, but when such events as surprise attack by an aggressor are involved it is possible and, frankly, necessary under any conditions not to permit the moment of surprise whose consequences might at the present time be difficult to overcome. It is absolutely clear and beyond argument that Marxist-Leninist science is fully capable of foreseeing such a significant phenomenon in the life of society as the transition from a condition of peace to a condition of war.[33]

In this statement Rotmistrov added two new facets to the doctrine of the pre-emptive strike. First he made the point that the consequences of a successful surprise attack might be difficult to overcome. This was a corollary of his proposition, made earlier in the year, that surprise might be one of the decisive factors affecting not only the course but also the outcome of the war. More novel, and more important for the formulation of a pre-emptive strategy, was his second point, that the Soviet Union could reasonably expect timely warning of the enemy's preparations for a surprise attack, so that it would not be surprised. In the absence of a belief that timely warning was possible, the whole pre-emptive strategy would be meaningless.

By definition and by logic "pre-emption" required the receipt of warning.

These points were reiterated in 1956 in a long, ambitious book entitled *Militarism,* also published by the Ministry of Defense. The author, Skopin, re-emphasized what had become the standard Soviet line, that strategic surprise could be of tremendous importance and that the Soviet Union, if threatened with attack, would find some way of getting in the first blow. Skopin argued: "Thanks to nuclear weapons strategic surprise has become unusually and unprecedentedly dangerous. Any other evaluation would be blind and naïve. But from this follows not the victory of militarism [that is, the initiator of aggression], but only the very great price of victory over militarism." The capitalists, he continued, thought a surprise nuclear attack the only promising way to win the duel between Capital and Labor. But monopoly capital underestimated both the military strength of the Soviet bloc and its constant readiness to deal with surprise. Furthermore, "the massive popular genius always finds new infallible ways and means for rebuffing treacherous surprise attacks of any size." Then Skopin rhetorically affirmed what had now become an article of faith, that the Soviet Union would always have timely warning of attack: "Just as the chain reaction within the atom produces the sudden splitting of the nucleus, so the surprise attack by militarism produces a 'chain reaction' of retaliatory activity."[34] Virtually the same statements were made as late as October, 1957, when a second edition of Skopin's book was in galleys.[35]

Once it became official doctrine that a successful surprise attack could determine the ultimate outcome of the whole war, the Soviet version of the events of 1941 had to be revised. The very editorial in *Military Thought* that praised Rotmistrov's article and repeated his advocacy of "pre-emptive actions" started a campaign against the then-current doctrine that a planned "active defense" had held off defeat in 1941 and 1942. The relevant passages read:

> The authors of many works [on the war] do not give a correct objective evaluation of events, but give a one-

sided account of the course of the war, seek to embellish and idealize many of the phenomena of the war, do not treat the difficulties adequately, and either maintain silence on our mistakes and shortcomings or minimize them. In research on the war the chief attention has been erroneously devoted to the military events of the second half of the war and to the offensive operations of the Soviet Army . . . in 1944 and 1945 . . . when the enemy had lost the initiative and the ability to conduct offensive operations on a more or less large scale.

As a result of its treacherous invasion the German Fascist Army, as is well known, succeeded in the initial period of the war in gaining important successes. . . . However, people are to be found to this day in our scientific institutes, academies, and the editorial boards of our military journals who represent the failure of 1941 as a victory, characterizing this as the period of the classic form of the so-called "active defense. . . ."

The paeons to active defense and its misinterpretation as something planned in advance lead not only to the distortion of what really happened in 1941 but also to the idealization of this form of war, and incorrectly orient our cadres to the possibility of its repetition in a future war.

The very designation of the initial period of the war as the "period of active defense," which has wide currency in military literature and has entered the programs of instruction of our military-pedagogical institutes, incorrectly represents the actual character of that period, since the military activities of our troops for the most part had the character of withdrawal operations.[36]

Here the editors of *Military Thought* drew attention to a particularly striking example of the danger of falling victim to one's own propaganda, that is, of accepting as guiding principles statements made only for political purposes. Marshal Rotmistrov, obviously a leader in the fight for more realism, took issue with a writer who had written in the traditional way that the German surprise attack had turned into an unexpected catastrophe for the Germans and that the planned retreat of the

Soviet army had surprised the enemy by turning into a victorious advance. Rotmistrov commented sarcastically:

> Thus the [German] surprise attack is converted into an advance into catastrophe, and the unexpected [Soviet] withdrawal becomes a victorious advance for that side. Such conversions and transitions do not occur in life. A surprise blow is a surprise blow and a withdrawal is a withdrawal. One cannot be converted into the other. If it is admitted, as apparently the author of this book wants to say, that similar conversions might recur and should be expected, then nothing remains but to present the opponent with freedom to deal surprise blows and turn them into a sure path to his downfall. These enemy blows would represent no danger for us since they would not be supported by superiority in the permanently operating factors. (According to the author, surprise not backed up by the permanently operating factors is not effective.)[37]

After March, 1955, many writers echoed the editorial position of *Military Thought,* sometimes using the same phrases. On May 6 an editorial in *Red Star* chided Soviet writers and thinkers for having concentrated only on the successful battles and operations of the last war and for not having reviewed Soviet mistakes and failures.[38] In an article on the tenth anniversary of the victory in Europe Marshal Sokolovskii also referred to the necessity of studying the experience of the first difficult months of the war.[39] General Shatilov was explicit on this point. He insisted that the German advantage of surprise, although temporary, made the war develop very differently from the way it would have done otherwise. He complained that Soviet literature

> . . . often idealizes the first period of military operations and presents it as the so-called classic form of "active defense" in operation. Furthermore the authors, contrary to the true facts, try to present "active defense" as if it had been planned in advance and had been included in the calculations of our command. In fact the initial period of the war, in view of the suddenness of the enemy attack and

his numerical superiority in tanks and airplanes, was very
unfavorable for our country and for our army which suffered the bitterness of retreat despite the stubbornness and
bravery of her fighters, who defended every inch of native
soil.

Such a view, Shatilov pointed out, "distorts the historical truth
and incorrectly orients our people by creating the impression
of the possibility and even of the desirability of treating these
events as precedents for the future."[40] Shatilov was clearly
castigating those who minimized surprise on the ground that
the Soviet Union had undergone a surprise attack and yet had
emerged victorious from the war. Since the spring of 1955 this
view has been out of favor and military journals and books have
continued to describe "active defense" as complacency.

Only once has there been a significant variation in this
theme, and the occasion was a difference on political rather
than strategic matters. In April, 1956, the editors of *Military
Herald*, the journal of the ground forces, wrote that the defeats
in the initial period of the war were largely Stalin's fault.
Furthermore, "one of the most important reasons for our military shortcomings in the initial period of the Great Fatherland
War was that Soviet industry had not been promptly and properly mobilized for the production of the necessary weapons and
munitions. As a result, despite the fact that industry had attained a level of development adequate to guarantee completely
everything the troops required and even before the war had
produced excellent pieces of military equipment, the Soviet
Army until the end of 1942 suffered shortages in artillery, tanks,
and aircraft."[41] The implication of the whole editorial was that
Stalin and the political leaders, not the armed forces, bore
responsibility for the early defeats. The editors of *Red Star*,
no doubt in response to pressure from party leaders, protested
the opinions of *Military Herald:*

One cannot but be shocked and pained at the completely
incorrect and harmful judgments appearing in the editorial article of the fourth issue for 1956 of *Military
Herald*. The article asserts that our army had to retreat

and wage difficult defensive battles allegedly because the
troops had not been put into fighting readiness. . . . The
article crudely distorts the mobilized readiness and the
potentialities of our industry.

Whether or not they wanted to, the authors of the article
just cited from *Military Herald* have minimized the significance of our victory in the past war and have minimized
the decisive role of the Soviet people and their Armed
Forces in the winning of that victory.[42]

These incorrect judgments, the *Red Star* writers added, were
advanced in the guise of criticism of the cult of personality,
which had been one of the main features of the Twentieth
Party Congress: "But it is impossible, under the guise of un-
masking that cult, to minimize the role of our Party and its
Central Committee, the role of our people and of the Soviet
Government, both in strengthening the defensive capability of
our country and in the organization and accomplishment of the
defeat of Fascist Germany."[43] The Party leaders apparently felt
that the military were carrying things too far in implying that
the Party and its Central Committee had let the country down.
The army seemed to be challenging the good judgment of
several of the present Party leaders as well as of Stalin, in
economic matters as well as military, and to be claiming more
of a voice in the sphere of state policy. Nevertheless, *Red Star*
soon modified its shocked reaction to the editorial in *Military
Herald*. On July 19 the editors wrote a new article[44] about
Party leadership of the armed forces that made no reference to
their May editorial, but that was clearly a revision of it. In
defense of the Party, they stated that it had always been aware
of the danger fascism represented, had preached vigilance, and
had ultimately led the army to victory. Only Stalin had failed
to take the necessary measures. So far the article seemed to
make no retreat in its championship of the Party. But when it
admitted that "industry was not promptly and properly mobilized so as to insure to our army an adequate quantity of
military equipment and munitions," it was paraphrasing the
very sentence that *Red Star* had characterized as a distortion

SURPRISE AND THE INITIATION OF WAR   **199**

two months earlier. Moreover the article went on to flatter the
generals: "Certain important factors, particularly the role of
the Soviet army generals in determining the outcome of the
war, had been underestimated."

The reason for *Red Star*'s change of attitude is not hard to
find. Marshal Zhukov, who had recently become Minister of
Defense, had raised the whole question of the honor of the
armed forces and the responsibility for early Soviet defeats in
World War II in a manner that could not but reduce the prestige of the Communist Party. This was probably a major
reason for his ultimate dismissal in 1957, when he was taken to
task for vainglory and for trying to deprive the Party of its due.
In 1957 there was not a word about the army's criticism of
"active defense." Any revision of the now-official policy of attacking active defense could easily have been interpreted as a revival of the idea that surprise was of secondary, not crucial,
significance. The party leaders had no intention of taking such
a backward step in military doctrine. Zhukov's dismissal was
inspired by political differences, not by any disagreement between Party and army on basic military thought.

In the first half of 1955, as we have seen, the Soviet leadership adopted a basic innovation in military strategy. The requirement that the Soviet Union be prepared to strike a pre-
emptive blow in order to forestall an enemy attack was bound
to affect military planning, procurement, and training. In addition, suitable ways had to be worked out for presenting the new
policy to domestic and foreign audiences.

What did the Soviet Union have to do in order to bring
her military posture into line with the new requirement? In
crude terms, she had to be able to beat the enemy to the draw.
But when nuclear weapons are to be delivered by aircraft, by
intercontinental ballistic missiles, by cruise missiles from submarines, or by a combination of these vehicles, "the draw" is an
enormously complicated act. When the aim is pre-emption, the
act of drawing is further complicated by the need to interpret
the enemy's moves and to learn his intentions.

A modern strategic air force always has some fraction of its
aircraft ready to start instantly on a bombing mission. The

fraction grows larger during alerts and practice maneuvers. An increase in the number of aircraft at maximum readiness is not necessarily an indication of intention to start hostilities. Even detailed information on the activities of an opponent's air force does not yield unequivocal conclusions about the orders being executed by that air force. These considerations apply even more strongly to ballistic missiles than to manned bombers. How is one to know the exact time to pre-empt, and can one be ready by then?

Let us assume that a decision to strike pre-emptively has been taken on the basis of what is considered adequate warning. How much time is then required to make the strike pre-emptive rather than merely retaliatory? When aircraft are the chief means of delivery, one must count as a minimum the time of flight. It is more realistic to add the time required to make ready more crews and planes than those available at the moment of warning. Even if the main delivery system is intercontinental ballistic missiles, time is required for a count-down on those at maximum readiness and more time to get other missiles into firing position. These necessary time lags mean that even unequivocal warning may not permit an effective pre-emptive blow, that is, one that knocks the opponent's weapon from his hand.

If the chances of getting in a telling pre-emptive strike are so poor, why, one is bound to ask, did the Soviet leaders lay down the requirement for one as their guiding principle? A nation will surely adopt the strategy that seems to offer the best chance of victory. It does not follow, however, that even a very powerful nation is at all times in a position to devise and employ a promising strategy. There may be periods in a country's history, especially transitional ones, when her official strategy must be merely the best of several poor alternatives.

What were the Soviet alternatives at the beginning of 1955, when the policy of pre-emptive capability was announced? The traditional aim had been to avoid war with any great power. This policy assumed the military weakness of the Soviet Union and the probable loss of such a war. To ward off calamity no concession was too great; no insult too humiliating. In the months before June, 1941, Stalin appeased Hitler on almost every issue. Hoping that German mobilization was a bluff, Stalin feared that preparations against a German attack might provoke it and felt that passivity might prevent it. This seems to be the explanation of his otherwise inexplicable failure to heed the most unequivocal of warnings. To Soviet leaders in 1955 a policy of appeasement seemed indefensible. First, it had failed miserably in 1941; second, Eisenhower presented no such threat as Hitler; and third, the Soviet leaders felt immeasurably stronger in 1955 than in 1941. Moreover, to leave the initiative to a possible enemy, as Stalin had done, would be far more dangerous under present conditions. If nuclear weapons were used, the victor in the first campaign might well be the victor in the whole war. If the Soviet Union were to suffer the first strike she could not count on a repetition of her successful recovery and counterattack in World War II. Traditional passivity was no longer a workable basis for military planning.

Another alternative was to ensure Soviet priority by initiating a strike against the United States. The object of a war thus begun had to be at least an improvement of the prewar position. The weapons balance could not hold out such a promise to the Soviet leaders. Although it is impossible to say exactly what the weapons balance was in 1955, or what the Soviet leaders thought it was, it is clear enough that American retaliation to an initial Soviet strike would have been devastating. No matter how many nuclear weapons the Soviet Union then possessed, she had a delivery system much inferior to the American one. Even if the Soviet leaders counted on all accidents and unforeseen circumstances favoring them, they could not confidently expect to obviate American retaliation by making a surprise nuclear attack on Western bases. We have no reason to think that the Soviet leaders ever seriously contemplated any such reckless solution to their problems. A preventive war, at a time of their own choosing, was not an acceptable policy in 1955.

The third and last alternative strategy, and the least unsatisfactory, was that of the pre-emptive blow. The requirements for a successful pre-emptive blow were unequivocal and timely warning of an impending enemy attack, and the ability to destroy the enemy striking force before it could get in its strike. As far as unequivocal warning was concerned, Soviet leaders took a very sanguine view. Talenskii, in his opening article, pointed out that the advantages accruing to an aggressor could be minimized "by a skillful and vigilant intelligence."[45]

In May, 1955, the editors of *Military Thought,* in the same editorial in which they advocated preparatory measures for a pre-emptive blow to prevent an enemy surprise attack, dealt with the problem of warning. Marxism-Leninism, they wrote, taught that wars are always preceded by the formation of aggressive military coalitions, and history has demonstrated quite clearly that "not a single modern war began without a series of provocations preceding it."[46]

In his "secret" speech on Stalin, delivered at a closed session of the Twentieth Party Congress, Khrushchev reviewed the warnings of a German attack in 1941. On April 3 Churchill warned Stalin through Cripps, but "Stalin ordered that no credence be given to information of this sort, in order not to provoke the initiation of military operations." Khrushchev cited two separate warnings from Soviet military attachés in Berlin on May 6 and May 22, and a new warning from the British on June 18. On the eve of the invasion a German citizen crossed the border and told of the coming invasion.[47] Khrushchev might also have mentioned even sharper warnings from Soviet intelligence sources in Japan and Switzerland.[48] From these warnings the editors of *Military Herald* argued that the German attack should have been expected:

> The very ideology of fascism and also the whole prewar policy of the Hitlerite clique was irrefutable evidence of the preparation for an attack upon the U.S.S.R. and, moreover, the fascists did not even conceal their plans. Thus, despite the conclusion in 1939 of a non-aggression pact, there was no doubt of the possibility of a treacherous blow against the Soviet Union by Hitler. In the spring of 1941 this possibility was converted into a real threat. Numerous facts revealed in good time by Soviet military

intelligence* testified to this threat. In particular it was
learned in good time that a tremendous number of German fascist troops, including strong tank units, had been
concentrated along the Western U.S.S.R. border.

But the German fascist attack was a surprise to the Soviet
Armed Forces all the same, although it cannot possibly
have been a surprise to the highest leadership of the country—which at that time was concentrated entirely in the
hands of J. V. Stalin. The main point is that, despite every
obvious sign of the preparation of aggression, the measures
of readiness necessary to exclude surprise were not taken.[49]

Statements of this kind often did more than throw the blame
for the defeats of 1941 on Stalin: they also expressed the confidence that similar failures to heed warnings need not recur.

Nevertheless the analogy between the events preceding the
German attack on the Soviet Union and those likely to precede
a third world war was obviously far from perfect. The deployment of more than a hundred German divisions along a two-
thousand-mile frontier was hardly comparable to the preparation of a nuclear air strike. On the other hand the Soviet leaders
might expect that no Western parliamentary democracy would
go to war without giving some kind of notice or warning.
It will be recalled that in November, 1954, when the magazine
Kommunist pointed to the growing danger of war, one of the
arguments adduced was the curtailment of liberties in the
United States and the strengthening of fascist tendencies. As
long as the present system of government prevails in the United
States, the Soviet leaders will probably not worry very much
about a "bolt from the blue." For all these reasons, the Soviet
policymakers are optimistic about the feasibility of receiving
timely warning of any nuclear attack.

As for the likelihood of a Soviet pre-emptive blow to destroy
the American striking force before it can get to its targets, one
can do little more than isolate the elements that would enter
into a Soviet decision to attempt a pre-emptive nuclear blow
against the United States. If this capability be poor, the need

* Such Soviet references to their own espionage are extremely rare.

for reliable warning signals will rise. In other words, the
greater the risk of retaliation, the greater the desire not to risk
a nuclear exchange. If minimal retaliation is expected, the attacker may think it worth while to strike pre-emptively, even
though he is far from certain of the putative enemy's intentions.
If we assume (as we have suggested the Soviet leaders assumed)
that in 1955 a nuclear war could have been a disaster for the
Soviet Union no matter who enjoyed the advantage of the first
strike, then we must also assume that it was Soviet policy to
wait until the very last moment before initiating such a war.

In the unlikely event that the Soviet Union should ever
acquire a striking capability so strong and sure as to preclude
retaliation, a Soviet pre-emptive blow would assure a Soviet
victory, at little or no cost in terms of damage to the homeland.
In that case it is difficult to imagine Soviet leaders risking a
seizure of the initiative by the enemy. At best, a policy of waiting would raise the cost of an ultimate Soviet victory; at worst,
it would result in final defeat. Let it be emphasized, however,
that the circumstances of this hypothetical case are unlikely to
occur.

Since a "retaliation-proof" attack is out of the question in
the foreseeable future, the Soviet leaders are likely to be influenced by various subtle political factors in defining the conditions under which a pre-emptive blow would be justified.
They will certainly take into account the character of the
American presidential incumbent and the domestic situation
in the Soviet Union. The possibility cannot be excluded that
in certain circumstances a Soviet political leader or faction,
convinced of Soviet ability to win a nuclear war, will overestimate the indicators of a possible American attack and underestimate the danger from American retaliation. As we have
seen, Khrushchev has not hesitated to provoke war scares for
partisan political advantage.

The difficulties of coming to a decision to make a pre-emptive strike are so obvious that the Soviet leaders must have
realized them in 1955, at or about the time they adopted a
policy of readiness to strike pre-emptively. These reflections
pointed to something more than a generalized military ex-

pansion; they pointed to the kind of military program that would aim at a retaliation-proof capability. This capability could be used to strike "preventively" and thus circumvent the weakness of the pre-emptive strategy, with its dependence on unequivocal warning. Ideally this capability would preclude damage to the country possessing it. Obviously this was a goal worth shooting for.

Without assurance that warning of an enemy attack will come in good time and that pre-emptive action will be speedy, dependence on pre-emption becomes effectively only dependence on retaliation. The only real guarantee that a nuclear strike will be early enough to damage the opponent's striking force before he can employ it is to hit the opponent before he has begun to prepare a strike of his own. This is the long-established and widely excoriated principle of preventive war.

Whatever the possible advantages of preventive war, American public opinion and the American political system do not permit an unprovoked, or even pre-emptive, attack. Therefore the United States has to rely mainly on her capacity to retaliate if she or her allies are attacked. In the Soviet Union, however, the Party controls military policy and is a law unto itself. The leaders have only to be convinced of the correctness of aggressive policy; it requires no popular mandate. This basic characteristic of Soviet politics makes it legitimate to inquire whether the Soviet leaders are employing the phrase "pre-emptive blows" as a euphemism for preventive war.

Preventive nuclear war makes sense for the Soviet Union only if that country can be reasonably sure to emerge unscathed. Even if the Soviet leaders were convinced that they possessed the required military preponderance, they would not necessarily decide to start a preventive war. That decision would depend on many other circumstances that cannot now be foreseen. It is possible, however, to list some factors that would tend to produce such a decision and some that would work against it.

The Soviet leaders, whether or not in command of a retaliation-proof capability, might conclude from available evidence that the United States would soon have such a capability. Preventive war might then seem a worth-while gamble.

It would be oversimplification to suggest baldly that the Soviet political leaders may seek to extricate themselves from domestic or foreign difficulties by seeking victory in a nuclear war against the United States. But the prospects of such a victory can be readily imagined as influencing their judgment about the certainty of warning needed to trigger a pre-emptive strike. Again, it is not difficult to picture a situation in which the Soviet leaders, agitated by setbacks and eager to regain lost ground, might undertake some limited aggressive action, giving rise to Western counteractions that could be interpreted as warning of an intention to make a nuclear strike. In this connection, contrast Soviet nonintervention in Yugoslavia in 1948 with Soviet intervention in Hungary in 1956. In 1948 Stalin was the unchallenged dictator of the Soviet Union. His failure to prevent Tito's defection and his subsequent failure to force Yugoslavia back into the Soviet camp did not appreciably diminish his position at home. In 1956 Khrushchev could have been, and probably was, blamed for creating the conditions that led to the Hungarian revolution. Even his ruthless suppression of the revolution does not seem to have silenced the opposition to him within the Party. In 1948, either because of the established pattern of caution in foreign policy, or because of a sense of military inferiority, Stalin did not risk a general war by a direct invasion of Yugoslavia. He satisfied himself with the hope that "loyal" communists within the Yugoslav Party would overthrow Tito. In 1956 the Soviet leadership placed no such faith in the Hungarian communists and accepted whatever risk of general war Soviet intervention in Hungary entailed. Presumably they felt that greater Soviet military power reduced the risk of general war.

The contrast between 1948 and 1956 suggests that growing Soviet military strength, by increasing Soviet confidence, will encourage bolder Soviet political activities. Before Stalin's death Soviet expansionist tactics were always applied in areas bordering the Soviet bloc. Today, however, the Soviet Union has leapfrogged some allies of the West to establish close relations with countries like Egypt and Indonesia. The number of points at which friction with the West can take place has increased. Furthermore, failures in Soviet foreign policy threaten the domestic position of the leaders, and successes bolster it. We should not necessarily conclude, however, that Soviet aggressiveness and willingness to run risks are always greater under "collective leadership" than under an autocrat. In the present stage of collective rule, where a leader who is *primus inter pares* must listen to the advice of his associates, hasty judgments are less likely than they might be under a single dictator. Hence it is less likely that the Soviet leadership of today will rashly and falsely assume that they have a retaliation-proof striking capability or that they must initiate nuclear war in order to forestall an imaginary plan of the enemy's.

None of the above considerations goes far toward answering the question, Is the Soviet Union planning preventive war? They suggest, however, that the initiation of a "preventive" nuclear war by the Soviet Union will not be seriously considered by the Soviet leaders unless the Soviet Union's military strength promises to be able to destroy the enemy while limiting destruction in the Soviet Union to an acceptable level. They also suggest, to the extent that Soviet political and economic expansion abroad is unopposed and successful, that the political leadership within the Soviet Union will improve its position, so that the need for desperate foreign adventures to recover lost prestige will be correspondingly less.

No single factor is likely to bring about a Soviet decision to initiate war against the United States. Soviet prospects for peaceful expansion, the Soviet domestic situation, and the Soviet estimate of opponents' intentions will all enter into any such decision. Yet if all these factors are favorable to aggression, they cannot lead to a decision to attack except in the unlikely event that the Soviet Union has developed a military pre-eminence that the leaders are confident will limit damage to their country to an acceptable level. The Soviet leaders cannot count on achieving such pre-eminence as long as the United States and its allies continue their efforts to improve their military position.

In 1955 the Soviet Union was probably too weak to consider seriously a policy of seeking nuclear war with the United States, no matter how much advantage they could derive from surprise. Is it justifiable to conclude from the subsequent efforts of the Soviet Union to improve her military strength that she is planning to initiate a nuclear war in circumstances where surprise would be maximally assured—that is, preventively? It is far more likely that the Soviet Union is seeking a retaliation-proof capability in order to give herself freedom of action, should a wide variety of other circumstances favor a Soviet surprise attack.

So far we have been attempting, with little concrete evidence to go on, to discover the actual intentions of the Soviet leaders in relation to their policy of readiness to strike preemptively. It remains to examine the public statements that have been made about Soviet intentions. How has the new Soviet military doctrine been presented to audiences at home and abroad? The answer to this question, of course, can throw only a little indirect light on the problem of actual Soviet intentions.

In making their strategies effective, the Soviet leaders must indoctrinate their fighting men. A new strategy has to be presented in such a way that its weaknesses will be minimized and its strengths emphasized. For the sake of good morale a certain amount of distortion may have to be introduced. In this field of activity the Soviet leaders obviously enjoy an advantage over their democratic counterparts. Military leaders in the democracies must point to, sometimes even advertise, deficiencies in military posture in order to raise funds from elected representatives. They may even reveal aspects of future development that have deleterious consequences for service and civilian morale. In the Soviet Union, of course, deficiencies in the armed forces are discussed either in private or in a guarded way before the public. The morale of the Soviet armed forces is an important consideration in the official promulgation of strategy. The members of the armed forces want to believe, and are told, that they will not have to fight unless attacked, and that if attacked they will be victorious. These traditional ingredients of military indoctrination, designed for purposes of morale, are not easy to reconcile with the new official doctrine that striking first offers great if not crucial advantages to the attacker. The awkwardness is compounded by the requirement that the Soviet armed forces be ready to repulse a surprise nuclear attack, no matter how remote that contingency. To inculcate such readiness the importance of surprise attack cannot be minimized. The only way to harmonize all these requirements is to insist on the possibility of timely and unequivocal warning of an enemy attack. Then it is possible to argue with some consistency that surprise attack with nuclear weapons is very important, perhaps decisive, and that although the Soviet Union will fight only after being attacked she will be able to retaliate instantly, or to strike pre-emptively, so as to assure victory.

Foreign policy and military security obviously must affect the manner in which strategic formulas are presented in the open press. The Soviet Union never initiates an aggressive war; it fights only in self-defense. Soviet propaganda has been absolutely consistent although not always convincing on this point. Even the conquest of the Ukraine and the independent Caucasian states in 1920-1921 was carried out in the name of native self-determination. The Baltic states were absorbed "at their request." The Soviet war against Finland in 1939-1940 was "provoked by the Finns." In keeping with this picture of spotless virtue Soviet writers must insist that any future war will be precipitated by the capitalists, not by the socialist camp.

The difference between actual and professed Soviet intentions is well illustrated by General Kurasov's article, "On the Question of the Pre-emptive Blow." First Kurasov charges the West with planning "preventive" war, and denies that the Soviet Union plans "pre-emptive" war. He argues that the Soviet Union's policy has always been peaceful. She has reduced her armed forces, unilaterally ceased atomic weapons tests, and sought a meeting at the summit to dissolve international tensions. The Soviet Union cannot be complacent, however, because she has suffered in the past from surprise attacks. The enhanced importance of surprise in the nuclear age has been

discussed by individual authors in the Soviet Union. Their
theoretical statements on measures to frustrate surprise have
been misinterpreted in the West "as a summons to pre-emptive
war":

> The Soviet Union was never the first to start a war and in
> all cases has only taken up arms to defend itself after suf-
> fering the attack of the enemy.
>
> The ideas of "preventive war" and the dealing of a pre-
> emptive blow as a means of attack and of unleashing war
> are incompatible with the peaceful policy of the Soviet
> state. . . .
>
> The Soviet people cannot forget that imperialistic coun-
> tries still exist whose ruling circles have not given up hopes
> for the annihilation of the socialist states. This forces the
> Soviet Union to strengthen its defensive capability in every
> way and constantly to maintain the armed forces in full
> fighting readiness to repel an attack of the imperialist ag-
> gressors at any moment. . . .
>
> But the Soviet Union has never threatened anyone with an
> attack, "preventive war," or dealing a pre-emptive blow.
> Always, beginning with the first days of the existence of
> the Soviet Union, the leaders of the Communist Party and
> of our state have said that, in the event of an attack upon
> us, an immediate retaliatory blow will be dealt to the ag-
> gressor.
>
> Naturally, the idea of dealing a retaliatory blow does not
> mean conducting only defensive actions. If any aggressor
> tried to make an attack upon us, the Soviet armed forces
> would conduct the most resolute offensive action against
> him.
>
> The great Lenin, foreseeing the possibility of an armed
> attack against our country because of the constant danger
> of war for us from world capitalism, showed that it was
> impossible to say we would only defend ourselves. "If we,"
> he said, "in the face of constantly and actively hostile forces,
> should give the promise they propose, that we would never
> have recourse to certain actions which in the military

strategic sense could be considered offensive, then we would not only be fools but criminals too. . . ."

The Soviet armed forces must constantly improve their military readiness so that at any moment they can not only repel an aggressor's surprise attack against our country but can immediately deal him a retaliatory blow of the kind that will once and for all put an end to any and all attempts to disturb by armed force the ordained movement of the Soviet people to communism.[50]

In this article can be found all the themes suited to the various purposes that a public enunciation of strategy must serve. The Soviet Union is peaceful; the capitalists are hostile; the Soviet Union will never start a war; surprise with nuclear weapons is very important; Lenin said that it would be criminal to promise not to "have recourse to certain actions which in the military strategic sense could be considered offensive"; the Soviet Union must be vigilant and will repel a surprise attack; if attacked, she will win the ensuing war. These themes are considered suitable fare for both domestic and foreign audiences.

It is worth noting that General Kurasov lumps together the terms "preventive" and "pre-emptive," using them side by side more than once in a kind of jingle. He not only denies categorically that the Soviet Union is capable of initiating a preventive war; he also denies that it is Soviet policy to deal a pre-emptive blow. He defines neither term. It will be recalled, however, that Marshal Rotmistrov drew a clear distinction between the two kinds of attack and denied only that the Soviet Union would resort to the preventive kind. Evidently subtle or controversial distinctions are considered unsuitable for propaganda purposes. The easiest way out is to cut off discussion by denying the intention to initiate war under any circumstances whatsoever. Just as it is now Soviet official policy to be ready to deal a pre-emptive blow on receipt of timely and reliable warning of a planned enemy attack, so it is also official policy publicly to deny the existence of any such military doctrine.

That this denial is worthless as an indicator of Soviet intentions we have tried to demonstrate by presenting evidence to the opposite effect from the Soviet military press and official statements. It is now time to examine the evidence of developing Soviet military posture to find out whether or not this sustains our thesis that the strategy of pre-emption is now officially accepted in the Soviet Union.

NOTES

1. Editorial, "On Some Questions of Soviet Military Science," *Voennaia mysl' (Military Thought)*, No. 3, March, 1955, pp. 3-17.
2. C. L. Sulzberger, "Russia Deplores 'Challenge' by U.S.," *The New York Times*, April 18, 1947.
3. *Report of Joint Committee on Atomic Energy Created Pursuant to Public Law 585—Seventy-ninth Congress*, Report No. 1169, 81st Congress, First Session, October 13, 1949, p. 13.
4. Colonel G. A. Tokaev, *Stalin Means War*, London, 1951, pp. 91-122.
5. Colonel I. N. Nenakhov, "The Policy of the Communist Party in Strengthening the Active Defense of the Soviet Union," *Voennaia mysl'*, No. 10, October, 1953, p. 16.
6. Major General N. Pukhovskii, "The Creative Character of Soviet Military Science," *Voennyi vestnik (Military Herald)*, No. 1, January, 1954, p. 18.
7. Marshal of the Soviet Union A. Vasilevskii, "On Guard over the Security of Our Soviet Motherland," *Red Star*, February 23, 1954.
8. Colonel S. Mazhorov and Colonel I. Tikhonov, "The Advanced Character of Soviet Military Science," *Red Star*, February 28, 1954.
9. Colonel A. Piatkin, "Some Questions of the Marxist-Leninist Science of War," *Voennaia mysl'*, No. 3, March, 1954, p. 23 *et passim*.
10. Marshal of the Soviet Union A. Vasilevskii, "The Great Lesson of History," *Red Star*, May 7, 1954.
11. "On the Question of the Character of the Laws of Military Science," *Voennaia mysl'*, No. 11, November, 1954, p. 44.
12. Colonel V. Kargalov, Candidate in the Pedagogical Sciences, "Military Questions in the Decisions of the Communist Party," in *Marksizm-Leninizm o voine, armii i voennoi nauke (Marxism-Leninism on War, the Army, and Military Science)*, Moscow, 1955, p. 20. The original appeared in *Red Star*, April 16, 1954. The manuscript of the book was delivered to the printer on October 8, 1954, and the galleys were ready for printing on February 3, 1955.
13. Major General N. Pukhovskii, "The Creative Character of Soviet Military Science," in *Marksizm-Leninizm o voine, armii i voennoi nauke*, Moscow, 1955, p. 100.
14. *Ibid.*, p. 107.
15. Colonel V. Vasilenko, "The Reactionary Essence and the Aggressive Character of Imperialistic Military Ideology," in *ibid.*, p. 213.
16. Marshal of Tank Forces P. Rotmistrov, "On the Role of Surprise in Contemporary War," *Voennaia mysl'*, No. 2, February, 1955, p. 14.

17. *Ibid.*, p. 17.
18. *Ibid.*, p. 18.
19. *Ibid.*, pp. 18-19.
20. *Ibid.*, p. 20.
21. *Ibid.*, p. 21.
22. General of the Army V. Kurasov, "On the Question of the Preemptive Blow," *Red Star*, April 27, 1958.
23. Editorial, "On Some Questions of Soviet Military Science," *Voennaia mysl'*, No. 3, March, 1955, p. 5.
24. Tank Marshal P. Rotmistrov, "For Creative Examination of the Questions of Soviet Military Science," *Red Star*, March 24, 1955.
25. Editorial, "The World-Historical Victory of the Soviet People," *Voennaia mysl'*, No. 5, May, 1955, pp. 12, 13.
26. Colonel General P. Kurochkin, "The Victory of the Soviet Military Art in the Great Fatherland War," *Voennaia mysl'*, No. 5, May, 1955, p. 18.
27. Marshal of the Soviet Union A. Vasilevskii, "The Great Victory of the Soviet People," *Izvestiia*, May 8, 1955.
28. Lieutenant General of Aviation P. Braiko, "Soviet Aviation in the Great Fatherland War," *Vestnik vozdushnogo flota (Herald of the Air Fleet)*, No. 4, April, 1955, p. 19.
29. Editorial, "The Great Strength of the Leninist Idea of the Defense of the Socialist Government," *Vestnik vozdushnogo flota*, No. 4, April, 1955, p. 8.
30. Lieutenant General B. S. Shatilov, "An Important and Noble Theme," *Literaturnaia gazeta (Literary Gazette)*, May 28, 1955.
31. Colonel General V. S. Popov, *Vneznapnost' i neozhidannost' v istorii voin (Surprise and the Unexpected in the History of War)*, Moscow, 1955. The manuscript was delivered to the printer on November 1, 1954, and ready in galleys on June 10, 1955. Rotmistrov's review was an article entitled "Surprise in the History of Wars," *Voennyi vestnik*, No. 11, November, 1955, pp. 90-96.
32. Colonel General V. S. Popov, *Surprise and the Unexpected in the History of War*, Moscow, 1955, p. 31.
33. Tank Marshal P. Rotmistrov, "Surprise in the History of Wars," *Voennyi vestnik*, No. 11, November, 1955.
34. V. I. Skopin, *Militarizm*, Moscow, 1956, p. 431. (Manuscript delivered to the printer on July 25, 1956; in galleys on August 3, 1956.)
35. V. I. Skopin, *Militarizm*, 2d ed., corrected and expanded, Moscow, 1957, p. 503. (Manuscript delivered to the printer on July 5, 1957; in galleys on October 5, 1957.)
36. Editorial, "On Some Questions of Soviet Military Science," *Voennaia mysl'*, March, 1955, pp. 7-8.
37. Tank Marshal P. Rotmistrov, "Surprise in the History of Wars," *Voennyi vestnik*, No. 11, November, 1955, p. 94.
38. Editorial, "Study the Experience of the Great Fatherland War Creatively," *Red Star*, May 6, 1955.
39. Marshal of the Soviet Union V. Sokolovskii, "The Tenth Anniversary of the World Famous Historical Victory," *Red Star*, May 8, 1955.

40. Lieutenant General V. S. Shatilov, "An Important and Noble Theme," *Literaturnaia gazeta*, May 28, 1955.
41. Editorial, "Glorious Anniversary," *Voennyi vestnik*, No. 4, April, 1956, p. 6.
42. Unsigned article, "The Great Victory of the Soviet People," *Red Star*, May 9, 1956. An unsigned article is more authoritative than a signed one, since presumably it has the sanction of the editors.
43. *Ibid.*
44. Unsigned article, "The Leadership of the Communist Party Is the Source of the Power of the Soviet State and Its Armed Forces," *Red Star*, July 19, 1956.
45. N. Talenskii, "On the Question of the Character of the Laws of Military Science," *Voennaia mysl'*, No. 9, September, 1953, p. 38.
46. Editorial, "The World-Historical Victory of the Soviet People," *Voennaia mysl'*, No. 8, May, 1955, p. 11.
47. "Secret Speech of Khrushchev Concerning the 'Cult of the Individual' Delivered at the Twentieth Congress of the Communist Party of the Soviet Union, February 25, 1956," in *The Anti-Stalin Campaign and International Communism: A Selection of Documents*, edited by the Russian Institute, Columbia University, New York, 1956, pp. 44, 45, 48.
48. Charles Andrew Willoughby, *Shanghai Conspiracy: The Sorge Spy Ring, Moscow, Shanghai, Tokyo, San Francisco, New York*, New York, 1952; Alexander Foote, *Handbook for Spies*, New York, 1949.
49. Editorial, "A Glorious Anniversary," *Voennyi vestnik*, No. 4, April, 1956, p. 6.
50. General of the Army V. Kurasov, "On the Question of the Pre-emptive Blow," *Red Star*, April 27, 1958.

CHAPTER SEVEN

THE CONDUCT OF A NUCLEAR WAR

The Soviet Union, like all other great powers, undoubtedly requires her Ministry of War to maintain an up-to-date series of war plans to meet various military contingencies. Such plans are periodically revised as the military strength and political goals of the major powers change. Less often they are altered to conform to new ideas about the nature of war. When, early in 1955, the Soviet leaders officially adopted the doctrine that the first blow could be decisive, it is more than probable that this led to a major revision of the plans for a large-scale nuclear war. To draw up satisfactory plans for such a war, the planners would need to know whether Soviet military doctrine emphasized primarily the possibility of recovery from a first blow (with the further possibility of going on to victory) or, on the other hand, the likelihood that the initial attack would determine the whole subsequent course of the war in the attacker's favor.

There is a good deal of evidence that Soviet plans for the conduct of a major war have undergone radical revision in recent years. An outline of present war plans emerges from various Soviet statements that while not numerous, are quite explicit. Moreover, there is a very extensive Soviet literature on the role of particular arms in the execution of the over-all plan for nuclear war.

At the Twentieth Party Congress, Marshal Zhukov's speech

set forth in general terms the revised Russian ideas on the conduct of war. Zhukov gave the highest official sanction to the prediction already adumbrated by lesser figures that nuclear, chemical, and bacteriological weapons would be widely employed in the war of the future. The existence of these new weapons, he said, did not reduce the decisive importance of the ground forces, but increased the importance of the air forces and active air defense. The air force, he concluded, was a most important means for ensuring the security of the Motherland. Never before had a high Soviet official assigned such importance to the air force.[1] The implication of Zhukov's remarks was unmistakable: delivery systems for nuclear weapons and defense against them were of the first importance.

Zhukov's thoughts were expanded and made explicit by General Krasil'nikov in an article written for an anthology on warfare published in 1956. Krasil'nikov, going farther than anybody else had to that time, asserted that a future war, if it came, could encompass not only Europe and Asia but also America and Africa, and consequently could "lose its former land character." The significance of aircraft and unmanned means of aerial attack and the significance of navies, especially submarines, had grown. Krasil'nikov emphasized, as do all Soviet writers, that air attack, though it had become terribly important, was not the be-all and the end-all of war. Its great importance, however, required the ability to strike a pre-emptive blow: "In order always to be ready to retaliate to possible enemy blows with even more destructive blows or *to frustrate the blows he is preparing* it is necessary to have a tremendous quantity of conventional weapons and weapons of mass destruction [author's italics]."[2] The new situation imposed the necessity to defend the entire territory of one's country from air attacks. The possibility of extensive damage to the rear through the action of aircraft made the initial period of the war more important than before. Surprise attack by a country better prepared for war than its victim had always given the attacker real strategic superiority, "at least during the first period of the war."[3]

Modern means of attack, Krasil'nikov continued, especially

aircraft, nuclear and chemical weapons, and airborne and mechanized troops, made it easier to carry out a surprise attack and also made "such a blow more dangerous than before." Surprise attack, widely employed in the Second World War, was now a typical device of warfare, and in preparing for war it had to be taken into account: "The seizure of the strategic initiative by the opponent is now fraught with exceptionally grave strategic and military-political consequences for the country suffering a surprise attack."[4]

One method of conducting a world war, continued the general, was to deliver a single massive blow in order to destroy the enemy's armed forces. Lightning war was the common name for this strategy. A second method was to destroy the opponent by a series of mighty blows. A third method was to concentrate the main forces on the destruction of the enemy's economy, cities, and political and administrative centers, and to combine this with decisive blows against his armed forces (that is, blows designed to finish off his already undermined forces). The first two were counterforce strategies; the third might be called the strategy of intensive and massive attrition.

Krasil'nikov then assessed the three strategies. The lightning war so frequently excoriated in Soviet military writing could, he admitted, bring victory after one or two blows, but only if the country or coalition so attacked was militarily weak and badly prepared for war. The examples selected by the Soviet writer—Poland in 1939, Belgium, Holland, and France in 1940—make it clear that he did not regard the Soviet Union as falling into the class of nations that could be beaten easily in a lightning war. The lightning war, he implied, could be successfully employed under modern conditions to knock a member out of a military coalition, and so to gain a very great strategic advantage, but not necessarily to win the war as a whole. An attempt to win the war by a single blow was doomed to failure against a strong coalition possessing great territory, modern military equipment, and good air defenses. The author expressed all this in a general frame of reference, so that he could have been talking about a Soviet attack on the United States, or an American attack on the Soviet Union.

Concentration of the attack against the deep rear was not considered by Krasil'nikov to be a winning strategy in itself, but an important contribution to the whole conduct of the war. He insisted that the only winning strategy was one adapted to an extended war with many campaigns, but emphasized at least as strongly the importance of the initial phase of the war. Mistakes in the early part of the war could lead to the loss of the war. The Soviet Union would not make such mistakes, implied Krasil'nikov. Thus he did away with an apparent inconsistency in his argument and left open the possibility of phases of nuclear war subsequent to the first.

Soviet military writers are obliged to make a special case of the defense of the Soviet Union whenever they are discussing a war initiated by another country. To say flatly that the opponent's surprise attack can win the war would be to surrender to pessimism and to undermine the morale of the armed forces. The Soviet position, therefore, does not minimize the problem of coping with an opponent's surprise attack, but holds out hope for a successful defense against it.

The following quotation from Krasil'nikov is the most detailed and explicit statement of the Soviet strategic plan for the first phase of a major war that has turned up in the research for this book:

> The employment of modern means of conflict, allowing for the constantly growing range of aircraft, the further development of military equipment, and the complete motorization of the army, can give to military activities in the initial phase of the war a completely new character and an exceptional intensity. It is in this stage of the war that the most critical situations and special conditions of the armed conflict, determining the character of its later stages, can be created. The initial phase of the war can, in contemporary conditions, include one and often even two campaigns simultaneously conducted on different strategic fronts or in different theaters of military operations. The campaigns of the initial stage of the war are conducted in conditions differing from those in which the subsequent operations are conducted. [Among the conditioning factors] strategic sur-

prise in starting the war is specially characteristic and it has a definite influence on the character of operations and on the mobilization of the country and the armed forces. The successful employment of strategic surprise in the initial phase of the war can lead to disruption of the opponent's existing plan for the strategic deployment of his main forces and to the possibility of a rapid piecemeal destruction of the troops concentrated by him. . . . An especially intense struggle to pre-empt the opponent and seize the strategic initiative will take place in the campaign of the initial phase of the war. The seizure of the initiative secures an opportunity to exploit the lack of readiness of the enemy's armed forces and to deal crushing destruction to the troops of his first strategic echelon. This is very important from the point of view of reducing his military economic resources and personnel contingents.

Especially characteristic of the initial campaigns, also, is an exceptionally intense struggle for the air, both on the front and over the territories of the contending countries and in the deep rear of these countries. Inasmuch as air forces have the greatest readiness for action and dispose of means for dealing powerful blows, campaigns will obviously be started by their active employment. In the campaign of the initial phase both sides will first seek to deal crushing destruction to the opponent's air forces, and his sources for the production of atomic weapons, and to seize mastery in the air.[5]

Krasil'nikov clearly believed that the first phase of the war was the most important, and that both sides would consequently try to seize the initiative. He divided the first phase into several major parts: the simultaneous destruction of the enemy's air forces, his stocks of nuclear weapons, the establishment of command of the air, and the disruption of the enemy's war plan: "Strategic surprise in starting the war" in this first phase could strongly affect the course of subsequent phases.

In March, 1957, Marshal Zhukov again expressed himself in general terms. Since atomic weapons would soon increasingly replace conventional weapons, the former "would inevitably be employed [in a future war] as the basic means of conflict. . . .

Atomic weapons . . . will be widely employed as organic weapons in the armies." One of the most important duties of the Soviet armed forces, especially the air force and active air defense, was to be "always ready to frustrate any attempt by the aggressor to accomplish a surprise attack upon our country."[6]

In June Marshal Zhukov made even more explicit the distinction between the first and subsequent phases of the war in a speech made in India when he said that

> in order not to be mistaken in the military strategic aspects, it is necessary to clarify the influence exerted on organization, tactics, and strategy by the new weapons and equipment which possibly will be employed both in the beginning and in the course of the war.[7]

As time passed, increasing emphasis was placed on the importance of forces-in-being deployed for immediate action, an obvious consequence of the doctrine that the first phase of nuclear war can be decisive. Colonel Petrov, in an article published in May, 1958, pointedly emphasized the importance of forces-in-being. His views are particularly interesting because they were offered as background material for students of doctrine in the armed forces.

Following the pattern established by Talenskii and Rotmistrov, Colonel Petrov stressed the importance of the first phase of a nuclear war without denying the importance of subsequent phases. He presented the successful defense of Soviet territory against enemy attack as a condition for the "speedy mobilization of the strategic reserves." By accepting the possibility of phases of the war subsequent to the first, he was remaining faithful to the new doctrine that the first phase of the war *could* but not necessarily *would* be decisive.

In his treatment of the forces-in-being, however, Colonel Petrov introduced a new note by restricting the definition of war potential in an unprecedented way. While recognizing that war potential had often been broadly defined as a combination of economic, political, and military factors, Petrov felt that a narrower definition would be more useful. "Since," he argued, "the fate of a war is directly determined by the fierce clash of the armed forces of the contending sides, war potential is understood to be only that portion of the potentialities which are incorporated into the country's armed forces themselves."[8] Forces-in-being now had the same importance that mobilizable potential once possessed. Consequently their readiness was of paramount importance. One's own forces "should be ready for the immediate conduct of military operations against the opponent's ground and air forces in case of a surprise attack."[9]

Although the fate of a war is determined by the fierce clash of the armed forces and although the most useful definition of war potential is forces-in-being, mobilization after the outbreak of hostilities and reserves are accorded great importance. The apparent inconsistency is resolved if we add that such mobilized reserves can only influence the outcome of a war if the forces-in-being are victorious at its outset. If the Soviet Union strikes first and destroys the bulk of the opponent's forces-in-being, the problem is relatively simple. If the opponent strikes the first blow, the Soviet forces-in-being must blunt that blow sufficiently to render it indecisive. Obviously the second task is immensely more difficult than the first, but Soviet military writers cannot admit that it is an impossible task. Hence Petrov's assignment of importance to both the first *and* subsequent phases of war. The novelty of his presentation is this: whereas formerly victory was to be won mainly by resources, arms, and troops mobilized after the outbreak of hostilities, now victory depends mainly on forces-in-being properly deployed to deal with (or perhaps deal) a surprise nuclear attack.

By examining the mission assigned to each arm of the Soviet forces, we can judge to what extent changes in the structure of these forces reflect the changes already traced in military doctrine. In doing so, however, we must remember that military forces have rarely been perfectly suited to the execution of the strategies favored at any particular time. Military thought may outpace military capability. The complexity of modern equipment, for example, brings long time lags between weapons design and operational readiness. The very pace of technological development tends to make much equipment obsoles-

cent. On the other hand, technology may get ahead of military
doctrine, as it did in the early history of nuclear weapons. It
would be misleading, therefore, to draw conclusions about
Soviet strategy from an examination of any individual weapon
system, or even from a complex of such systems designed for a
particular mission. We must keep in mind the whole picture,
even while we are discussing isolated portions of it.

Before we look into what the Soviet military writers have
asked of the several arms in nuclear warfare, we must pause to
note the impact of the H-bomb on Soviet thinking. The
H-bomb differed so greatly from the A-bomb that its development really constituted a second military revolution within a
decade. Its very-much-greater blast effect; its lethal fall-out,
which could persist for a long time and spread over great areas;
and its relative lightness and compactness vastly increased the
possible destructiveness of a nuclear war. It could be carried
by many aircraft already operational in the Soviet and American air forces. It could be built into missile warheads, making
the long-range guided missile far deadlier than had previously
been thought possible. The fall-out effect of the H-bomb was
especially important to the Russians because they had com-
forted themselves with the belief that their vast territory made
them less vulnerable than other peoples to A-bombs. Even
before the American tests of March, 1954, established the widespread fall-out effects of the H-bomb, some Russian thinkers
were already arguing that atomic weapons had changed the
whole character of war. The appearance of thermonuclear
weapons certainly reinforced their arguments.

The results of the March tests of the H-bomb were quickly
made known in the United States and the rest of the world and,
by August, 1954, were published in the Soviet Union. For instance, a *Pravda* news story repeated some statements made by
Drew Middleton in an article written for *Collier's* magazine.
Middleton was quoted as saying that since from two to six
H-bombs could destroy all of England, the question for the
English people was not one of victory or defeat, but what small
percentage of the population would survive.[10] The Soviet air
force magazine described the three stages of the H-bomb reac-

tion, its yield of ten megatons or more, and the secondary radiation at ground level, derived from wind-scattered fall-out. Despite the magnitude of its reported effects, the H-bomb was said to be a terror and propaganda weapon and not a tried means for the conduct of war.[11] This unconvincing conclusion, however, was excised from the second edition of a book in which this article was reprinted in 1955.[12]

It was soon admitted freely in the Soviet Union that the H-bomb had military utility. The question then arose of how best to deliver it to a target. Aside from manned bombers, the obvious delivery vehicle was the long-range missile, and the Soviet leaders must have been glad that they had not waited for the introduction of compact high-yield bombs before taking steps to develop what they now call the "decisive weapon."

The ballistic missile—when it becomes operational and has, in a satisfactory combination, accuracy, numbers, and reliability—will indeed be a formidable weapon of strategic surprise. As early as 1956, Major General Pokrovskii, who is prominent in military research and writing, was most enthusiastic about the ballistic missile on several counts. First, he considered that the accuracy of long-range missiles could be made greater than that of conventional artillery. The distance of the shell burst from its target is measured in hundredths of the range, sometimes in thousandths; a significantly smaller deviation could be expected with long-range missiles.[13] Pokrovskii, writing after the announcement of the launching of the first Soviet intercontinental ballistic missile, talked about a maximum deviation from the target of six to twelve miles. Maximum deviation is a vague term, and very probably deliberately vague.

Two other articles written about the same time gave roughly similar estimates of accuracy. A Doctor Kazakov, for example, gave 0.0002 of the distance traversed as the maximum possible error for intercontinental ballistic missiles armed with hydrogen-bomb warheads, when employed against military targets as large as cities. For a range of five thousand miles this would mean an accuracy of something like ten miles.[14] But a major general and professor in the most important technical academy of the air force, writing on September 14, talked in terms of even greater accuracy, giving five or six miles as the expected deviation from the target.[15] Whatever accuracy the Russians privately expect of ballistic missiles, they are probably justified in their expectation that eventually the accuracy of missiles will suffice for most purposes because of the great areas destroyed by H-bombs. Pokrovskii had such confidence in the accuracy and reliability of long-range, thermonuclear missiles that he believed, "at least in principle," in the effectiveness of single firings.[16]

Despite the great problems of the attainment of accuracy, the Russians view the missile as an important element in a counterforce strategy because it is difficult to detect and intercept in its brief flight. As the Russians themselves have pointed out in a technical article on the subject, it will be enormously difficult to detect the firing of ballistic missiles, even if certain suggested devices sensitive to infrared radiation are fully developed. Detection may be technologically feasible, yet prohibitively costly. Even if the firing of the ballistic missile could be detected, very little time would remain to act on this knowledge.[17] Before defending forces can take effective countermeasures in fifteen or twenty minutes, the maximum warning that could be hoped for, great technical advances must take place.

Ballistic missiles are probably still too unreliable in performance for reliance on them alone to execute the counterforce mission. There is a great likelihood that their very complex equipment will fail to function altogether. This difficulty, however, may be overcome by assigning sufficient missiles to each target to compensate for their unreliability. For a long time to come the number adequate to compensate for unreliability may be so large as to constitute an unacceptable cost. Although the individual ballistic missile is seemingly such a blunderbuss, in time it can be made a militarily effective weapon, and it is certainly one that presents formidable problems to the defense.

If the Soviet military planners were interested in these weapons only for their value in deterring the United States, they would surely accept missiles with errors four or five times as large as the maximum actually designated as permissible in Soviet public writing. In a strike against the United States, errors of such magnitude might leave the American retaliatory force largely untouched. The Soviet accuracy requirements indicate that the ballistic missile is intended at least as much to strike actual military targets as to deter an enemy attack.

Another advantage of the ballistic missile stressed by Pokrovskii is the relative ease of constructing, dispersing, and camouflaging the launching platforms. They probably will be less difficult to conceal than airfields, as Pokrovskii insisted. One side will find it all the more difficult, therefore, to prevent missile launchings by the other.[18] Without international weapons inspection, the advantages of concealment would benefit mainly the Soviet Union, for few American installations where considerable numbers of people work can be kept secret. The Soviet Union is able to use methods to ensure secrecy that would not be permissible in the United States.

Missiles with thermonuclear warheads obviously do not have to be as accurate as conventional, high-explosive weapons. This was pointed out by the Commander-in-Chief of the Soviet Air Forces, Marshal of Aviation Vershinin, in a rare interview with the press. His published remarks provide a glimpse into the official Soviet estimate of the importance of the ballistic missile. The essential points are contained in the following excerpts:

> The modern destructive means for the conduct of wars do not require aiming aircraft or rockets precisely at a military base. It is no longer a matter of artillery duels or aerial bombing in the sense of the last war. Nevertheless bombers were frightful then too. . . . But the bombers and the terrible raids of the past can by no means be compared with what a future war would bring if some madman should begin it. Atomic and hydrogen weapons have appeared, as have various types of missiles with atomic and hydrogen warheads, including intercontinental ballistic missiles. These are weapons of terrible power.
>
> It is not appropriate to joke about such a serious matter, but friends who have been in England have told me of this

joke, now current in England. They say that the people in England are divided into optimists and pessimists. The pessimists believe that three hydrogen bombs exploded over the British Isles would be enough to knock them out completely. The optimists say this is not so; that not three but six bombs must be exploded. . . .

Now the expectation that America's remoteness will spare her military blows in the event of a new war is no longer tenable. In the age of jet technology and atomic energy, great distances will no longer play a decisive role. What was once inaccessible has now come within easy reach. The modern means for aerial attack, characterized by great speed and range, are capable of delivering blows to military targets anywhere on earth. Intercontinental ballistic missiles can deliver the most terrible weapon, the hydrogen bomb, instantly to the remotest regions of any continent on earth.

In present conditions, bombers are naturally still being built. The United States especially emphasizes this kind of weapon. But missiles now call into question the expediency of further developing bomber aircraft, since the former are more reliable and dependable. From the history of World War II we know how many bombers returned of those sent out on missions, and how many did not reach the target. It is almost out of the question for a missile not to reach the target. Modern anti-air defense is ineffective against these missiles.[19]

The implication of all this was unmistakable. The United States was now as vulnerable to attacks by the new Soviet missiles as the Soviet Union had been in recent years to attacks by American bombers from numerous, encircling bases. Vershinin said that manned bombers were not the ideal vehicles to carry nuclear weapons to the United States. Perhaps he meant, although obviously he could not say so, that the forward bases of SAC made American bombers a much greater threat to the Soviet Union than Russian bombers could be to the United States. Soviet ballistic missiles, however, he implied, deprived the United States of whatever advantage she might have enjoyed in manned bombers.

Although Soviet commentators carefully avoided committing themselves to a statement that the United States would take a long time to develop intercontinental ballistic missiles, they implied strongly that until this happened the Soviet Union would have a great over-all advantage.

A few days after the Vershinin interview, General Pokrovskii attributed to the ballistic missile an accuracy and destructive power that made it possible to destroy any strategic target on the earth's surface. In accordance with Soviet tradition, however, no weapon should be characterized as decisive in itself, so Pokrovskii added: "Without in any way denying the power of the intercontinental missile, even this weapon cannot be considered absolute and invincible."[20] This almost standard reservation was dropped in March, 1958, when Major General Talenskii said in so many words that the intercontinental ballistic missile was a decisive weapon. By this time there could be no doubt that Talenskii spoke for others beside himself:

> For the time being the Soviet Union has monopoly possession of the super-powerful intercontinental missile. . . . Yet the Soviet monopoly possession of *the decisive weapon of our time* has not given rise to a single aggressive feature in the foreign policy of the USSR. . . .*
>
> The Soviet Union employs the major advantages it has gained from possession of the *decisive modern weapon* to intensify its foreign-political efforts for lasting peace and security. . . .
>
> The military significance of having solved the problem of creating a powerful, super-long-range, ballistic missile, capable of entering cosmic space and hitting any designated point, is exceptionally great. It is not only a quantitative increase in the potentialities of military strategy; it

---

* The Soviet English-language version of the article where these passages appear renders the Russian word *reshaiushchii* as "ultimate," whereas here the standard rendering, "decisive," has been retained. Using "ultimate" obscures the significance of the abandonment of the old formula that no decisive weapons exist. For the official English version see Major General N. Talensky [sic], "Military Strategy and Foreign Policy," *International Affairs*, No. 3, 1958, pp. 26, 27.

is a qualitative leap which fundamentally changes the methods and forms of the armed conflict. The intercontinental ballistic missile changes military strategy and its potentialities to an immeasurably greater degree and much more rapidly than, for example, the appearance of firearms or of aircraft in the past [author's italics].[21]

It is difficult to exaggerate the importance of the epithet "decisive" when employed to characterize ballistic missiles. For more than a quarter of a century Soviet military discussions had branded as an "incorrect" tenet of "the aggressors" the notion that a single weapon could be decisive in war. Almost every mention of the blitzkrieg theory of war was coupled with a reference to the principle that no decisive weapon existed. For Talenskii to say that ballistic missiles were decisive weapons was to announce the lapse of an established law of war. In Marxian theory, laws of war like laws of society are not eternal but lose their force when one period of history gives way to another. Talenskii undoubtedly had just such an historical upheaval in mind, because he described the potentialities of military strategy as increasing qualitatively rather than quantitatively. In Marxian theory, which in this case borrows directly from Hegel, quantitative changes in the relation of social forces occur *within* an historical period; when the quantitative changes become so great as to constitute qualitative changes, a new epoch in history is marked. It is in the light of this communist dogma that one should interpret a statement, made by Chou En-lai on February 10, 1958, to the effect that the Soviet launching of two earth satellites constituted "a new turning point in the world situation."[22] That Chou En-lai's speech preceded Major General Talenskii's article suggests what one might have guessed in any case: Talenskii's announcement that the intercontinental ballistic missible was a decisive weapon reflected a party decision on the highest level.

Perhaps the Soviet leaders chose to express their full appreciation of the basic changes wrought in warfare by the advent of nuclear weapons at a point in weapons development when they had jumped ahead and acquired a monopoly, even if only a temporary one. Political and psychological considerations argue strongly in favor of this explanation, but other reasons of equal cogency can be suggested. These arise from the nature and capabilities of the ICBM. The intercontinental ballistic missile is the weapon of surprise *par excellence.* No other vehicle can deliver an H-bomb with such good chances of achieving surprise. At present the outlook for effective anti-missile missiles is not good; certainly no claims are made that they already exist. The intercontinental ballistic missile, as the Soviet writers reiterate, is only useful against fixed targets whose coordinates are known. Thus it is suitable for employment against airfields with their aircraft, missile bases with their missiles, naval bases with their ships, atomic centers, administrative centers, and industrial complexes. It is not suitable for firing at aircraft aloft or ships at sea. If it is to be used in a counterforce role, it must be used pre-emptively or preventively, unless it is to destroy only vacant airfields and naval bases.

The Russians, as we have seen, stress the ease with which missiles can be relocated and concealed. These characteristics greatly enhance the likelihood that numbers of these weapons would survive a surprise attack to retaliate against the opponent. This likelihood, in turn, is a deterrent against such a surprise attack. It seems that the Russians value the deterrent power of the ICBM, but consider it mainly as a weapon of surprise. Accuracy is not required for purposes of retaliation and deterrence, yet the Soviet military writers demand accuracy. Thus, it seems reasonable to believe that the Soviet ICBM system is now assigned essentially, although not exclusively, to a first-strike mission.

Manned bombers will obviously be important for some time to come. Soviet views on air bombing have changed a great deal in the past twenty years. Before World War II, the Soviet air force was essentially an adjunct of the army, designed mainly for infantry support, interdiction, and reconnaissance. During the war it was also employed to support partisan activity, which had no more been foreseen than the retreats of the Red Army. When the Russians analyzed the experience of aerial bombing in World War II, they decided that it had not contributed

much to the collapse of Germany. A different conclusion would
have left them at an admitted disadvantage, for the best bomber
until the end of the forties, the B-29, could be used by the
United States from forward bases to attack Russia, while the
Russian copy of this machine lacked the bases that would
enable it to reach the United States.

The Russians seem to have retained for quite a long time
their low estimate of the power of strategic bombing. They
failed to take certain feasible measures to reduce, if not eliminate, the American superiority in bomb-delivery systems. They
were backward, for example, in developing an aerial refueling
capability. The refueling of aircraft aloft was achieved on a
small scale more than twenty years ago. In the Soviet Union
experimental refueling took place as early as 1933. Sir Alan
Cobham's refueling system had been carefully described in the
technical literature before World War II. Not until 1955, however, did an article appear in the Soviet press describing aerial
refueling as an essential component of an intercontinental
bombing system, and not until 1957 did the Soviet Union
demonstrate a bomber refueling capability in practice.[23] Refueling in the air could not in itself have eliminated the American advantage in bomb-delivery capability, but it would have
helped a great deal. Refueled planes could fly further with
heavier loads. Even when the Soviet Union replaced her copies
of the B-29 with longer-range planes, refueling could have increased their effectiveness. The Russians may have been slow to
develop refueling for many reasons, but one of them was probably the persistent assumption that even a major war would not
involve Soviet bombing of the United States. It is tempting to
believe that the basic changes of 1955 in Soviet military thinking either stimulated or accelerated the rapid advances in refueling that took place in the next two years.

Other evidence of a more direct kind sustains the thesis
that the Soviet evaluation of strategic bombing changed radically some time in 1955. For example, in January, 1955, the
Soviet air force magazine carried an article on the effects of
atomic radiation that discussed atomic weapons largely in terms
of their tactical employment. Pointing out that aircraft were

the vehicles most suited for nuclear weapons, the writer envisaged the chief targets as troops in the field, naval vessels,
industrial areas, and air fields. Since it was so difficult to hide
atomic artillery in position or on the march, and since the
accuracy of both guided and unguided missiles was poor (despite the difficulty of defense against them), aircraft would be
the basic vehicles for atomic weapons. Accordingly, a prime
purpose of bombing would be to deny the opponent the use
of his airfields, so as to weaken the air support of his ground
forces. In this scheme, atomic weapons would be used to interdict the enemy's airfields, and to influence the ground or naval
battle. They were not strategic weapons to be used at long
range against the enemy's forces or industry.[24]

Before long other opinions were finding public expression.
There was a growing confidence that aircraft could carry bombs
against targets in the deep rear, even thousands of miles away.
One writer implied that American aircraft could successfully
deliver weapons to the Soviet Union. He thought the B-36 too
slow for that purpose, but admitted the superiority of the B-47,
which he described as rapidly replacing the B-29 and B-50,
and as able to carry a nine-ton bomb load at high speed over
the rather short range of 3600 miles. The comparatively short
range of the B-47, he continued, required SAC to introduce
tankers.[25] By 1956 articles in the Soviet press completely accepted this possibility. An article in *Red Star* about pilotless
aircraft with subsonic speeds estimated that they could accomplish long-range bombing missions quite successfully. These
vehicles that, said the article, accomplished the very same tasks
as ordinary aircraft, were designed to destroy great administrative and industrial centers, railroad junctions, seaports, bases,
and areas where troops and military equipment were concentrated. The advantage of this sort of vehicle was its ability to
operate in any weather and to take off even from mobile launching platforms. Pilotless aircraft could be guided in various
ways, either by automatic pilot, which in the opinion of this
writer curtailed accuracy, or by inertial guidance, preferable in
very long flights. This writer, and doubtless other more im-

portant persons, now saw large-scale war in terms of long-range bombing.[26]

A month later an article in *Red Star* discussed the employment of air-to-surface guided missiles. These, it was said, would solve "the problem of accuracy in bombing from modern aircraft" and reduce the loss of bombers. Other bombs might be released at a ground distance of perhaps fifteen kilometers from the target, but a guided air-to-surface missile could be released hundreds of kilometers away. If these missiles had atomic warheads, the simplest automatic guidance system would suffice because the radius of destruction would exceed possible errors in finding the target. If ordinary warheads were used, the greater accuracy provided by a homing system would be needed.[27]

A year later there was no longer even a lingering doubt about the role of air power in future wars. Air power, it was frequently urged, should not be developed at the expense of other branches of the armed services. A balanced growth was needed. Evidently there was at least a possibility that the air force would absorb too much of the defense budget.

Together with missiles, it was said, aircraft now had the task of achieving the first surprise blow in the initial period of the war and disrupting the enemy's military and economic potential. They must also, in a broad sense, command the air: "Without the attainment of mastery of the air, the rapid seizure of the strategic initiative in the initial period of the war and the successful development of military activities on land and sea are unthinkable." As a consequence of the long range at which air power can operate, "the boundary between the front and the rear in hostile coalitions is obliterated, which makes it possible to subject important enemy strategic targets in other continents to powerful attacks. Missiles, as well as aircraft, will play a large role in this activity."[28]

As soon as the first artificial earth satellite was up, however, the official Soviet attitude became one of ostensible contempt for bombing aircraft, at least for those of the Western countries. Khrushchev told two British Members of Parliament that the era of the bomber was now past; bombing planes could be

burned without further ado.[29] This remark was not reported
in the Soviet Union. In talking to James Reston of *The New
York Times*, Khrushchev referred to the obsolescence of aircraft in a much more restrained manner:

> A revolution of a certain kind is taking place at the present
> time. Military specialists believe that both bomber air-
> craft and fighters are in the twilight of their existence.
> The speed and ceiling of bombers is such that modern
> missiles can destroy them.[30]

Khrushchev could legitimately argue that missiles would sooner
or later partially replace bombing aircraft, but his comments
probably sprang from his eagerness to belittle the Western
advantage in strategic-bombing capability, now that he had a
plausible excuse for doing so. Khrushchev pushed the ballistic
missile as far as it would go, and further, in an obvious effort
to discredit the Western military posture:

> It should be plainly said that the time is not very far off
> when everyone will have to recognize that military bases
> on the territory of other countries no longer have the
> significance once assigned to them by some immoderately
> boastful generals and aggressively inclined statesmen of the
> Western powers. One must soberly and realistically assess
> the development of modern technology, as a result of
> which the situation has basically changed. By the creation
> of the intercontinental missile, the question of the possi-
> bility of delivering hydrogen bombs to any point on the
> earth's surface is solved. Distance is no longer a barrier.
> As far as military bases in Europe, Africa, and Asia are
> concerned, missiles have long existed which can be de-
> livered to any part of these continents. I do not think it is
> a secret that we now have a collection of such missiles
> capable of accomplishing one or another operational or
> strategic mission. Let us not play hide and seek, but look
> squarely at the state of affairs. Can it really be supposed
> that the locations of military bases are known only to
> those who constructed them? And if the location of these
> bases is known, then modern missiles and other equipment
> can rapidly put them out of commission.[31]

Khrushchev was obviously exaggerating the speed with which
ballistic missiles could replace aircraft, in order to gain the
maximum propaganda advantage from the latest Soviet technological achievements. The Soviet air force commander, General Vershinin, had spoken only of the possibility of ceasing
the development of bomber aircraft, not of stopping their
production. Khrushchev himself took a more sober attitude
when addressing professional audiences at home. In a short
speech to graduates of the aircraft engineering schools, he left
plenty of room for manned aircraft in the Soviet scheme of
things:

> The modern means of warfare are very powerful. Now, as
> you know, the role of winged aircraft piloted by individu-
> als is somewhat reduced; and jet aircraft and missiles are
> taking their place.

> Without denying existing weapons to ourselves, we should
> go forward to perfect all kinds of weapons and to master
> the new jet and missile technology . . . so as to be always
> ready to repulse an attack. . . .[32]

Two months later an article in the daily organ of the Soviet
air forces declared that aircraft would continue to be important
in joint operations with ground and naval forces, "but could
also annihilate the opponent's strategic targets, in the interests
both of the war as a whole and of particular campaigns." One
passage was considerably at odds with Khrushchev's remarks
about the obsolescence of manned aircraft:

> The logical process of the qualitative development of the
> modern means of air attack, especially intercontinental
> ballistic missiles and medium range missiles, does not
> mean . . . that aircraft have outlived their day and that
> missiles will completely replace them in the near future.
> The presence in the weapon systems of the air forces of
> jet bombers and supersonic fighters and of airborne mis-
> siles of the air-to-surface and air-to-air classes, and the
> [presence] of atomic and hydrogen weapons and other
> means of destruction, have significantly improved the
> battle potentialities of aircraft for the accomplishment of

THE CONDUCT OF A NUCLEAR WAR

varied missions. The newest means of radio contact, radar, cybernetics, guidance systems, and automatation free aircraft operations from the limits imposed by darkness and bad weather. The results already achieved in the development of aircraft and in the means of destruction employed by them, and also the ceaseless qualitative improvement of aircraft equipment, give a basis for supposing that aircraft will play a very important role in a future war.[33]

The writer of this passage then quoted Khrushchev's speech to the graduates of the aircraft engineering academy and concluded that there was no question of the "disappearance of aircraft as weapons [carriers] in the armed forces, but rather a question of the nature of their further development."[34] The continued development of jamming devices, air-to-surface missiles, and "over-the-shoulder" bombing was balancing improvements in antiaircraft measures; therefore aircraft would continue to play a very important role in future wars.

Here was a Soviet colonel directly contradicting the words of his commander-in-chief nine months previously. Evidently Vershinin—and Khrushchev—had been either hasty or insincere when they publicly minimized the manned bomber. The Soviet leaders, especially Khrushchev, seem to have been somewhat carried away by the excitement of the ballistic missile and to have "retired" the aircraft as a vehicle for nuclear weapons as soon as the first successful ICBM firings had occurred. Either they soon changed their minds, or they had never really believed what they said.

Aircraft possess still other important advantages over missiles that Soviet writers neglect: they can be recalled. As General Thomas S. Power, the Commander-in-Chief of the Strategic Air Command, explained in a press interview, "in the event of the real alert . . . our aircraft would be launched and their crews would be assigned predetermined targets. However, they would be launched under positive-control procedures which would insure that, if the emergency did not materialize, they would not proceed. . . . The positive control procedures insure that no SAC aircraft can pass beyond proper bounds far from the Soviet Union or its satellites without additional unequivocal orders that can come only from the President of the U.S."[35] This means that in a severe international crisis the nation with an efficient air force need not be trigger-happy. Without a flexible recall system for aircraft, and in all cases with missiles, only one of two decisions is possible: send or hold. The ability to recall aircraft gives more time for deciding whether an attack is really impending or not.

Whatever the missile was doing to the aircraft, there could be no doubt that it would further extend the usefulness of the submarine. The size and destructiveness of H-bombs made them adaptable as warheads for missiles that could be fired from submarines. If and when Russian submarines were extensively equipped with missiles carrying nuclear warheads, the Soviet Union would enter a new era in her naval history. Russia had always suffered to some extent from her limited access to the great oceans of the world. By the eighteenth century her coastal regions comprised four distinct areas, the Arctic, the Baltic, the Black Sea, and the Far East, of which the first three could easily be bottled up by a strong naval opponent. The Russian navy consisted of two, later three, separate forces that could not easily be brought together even in peacetime. Not unnaturally, therefore, naval warfare has played a relatively small role in Russian history. The United States, on the other hand, has been protected by oceans from any possible strong enemies. For nearly a century these oceans were commanded by the British navy. In effect this fact precluded any serious threat to the United States, except on the one occasion when Britain herself was hostile, that is, in the War of 1812. In 1814 British sea power made possible the burning of Washington and the assault on New Orleans. On the enclosed waters of the Great Lakes, however, the United States established complete mastery. After 1880 American naval strength grew rapidly, became much more flexible with the opening of the Panama Canal in 1916, and was able to carry the battle to distant enemy territories in two world wars.

With the advent of missiles that can be launched from the sea, the relative naval positions of the United States and Soviet Russia may be entering a period of change. Since the

Soviet Union's only long, exposed coast is in the Pacific area, where there are few cities of any importance, her largely land-locked geography makes her less vulnerable to attack from short- and medium-range seaborne missiles than the United States, most of whose cities lie within easy missile range of the Atlantic and Pacific coasts. The longer the range of the missiles employed on both sides, however, the smaller will be the advantage possessed by the Soviet Union in any exchange of seaborne missiles.

The Soviet leaders are favored in this field by the circumstance that a fleet of several hundred long-range submarines was laid down in and after 1945 as a commerce-raiding and counter-troopship force. Opinions may differ on the utility of such a force in a future nuclear war, but it is obvious that the arming of some or all of the existing submarines with nuclear missiles can greatly extend their mission in such a war.

The Soviet military press, in its discussion of the possible role of submarines in a future war, leaves no doubt that Soviet naval officers appreciate the potentialities of missiles launched from submarines. In 1957 a Soviet admiral flatly stated that the appearance of the missile with a nuclear warhead, together with its supporting systems, had given navies a new strategic significance. The possibility had arisen of employing long-range missiles from submarines against administrative and industrial targets. This had created a requirement for underwater launching, and the admiral reported that the United States was already working on this problem. The fundamental needs were for an increase in the range, accuracy, and blast effect of missiles with nuclear warheads.[36]

Another naval writer claimed for naval forces the ability to strike surprise blows from great distances in the initial period of war, by using nuclear explosives and guided missiles. He described the strategic potential of naval forces in terms of what an opponent could do to the Soviet Union, and called for defensive fleet units to repulse attack by sea.[37]

A Major General Boltin took an army point of view in an article on military science written for the naval newspaper, *Soviet Fleet*. He stressed surprise in the initial stage of the war, but said nothing about submarines. Indeed he questioned the continued utility of capital ships when aircraft and missiles could deliver nuclear weapons.[38]

The development of systems for delivering nuclear weapons from a great distance has induced the Soviet Union to devote close attention to problems of air defense. Even in the Second World War, when they felt that aerial bombing could not do decisive damage, the Russians considered air defense worth an important investment. Before they had arrived at a clear idea of the role and value of nuclear weapons, the Russians elevated their estimate of the importance of bombing and invested considerable sums in warning systems against enemy bombers, an enterprise made easier by the open publication of American radar techniques. The development of jet interceptors was hastened by the purchase of British Rolls-Royce Nene engines. The Russians then made massive preparations for active air defense. But even these did not bespeak a true appreciation of the requirements for defense against nuclear bombing. To repel an attack by bomb-carrying aircraft, the Soviet Union needed all-weather interceptors, equipped with tracking and fire-control radar. Adequately equipped fighter planes were not introduced into the Soviet air force until the beginning of 1955. Surface-to-air missiles, also a vital component in any modern air-defense system, appeared at about the same time. Many fiscal and technical problems may have delayed the production of these defense weapons, but in the light of Soviet weapons theory and development in the period 1945-1953 it seems equally likely that the Russians lacked the sense of urgency that a fuller appreciation of the role and power of nuclear weapons later produced.

The Soviet press started to emphasize the tremendous importance of active air defense as late as the beginning of 1955, when readers were warned that not a single enemy plane must be allowed to get through the active defenses. The great destructive effects of nuclear weapons made this imperative. Here was a sharp contrast to the doctrine of World War II, under which active defenses were expected only to reduce the effects of localized bombing raids and to exact as high a toll as possible from the enemy bomber forces. In the nuclear age, however, a very few bombs could wipe out even the largest target, and it became almost pointless thereafter to shoot down the bombers that had done the damage. After a successful raid en masse, the destruction of the empty bombers could make little difference to the strategic picture. The only worth-while active air defense was one that could limit urban destruction to an acceptable level.

An examination of the present Soviet air-defense system reveals much about Soviet objectives and expectations in the event of war. Defensive posture is often a guide to strategic intentions. A system of defense may fulfill any one of several strategic purposes. A well-nigh-perfect defense system, for example, can serve as an effective deterrent to an opponent's attack. Theoretically, a perfect defense in the nuclear age is possible, through massive quantities of electronic detectors, interceptor aircraft, and surface-to-air missiles. In the real world, however, it is extremely unlikely that a perfect or near-perfect defense system can be created. At present defensive systems are far from capable of holding off large-scale nuclear attacks, especially by ballistic missiles. Practically speaking, there seem to be absolute limits to the efficiency of defensive systems.

The human element can never be entirely excluded, and the demands for good judgment on short notice may be too much for certain sectors of a defense system. Add to this what has been aptly called the fog of war and the low efficiency of operations during first hostilities and it becomes difficult to see how any active air-defense system could ward off all nuclear weapons. If the defense permits hydrogen bombs to get through in considerable numbers, its value becomes questionable. Planners of today are bound to ask themselves whether big expenditures on active defense are really worth while. In this connection, the point is that Soviet active air defense does make good sense in combination with Russia's pre-emptive doctrine for the initiation of war. In itself Soviet active air defense makes little sense as a deterrent to an enemy's first strike.

A necessarily imperfect defense of urban complexes is not

an important deterrent, but the defense of one's own striking force is the essence of deterrence, since an undefended striking force does not constitute a deterrent, but only a potential first strike force. Many components of air defense, of course, are important for the defense both of cities and of one's own striking forces. As it happens, Soviet active air defense is clearly intended to prevent or reduce damage to cities. Its purpose is not only to deter a possible opponent by protecting retaliatory capability, but also to conduct war successfully should it break out. But Soviet planners are bound to realize that active air defense could save neither the cities nor the retaliatory force if the attacker achieved strategic surprise. Little is gained from air defense if the enemy achieves strategic surprise. Only if the weight and effectiveness of the opponent's blow can be reduced by a pre-emptive attack does an active air-defense system, such as the Soviet Union has been developing, hold out promise. In that case, the whole burden of reducing losses from enemy missiles and aircraft would not be borne by the defenses. A pre-emptive blow that destroyed part of the enemy's striking force would thereby reduce his retaliatory capability to proportions that Soviet active air defense could cope with. If destruction to the Soviet Union were kept within these limits, the tremendous investment in active air defense would be justified.

Soviet writings on air defense reveal that late in 1954 a tentative step was taken toward the official conclusion that aerial bombing against targets in the rear could be of decisive significance. Colonel Fedorov, writing in *Red Star* in January, 1954, remarked that popular morale would be very important in a future war because of "numerous and destructive bombings by enemy aircraft."[39] The standard line had been to depreciate the importance of strategic bombing. In reworking his article for inclusion in a book, Fedorov added that the population "suffered great difficulties and deprivations" from bombing.[40] About the same time another military writer went somewhat further, declaring that direct action against the military potential of the opponent coupled with active defense of one's own strategic rear constituted a new branch of military art.[41]

After the doctrinal changes of February, 1955, the official

organs of the armed forces made it quite clear that the question of attacks on industrial objectives had acquired a major importance. In the words of an editorial in the air force magazine, the imperialists intended to begin war "by dealing blows with atomic and hydrogen weapons on vitally important targets in our country and the countries of the peoples' democracies in order to put the basic industrial facilities out of commission in a few days, to paralyze transportation, and to demoralize the population." This estimate of the opponent's strategy was made in connection with the public advocacy of the pre-emptive strategy, now put forward as the only way to deprive an aggressor of the advantages of surprise.[42]

Using atomic weapons, a few airplanes could cause serious damage to targets deep inside the country. Hence, "the slightest mistake of an antiaircraft unit in conditions of atomic warfare can lead to very serious consequences."[43]

In February, 1956, at the Twentieth Party Congress, Marshal Zhukov spoke of the real threat from air attack, especially by long-range rockets and jet aircraft, and then reassured his listeners with the statement that a great deal of work had been done to build up the active air defenses of the country:

> At the present time the air defense possesses modern, supersonic fighter planes, high quality antiaircraft artillery, antiaircraft rocket weapons, and other means for insuring antiair defense. . . . The task of the defense of the rear of the country has never been as urgent as it is under modern conditions. In the interest of security the Soviet people demand further efforts for the improvement and organization of local antiair defense and the appropriate preparation of the whole population. . . .[44]

The sense of urgency with which the program of air defense, both active and passive, was pursued is conveyed in the opening paragraph of an article in *Voennye znaniia (Military Knowledge)*, a popular magazine:

> The armies of the imperialist states at the present time possess varied means of air attack which permit them to deliver blows against populated centers, industrial estab-

lishments, and engineering complexes of countries thousands of kilometers from their borders. . . . Even the most remote population centers in the hinterland of any state can be the object of an enemy air attack in existing conditions.[45]

As a consequence of this possibility, said an article in *Red Star* a few months later, a powerful air defense was required to protect not only troops but also targets in the rear. "Neglecting the demands of the military art," warned the writer, has "often led to very serious military destruction."[46]

The emphasis on active air defense continued and in 1957 the Soviet press became more specific about the means that would be employed against the kind of attack described above. In March Marshal Zhukov told an audience of crack troops that Soviet planners assumed their probable opponents to have an adequate number of nuclear weapons and the means to deliver them to Soviet territory: "This circumstance requires our armed forces, especially . . . the air forces, to be always in readiness to frustrate any aggressor's attempt to accomplish a surprise attack on our country."[47]

In 1957 the Soviet military press expected an air attack upon the Soviet Union to concentrate mainly on airfields and air installations. The United States, said one review of American published statements on the subject, planned to base her active air defense on the destruction of her opponent's bases and airfields with atomic weapons.[48] British and American military opinion, wrote a Soviet colonel in June, had maintained that the primary task in the initial period of the war was the establishment of strategic air supremacy by mass employment of nuclear weapons against the opponent's airfields.[49] This was the obvious rationale behind the desire to pre-empt, and it called for vigorous measures to safeguard the striking force. The best possible active defense against enemy aircraft and missiles, according to the Soviet press, must have many ramifications. A warning system should provide signals for the interception of both high- and low-flying vehicles. The destruction of enemy air vehicles could best be accomplished by a mixed system of supersonic fighter aircraft equipped with search radar, high quality antiaircraft artillery, and surface-to-air missiles.[50]

The "best possible" active defense system, however, does not, in Soviet eyes, dispense with the need for civil defenses. Soviet planners are fully aware of the blast and fall-out effects of nuclear weapons and undoubtedly realize the immense difficulty of saving a large part of the population by civil-defense measures. Theoretically, shelters can be so well built and equipped that millions could survive within them until the fall-out from nuclear weapons had dissipated of itself or had been mechanically removed. But the cost of a thoroughly effective system of this kind would probably be beyond the finances of even the richest country. A more modest system, however, will suffice to reduce greatly the effects of an attack whose weight has been cut down already by a pre-emptive blow, by active defenses, or by both.

The rate of progress of the Soviet civil-defense program is secret, but its character and effectiveness may be judged to some extent through a considerable body of literature prepared for training the population, all of whom must participate in civil defense. In 1954 the Soviet government inaugurated an extensive program of popular education in civil defense against nuclear weapons. Since that time literally millions of copies of elementary pamphlets on the subject have been distributed in all the main Soviet languages.[51] A recent pamphlet in the series[52] begins with a clear but somewhat subdued account of the effects of various kinds of weapons. A second section describes traditional civil-defense measures for dealing with fires; a third describes some simple shelters, protective clothing and equipment, and hygienic measures; a fourth gives the rules for behavior after an atomic alarm is sounded, what to do during the raid, the meaning of signs to be posted after it giving the level of radioactive contamination, and the standard first-aid measures for those hurt. The last section tells how to pass through and clean up contaminated areas.

The psychological and political effects of a nuclear attack are not touched on in the training manuals, but a recent book on Western "militarism" has been remarkably explicit about these effects. The militarists, says the author, count on the mental disturbances that nuclear attacks can produce in millions of people. The exhaustion of waiting for a nuclear attack, the fatiguing inconveniences of antiatomic defense, the hermetically sealed antiatomic clothing worn in heat, frost, dampness, and darkness, with the concomitant acceleration of breathing, perspiration, and bleeding of any slight wound will all contribute to the terrorization of the civilian population. The militarists also expect that the great fear of gradual radioactive contamination will be much multiplied by the delay with which the symptoms of radiation poisoning will appear. They expect to benefit from the intensification of alarming rumors and to foster these through their own propaganda. "Indubitably, such militaristic expectations can be justified in some cases," concludes the author, but these effects of atomic bombing will be more pronounced among the people of capitalist countries than among people with "full political awareness."[53]

The general tone in the literature about bombing effects is reassuring. A typical account declares that active air defense is reliable and assures its readers that, "with efficient and properly organized antiatomic [civil] defense of populated places and of industrial and economic targets, loss from atomic bombings can be kept to a minimum."[54] In an interview with an American newspaper correspondent Khrushchev argued that the Soviet Union would escape the worst effects of nuclear weapons because of her size: "We too, of course, will suffer great losses. But look at the vast spaces on our map and look at Germany, France and Britain. One does not have to be a strategist or a military man to see the difference."[55] When the American correspondent volunteered the statement that the United States had vast spaces, Khrushchev answered: "Not quite as vast, and it should be kept in mind that American cities, such as New York, Chicago, San Francisco and others, have a large concentration of industries. Our industries are much more widely dispersed."[56] Khrushchev then explained that the recent Soviet governmental reorganization would bring about greater dispersion of industry, although it was not designed primarily for that purpose.

In February, 1958, it was revealed that the first stage of the civil-defense education program had been completed. A ten-hour course on antiatomic measures inaugurated in 1955 had been attended by some 85 per cent of the whole Soviet population. In January, 1957, a twenty-two hour course was begun, which included material on defense against chemical and bacteriological as well as atomic weapons. This course, compulsory for the whole population, was scheduled for completion in the large cities by July, 1958, and in the smaller cities and rural areas by the end of 1958. References were also made to preparation of a third program of training to be completed by 1960.[57]

The Soviet civil-defense program, which one can reconstruct from training literature, is a rather modest one in relation to the destructiveness of thermonuclear weapons. If large-yield H-bombs should fall in the center of cities, the kinds of shelter depicted in the pamphlets would not be very helpful. If on the other hand the bombs should fall on airfields outside cities or leave some cities altogether untouched, the shelters would save many lives that otherwise would have been lost from blast or fallout. If the Soviet Union suffered extensive nuclear bombing, the measures advocated in the mass training programs would avail little. The Soviet civil-defense program seems to start from optimistic assumptions about the course of any war that might break out. That optimism is perhaps based on the belief that the Soviet Union, if faced with war, would be able to get in the pre-emptive strike to which her leaders are committed. In that event the present civil-defense program would have a valuable role to play in defending the Soviet Union against the expected retaliation. Even in this relatively limited role, civil defense is extremely expensive. One may assume that the Soviet leaders expect to get positive military dividends from the effort that they have invested in civil defense.

Nuclear weapons have transformed naval operations as much as other departments of warfare.[58] We have considered above the utility of missile-launching submarines. The submarine makes it possible to use missiles with less accuracy and shorter range than would be required of intercontinental weapons. The short flight time for missiles fired near the coast makes detection and counteraction more difficult. As the accuracy of missiles increases, the advantages of firing them from submarines rather than from land bases may be diminished, but submarines like other naval units will always possess the virtue of mobility. This is an important element in deterrence because no surprise attack can be expected to obviate retaliation by mobile and easily concealed units. We can expect that submarines will play at least as great a role in the Soviet posture as in the American, if only because of the large number of American cities within easy range of oceans.

The main strategic functions of naval forces in the past have been to keep the seas open for one's own commerce while denying their use to the enemy, and to transport men, weapons, and supplies to distant theaters of war with minimum loss by enemy action. Russian wars, both Tsarist and Soviet, have involved expansion overland into contiguous areas. Russian naval operations have mostly been confined to sheltered waters, have usually been undertaken reluctantly, and have been subordinate to land operations at all times. Even in coastal defense the Russian navy has made a poor showing. The Russians have never aspired, like the French, to first-rank power by sea as well as by land. Far from being able to attack island countries off the Eurasian land mass, the Russians were incapable even of denying the Straits of Tsushima to the Japanese supply ships in 1904-1905. Overseas expansion has always been a task beyond Soviet strength. This circumstance helps to explain Soviet reluctance to build aircraft carriers. Moreover, while World War II demonstrated that the aircraft carrier was a capital ship indispensable for command of the seas, ship-based aircraft did not then have sufficient range or size for effective bombing of the rear. Today's aircraft carriers, however, may serve as takeoff platforms for strategic bombers. Nevertheless, the Soviet Union is making no effort to build herself a carrier fleet. As we shall shortly see, the Soviet leaders are convinced that in the nuclear age particularly, large surface units are an unnecessary luxury.

Had war come before the Soviet Union acquired a significant arsenal of nuclear weapons, the Soviet strategy would have been to expel the United States and its allies from Europe and to prevent by commerce raiding the offshore buildup required for a landing on the continent. Russia's continuing naval weakness, combined with her temporary deficiency in nuclear weapons, made it impossible for her to carry the war to American shores. The United States, on the other hand, was strong in just those areas where the Soviet Union was weak. Her commitments to NATO were based on her command of the oceans, which gave her the ability to transport supplies and reinforcements to Europe. Her policies in the Far East required that she be strong in the Pacific as well as in the Atlantic and Mediterranean. In any war between the United States and the Soviet Union, therefore, it was obvious that the roles of the opposing navies would be as different as their compositions.

In the Soviet view the advent of nuclear weapons has made it harder for the United States to base her strategy on naval might and easier for the Soviet Union to frustrate the United States in the execution of that strategy. In late 1956 and early 1957 the Soviet press devoted detailed attention to the changes that nuclear weapons had produced in navies. The increasing vulnerability of naval forces, especially in groups, is the theme of the Soviet writers. In the Second World War, they say, surface warships were vulnerable chiefly to four kinds of weapons: first to naval or shore-based artillery; second to torpedoes; third to bombs dropped from ship- or shore-based aircraft; and fourth to mines. The appearance of nuclear weapons and the improvements in missiles, they continue, have seriously aggravated the problem of capital-ship survival. In past wars naval forces proceeded in groups and sought protection by throwing out a system of defenses against hostile aircraft, submarines, and capital ships. The most valuable ships were screened by other ships and by aircraft equipped with detection devices and various specialized weapons. Even with these elaborate measures, say Soviet writers, many capital ships were lost by the major fleets of the world in the last war.

Today the survival problem for surface ships is more difficult than ever before, because completely effective explosive charges can be dispatched from great distances, with the requirement for accuracy reduced because of the great blast effect of nuclear weapons. According to Soviet writers, it has become practically senseless to assemble task forces like those used in past wars. Concentrations of naval vessels are so vulnerable to the effects of nuclear explosions that vessels must proceed at great distances from one another, so great indeed that they are virtually proceeding as independent units. A modern naval force requires special radar ships far ahead of the capital ships to detect dangers from aircraft. A naval formation dispersed for nuclear warfare may be three hundred miles in diameter. Now that aircraft can launch guided missiles they can strike naval vessels from a great distance. The submarine menace to surface ships remains as great as ever. All this creates a dilemma for the defenders of naval vessels.

To sum up, Soviet writers say that naval task forces are a thing of the past, that capital ships are obsolete or obsolescent, and that much smaller vessels can execute naval tasks as well or better than the large ships of former wars.

From these premises it follows that the American fleet, with its many large surface vessels, is to a great extent obsolescent. The numerous submarines of the Soviet fleet are regarded as useful under present conditions, while the surface fleet is not large. In a future war, say the Soviet writers, their own ground troops will be fighting in areas contiguous with the Soviet Union, while the United States will have to fight in areas separated by oceans. Hence the increased vulnerability of fleets is a tremendous advantage to the Soviet Union.

Articles in the Soviet press point out the severe effects of German attrition on American and British shipping in the last war and insist that in a future war the United States will again be unable to avoid the need to supply her forces by water over great distances. These discussions leave little doubt that Soviet planners expect a much higher degree of success in submarine warfare than the Germans enjoyed.

The Soviet writers assert that landing operations will be much more difficult in future wars than in the past. Great naval forces, troop convoys, and even artificial harbors, like those concentrated to effect landings in the last world war will be extremely vulnerable to nuclear weapons. Landings across the sea must now be made by small units, dispersed over a great area. These units will have to depend for supply on single vessels. These requirements will tremendously complicate the task of landing forces of the size landed in Normandy in 1944. Nevertheless, the landing of small forces behind enemy lines flanked by the sea may sometimes be better effected by water than by air. While the Soviet writers think there may still be uses for the kind of leapfrog operation conducted along the Black Sea coast against the Germans, they consider very difficult the landing of large numbers in the face of nuclear weapons. They concede that the landing force derives some advantages from nuclear weapons. Nuclear air bursts over the point of landing can be used to clear the area without contaminating the ground. Simultaneous ground bursts on the enemy flanks and rear will restrict his movements while the bridgehead is being established. In general, however, the Soviet articles imply that landing operations across great distances will be almost impossible because both convoys and beach assemblies have become so vulnerable.

Before the Soviet leaders recognized the full power of nuclear weapons, they felt that the United States would have to come to the Soviet Union across the sea in order to win a war against her. They felt confident that their superiority in ground forces would either deter or frustrate such a strategy. Now the Russians are still confident that the American war strategy must fail, but for different reasons. Now they feel that nuclear weapons will give an edge to the Soviet cause by making it extraordinarily difficult, if not impossible, for American naval forces to transport large numbers of troops and great quantities of supplies to the continent of Europe.[59] The Soviet military leaders consider that the United States should be deterred from making war against the Soviet Union by a realization of her inability to bring the war to a successful conclusion by occupying the Soviet Union. The Soviet leaders are so convinced that occupation of the defeated side's territory must conclude a war that they rarely mention it. The few references to this con-

comitant of victory are usually presented as truisms. Here is
an example from *Soviet Fleet:*

> With the appearance of weapons of mass destruction, the
> opinion began to be expressed in the American military
> press that landing operations were no longer necessary and
> that atomic bombardment of the opponent by air forces
> would determine the outcome of the war. However, the
> Pentagon leaders rapidly condemned such expressions of
> view and laid it down that, despite the existence of new
> kinds of weapons, troops occupying the opponent's terri-
> tory would determine the outcome of war.[60]

To prove his point the writer of this passage described in great
detail the various American landing exercises conducted in
1955 and 1956.

In many ways nuclear weapons have made much easier the
attainment of one of the objectives of the Soviet postwar naval
program, namely to prevent control by a superior naval power
of the waters adjacent to the Soviet homeland. This the Soviet
writers call "operational" command of the seas, as distinct from
"strategic" command of the seas. As a naval captain expressed
it in the pages of *Military Thought:*

> In modern conditions, when atomic weapons are employed,
> the possibility is increased of gaining operational com-
> mand [of the seas] when strategic command is in the hands
> of the opponent. Skillful use of atomic weapons permits
> the rapid weakening of the opponent's fleet in a particular
> sector, the creation of a favorable relationship of forces,
> and, until the opponent is able by moving forces from
> other sectors to change this relationship, the attainment
> of the operational goals which were set.[61]

In the Soviet view, the advent of nuclear weapons has
affected land warfare rather less than naval warfare. Considerable changes, however, have been taking place in the Soviet
ground forces.

Despite some reductions, the ground forces far surpass
those of any other major power in size and are perhaps even
qualitatively superior. This large and well-equipped force repre-

sents a tremendous investment of resources, and its maintenance must continue to be a heavy charge on the Soviet budget.
How is one to reconcile such a force with the Soviet doctrine
that the first phase of war may be decisive?

Not until the Soviet Union acquired delivery vehicles of
intercontinental range could she hope to win victory in the
first phase of war. Until that time she could do no more in
the first phase than deny victory to her opponents. The Soviet
leaders decided that a nuclear strike could settle the outcome
of war even before they had the ability to deliver a telling blow
at the United States. Until their recent acquisition of this
ability, they had to deter or win a war with the forces that they
could bring to bear in Europe and Asia. The ability of the
Soviet army to conquer Europe rapidly was a deterrent to the
initiation of a war against the Soviet Union. For some years
after 1945 the United States nuclear capability depended on
overseas bases and her war policy has always been influenced
by the wishes of her European allies. In these years the Soviet
army could help to deter an outbreak of war, but it held out
small promise of victory over a powerful opponent whose
homeland lay outside the Eurasian land mass. The function of
the Soviet ground forces as a deterrent to the initiation of war
by the West—something Soviet Marxism maintains is always
possible—would be a sufficient explanation of the tremendous
investment in those forces. A second and historically important
function of the ground forces has been to suppress domestic
unrest, and Russian armies have been traditionally deployed
for this purpose. Soviet leaders have continued this practice
and have used Soviet troops in Hungary and elsewhere to maintain Russian hegemony. Moreover the Soviet army has so long
been the senior service that it is probably able to procure a
larger share of the national resources than military doctrine in
itself would require. In spite of their prestige and importance,
however, the Soviet ground forces have not been able, or have
not cared, to prevent those military changes that owe their
existence to nuclear weapons.

At first examination, strategic nuclear weapons seem to
make large land armies obsolete, and it is true that ground

forces would not be very important if either the Soviet Union
or the United States were knocked out in the initial stages of
a war by a first nuclear strike. But neither of these cases can
be very interesting to the Soviet military planner, for they
represent the simple extremes of a whole range of complicated
problems that he must solve. It is obvious to him that a large
ground army cannot help a country defeated by nuclear devastation and that a victory guaranteed by other means would dispense with the need for enormous ground forces. The more
interesting cases for study are those where the outcome of the
initial phase of war is less one-sided. The cautious military
planner is bound to give most of his attention to the latter.

Consider first a war in which the Soviet Union has destroyed
rather more of the United States striking force and urban
wealth than she herself has lost. Neither side knows how much
residual striking capacity the opponent possesses; both hope to
destroy the enemy's striking capacity early and completely
enough to preserve a worthwhile proportion of their urban
areas and resources. The role of the ground forces in such a
situation will depend on the current state of the art in nuclear
weapons. Obviously, the benefit to the Soviet Union of a rapid
advance of her ground forces across Europe would be greater
at a time when the only accurate Western missiles were based
in Europe. At a later stage in Western missile development the
significance of Soviet army successes might be less.

It may be argued that the most efficient means of eliminating a missile capability in Western Europe, which could do
strategic damage to the Soviet Union, would be to launch Soviet
missiles of medium range from Eastern Europe against them.
This would be no guarantee, however, against missiles from
newly established sites in Western Europe. The only sure way
to deal with such a threat would be to occupy Western Europe
rapidly. Missiles, as Soviet writers have pointed out more than
once, are primarily useful against fixed targets whose coordinates are known in advance. In eliminating mobile and
camouflaged targets, as General Pokrovskii has pointed out, the
best results can be obtained by ground forces.[62]

The Soviet Union could, as she has threatened to do, drop

enough H-bombs on smaller countries such as Denmark, Norway, and England to make military operations impossible,
owing to extreme radioactive contamination. On the other
hand, if she could take out enemy missile bases with her own
missiles without creating too much radioactive fall-out and then
secure the ground area, the industry and resources of the
enemy would assist her in the task of domestic reconstruction.
In any case, whether or not the Soviet leaders are optimistic
about the outcome of a future war, if it happens they will want
to occupy Western Europe speedily.

Whether or not nuclear weapons existed, the Soviet military
leaders were bound to require the Soviet armies to reach the
Channel quickly in the event of war. Nuclear weapons made
this task both more urgent and more complex. In the early
fifties many Western spokesmen insisted that NATO's possession of tactical nuclear weapons would outweigh the numerical
superiority of the Soviet armed forces. The argument ran that
the Soviet forces would have to concentrate in order to make
advances against smaller forces armed with nuclear weapons.
This very concentration would provide the best possible target
for nuclear weapons. The Western reasoning seems to have
impressed Soviet military planners, who in 1954 started a major
program to familiarize all ranks with the effects of nuclear
weapons. At the same time, or soon afterwards, they began to
introduce nuclear weapons into the ground forces. While the
Soviet Union advocated an international agreement to abolish
nuclear weapons, she was introducing them rapidly into her
army. By March, 1957, Zhukov frankly warned that, "in the
event of a great military conflict, atomic weapons would inevitably be put into use as the basic means of destruction. . . ."[63]

Now that both the Soviet Union and the Western powers
possess what have been called tactical nuclear weapons, the
possibility of a Soviet advance in the face of opposition presents
new problems for both sides. Both possess tactical nuclear
weapons, but the Soviet side has more men. Can the Soviet
Union use her numerical superiority to gain a rapid victory?

Where tactical nuclear weapons are employed, it will be
advantageous, if not completely to avoid the traditional con-

centrations of force, at least to concentrate as briefly as possible. Mobility is obviously necessary, and to gain it the Soviet ground forces have to be motorized, mechanized, and airlifted to an unprecented extent. In the Second World War the Soviet army was deficient in the desired mobility, flexibility, and rapidity of decision largely because it possessed too few vehicles. Since 1945, but more markedly since 1953, the Soviet planners have striven for improved mobility. Even leaving aside nuclear weapons, which Marshal Zhukov has said will be an organic part of the Soviet army, the requirements for increased mobility have greatly increased the cost of the Soviet establishment.

In gaining such mobility, airborne forces are of obvious importance. In the Second World War airborne forces were, as a rule, lightly armed, and their reinforcement by air with heavier weapons was generally unreliable. Their operations were carried out, typically, among or near heavy troop concentrations. In raids of strategic importance, like those on the bridges of Nijmegen and Arnhem, the airborne troops could accomplish little or nothing unless the main front moved up to them. Without a junction of forces, the gains of the airborne units could be neither exploited nor held. Given the ponderous movements of the Soviet ground forces, it is not surprising that their airborne operations were generally not marked by success. Airborne partisans, however, accomplished much good work, because they were not dropped into areas of heavy enemy troop concentration. To summarize, in the Second World War airborne troops sometimes played an important role, but one that was always ancillary to the part played by ground troops. The one great exception to this rule was the German conquest of Crete.

Since the introduction of nuclear weapons in the Soviet army, increased emphasis has been put on lifting troops by air. A military parade in Moscow on the fortieth anniversary of the revolution displayed a new helicopter with greatly increased carrying capacity. When nuclear weapons are used in the field, the dangers of troop concentration may result in such a dispersion of the enemy ground forces that airborne operations are facilitated. Moreover, if the enemy tries to concentrate against airborne troops who are destroying his dispersed forces piecemeal, he risks losing them to the action of nuclear weapons. In addition to the many special tasks performed in World War II, airborne troops of the future may be used to put newly established enemy missile bases out of operation. Urban targets, too, may invite airborne attacks, since the defending troops may be kept outside cities in order to make the latter less attractive as targets for nuclear weapons. Thus, airborne forces can now exploit various new types of vulnerability arising from the dispersion imposed by nuclear weapons.

Airlift by helicopter is recommended by Soviet writers as an aid to mobility and is being adopted by the Soviet forces. Larger aircraft with vertical or near vertical takeoff capability will permit the use of makeshift airfields, and thereby greatly increase the speed with which a given force can be airlifted, or the size of force that can be moved in a given time. If roads are badly damaged, the ability to move across country will be especially advantageous, and the Soviet forces want vehicles that can move independent of roads and cross rivers without pausing. Even more than in World War II earth-moving machines will be needed in a nuclear war to construct and repair airfields and roads.

The Soviet ground forces, then, possess numerical superiority and aim for superior mass mobility. In the West it was once maintained that if both sides had tactical nuclear weapons the numerical superiority of one side would count for less than it formerly did. Those who put forward this view did not raise the question of how to prevent a growing relative advantage accruing to the initially larger force in conditions of mutual attrition. Moreover, if superior mobility were added to superior numbers, the larger army might well achieve a major breakthrough and then exploit it to the full. The breakthrough, of course, would depend on adequate quantities of the latest offensive weapons. One Soviet writer has recently expressed the idea that nuclear warfare will require more, not fewer, ground forces and that large reserves will therefore continue to be important.[64] Difficult as it is to foresee what a nuclear ground battle will be like, the Soviet planners have chosen to emphasize mobility, and they are able to muster many convincing arguments for doing so. They can learn from the Western press, too, that the American army of today is aiming in the same direction.

If and when the Soviet army is fully equipped and trained in accordance with present plans, it would be reckless to suppose, as some Westerners have done, that Soviet troops will display less initiative and skill than Western troops simply because their political system affords less scope to individuality than those of the United States or Western Europe. Russian discussions of training for a war of the future give a general impression of openmindedness and readiness to examine problems objectively. The following quotation from an article by a Soviet general is characteristic of Soviet writing on the subject:

> The appearance of weapons of mass destruction in the weapon systems of modern armies, the qualitative perfection of military equipment, and the complete mechanization and motorization of infantry have worked essential changes in the character of modern warfare. As never before, war has become a thing of rapid movement, demanding rapid reactions to a rapidly changing military situation. Naturally, in such situations, it is very important to be able to execute in the shortest time various changes of formation on the battlefield: advancing columns to deploy to pre-battle positions, forming up on a fighting line, attacking the enemy from the march, pursuing the opponent in vehicles, etc.
>
> The most characteristic means of action in the offensive is to attack from the march. It results in approaching the opponent in vehicles and by rapid march and deployment into battle positions, and finally in the attack itself. Given favorable circumstances, the attack can be carried out by the uninterrupted movement of the motorized infantry into battle deployment. When atomic weapons are employed, then in the interests of saving personnel and military equipment the troops will operate in a basically loose formation, and will gather together into a striking force only at the moment of attack. Thus the contemporary offensive battle can schematically be viewed as a series of

attacks from a moving position into the battle situation.
. . . Naturally in this situation a significant portion of the
infantry's time will be spent in vehicles. . . . Thus in the
modern battle, victory will go to the side which, other
things being equal, possesses the greatest mobility and
maneuverability. It would be erroneous to suppose that
the mechanization and motorization of the army automatically introduces these qualities into its action. No
matter how perfected the technical equipment of the
troops, high mobility and maneuverability can appear
fully only where personnel are accustomed to maneuver
in vehicles, are well trained, and have the necessary technical preparation.[65]

Concern with the mobility of troops when nuclear weapons
are employed on the battlefield is only one of the many consequences of the changed Soviet conception of war. The revised
Soviet understanding of the nature of war has demanded, right
down the line, revisions in the doctrine governing the Soviet
armed services.

*   *   *

The Soviet forces are expected to deter or to repel aggression, but these defensive functions derive from the ability of
the forces to wage offensive war successfully. The guiding
Soviet principle is readiness to fight any kind of war in the
most effective way, no matter what the relative likelihood of
the different kinds of war. The Soviet leaders and planners
have not succumbed to the kind of defeatism that argues that
the destruction will be so great as to make it pointless to
prosecute a major war in the most vigorous and effective way.
The basis of the Soviet doctrine is that war would be a calamity
indeed, but that its most awful consequences can be reduced by
the creation and thorough training of a differentiated force
ready for every contingency. The Soviet leaders believe further
that in some circumstances it might be desirable to strike an
initial nuclear blow, and they mean to have a military establishment suited to that end.

NOTES

1. "Speech of Comrade Zhukov," in *XXth Congress Report,* Vol. 1, pp. 480-482.
2. Lieutenant General S. Krasil'nikov, "On the Question of the Character of Contemporary Warfare," in *Marksizm i Leninizm o voine i armii, sbornik statei (Marxism-Leninism on War and the Army, A Collection of Articles),* Moscow, 1956, pp. 152-154. Prepared for galleys on November 28, 1956.
3. *Ibid.*
4. *Ibid.*
5. *Ibid.,* pp. 160, 161.
6. "The Speech of the Minister of Defense of the U.S.S.R. Marshal of the Soviet Union G. K. Zhukov, at the All-Army Meeting of Crack Troops on March 16, 1957," *Pravda,* March 20, 1957.
7. Zhukov speech in India, quoted by Major General B. Boltin, "The Role of Experience in the Development of Soviet Military Science," *Sovetskii flot (Soviet Fleet),* June 6, 1957. This is the only source that has been found for any part of the speech.
8. Colonel V. Petrov, "On the Essence of War Potential. An Aid to Students of the Marxist-Leninist Theory of War and the Army," *Sovetskaia aviatsiia (Soviet Aviation),* May 20, 1958.
9. *Ibid.*
10. "An American Magazine on Anglo-American Discords," *Pravda,* August 30, 1954.
11. M. Krementsov, "Atomnoe oruzhie" ("Atomic Weapons"), *Vestnik vozdushnogo flota (Herald of the Air Fleet),* No. 8, August, 1954, pp. 65-70.
12. M. Krementsov, "The Hydrogen Bomb," in *Atomnoe oruzhie (Atomic Weapons),* Moscow, 1955, pp. 219-228.
13. Major General G. I. Pokrovskii, *Nauka i tekhnika v sovermennykh voinakh (Science and Technology in Modern Wars),* Moscow, 1956, p. 50.
14. Comrade I. E. Kazakov, "How the Guidance of the Intercontinental Ballistic Missile Is Carried Out: An Interview with Doctor of Technical Sciences, Comrade I. E. Kazakov," *Sovetskaia aviatsiia,* August 31, 1957.
15. Major General V. A. Semenov, Professor in the M. E. Zhukovskii Military Aerial Engineering Academy, "The Development of Rocket Technology," *Sovetskaia Rossiia (Soviet Russia),* September 14, 1957.
16. Pokrovskii, *op. cit.,* p. 51.
17. **Engineer Major V. Kriksunov, "The Problems of the Interception of Intercontinental Ballistic Missiles," *Sovetskaia aviatsiia,* April 25, 1957.**
18. Pokrovskii, *op. cit.*
19. "On the Bellicose Statements of Some American, British, and West German Generals. Answers of the Commander-in-Chief of the Air Forces of the USSR, Marshal of Aviation K. A. Vershinin to Questions by the *Pravda* Correspondent," *Pravda,* September 8, 1957.

20. Professor, Doctor of Technical Sciences, and Major General of the Engineering Technical Services, G. I. Pokrovskii, "Intercontinental Missiles and Other Vehicles for Strategic Weapons," *Sovetskii patriot* (*Soviet Patriot*), September 11, 1957.

21. Major General N. Talenskii, "The Question of Military Strategy and Foreign Policy," *Mezhdunarodnaia zhizn'* (*International Life*), No. 3, 1958, pp. 34, 35.

22. Chou En-lai, "The Present International Situation and China's Foreign Policy," a speech delivered to the fifth session of the first National People's Congress, February 10, 1958. I am indebted to Alice Langley Hsieh for this reference.

23. Engineer Major Iu. Rumiantsev, "Refueling Aircraft in the Air," *Red Star*, May 31, 1955.

24. Candidate in Technical Sciences, Lieutenant Colonel of Engineers, I. Naumenko, "The Penetrating Radiation Accompanying an Atomic Explosion," *Vestnik vozdushnogo flota*, No. 1, January, 1955, p. 83; I. Naumenko, "The Penetrating Radiation Accompanying an Atomic Explosion," in *Atomnoe oruzhie*, 2d ed., Moscow, 1955, pp. 170-171. The sentence on the poor accuracy of guided and unguided missiles was eliminated from the version published in the book, *Atomic Weapons*.

25. Lieutenant Colonel of Engineers P. Safonov, "Airplanes: Carriers of Atomic Weapons and Their Employment (A Review of the Foreign Press)," in *Atomnoe oruzhie*, pp. 241-255.

26. Lieutenant Colonel of Engineers A. Baldov, Docent, Candidate in the Technical Sciences, "Pilotless Aircraft," *Red Star*, July 14, 1956.

27. Lieutenant Colonel of Engineers V. Glukhov, Candidate in the Technical Sciences, "Guided Missiles and Torpedoes," *Red Star*, August 16, 1956.

28. Colonel Iu. Pshenianik, Docent, Candidate in the Military Sciences, "On the Role of Aviation in Modern War," *Sovetskaia aviatsiia*, March 17, 1957.

29. "Khrushchev's Triumph," *Neue Zürcher Zeitung*, October 10, 1957.

30. "Answers to the Questions of the Chief Diplomatic Correspondent of the American Newspaper, *The New York Times*, J. Reston, October 7, 1957," *Pravda*, October 11, 1957.

31. "Answers to the Questions of the Correspondent of the Canadian Newspaper, *The Toronto Telegram*, P. Dempson," in N. S. Khrushchev, *Za prochnyi mir i mirnoe sosushchestvovanie* (*For a Lasting Peace and Peaceful Coexistence*), Moscow, 1958, p. 216.

32. "N. S. Khrushchev's Speech," *Vestnik vozdushnogo flota*, No. 4, April, 1958, p. 6.

33. Colonel A. Lapenin, "Aircraft in Modern War," *Sovetskaia aviatsiia*, June 3, 1958.

34. *Ibid.*

35. "H-bomb Flights Toward Russia?" *U.S. News & World Report*, June 6, 1958, p. 76.

36. Professor, Rear Admiral N. Pavlovich, "The Naval Art and the Development of the Military Equipment of the Fleet," *Sovetskii flot*, March 6, 1957.

37. Captain N. Nikolaev, "The Navy in the System of the Armed Forces of the U.S.S.R.," *Sovetskii flot,* May 29, 1957.
38. Major General E. Boltin, "The Role of Experience in the Development of Soviet Military Science," *Sovetskii flot,* June 6, 1957.
39. Colonel G. Fedorov, Candidate in the Philosophical Sciences, "Marxism-Leninism on War and the Army," Part 1, "The Origin and Essence of Wars," *Red Star,* January 6, 1954.
40. G. Fedorov, "The Origin and Essence of Wars," in *Marksizm-Leninizm o voine, armii i voennoi nauke, Sbornik statei (Marxism-Leninism on War, the Army, and Military Science, A Collection of Articles),* Moscow, 1955, p. 33. (Delivered to the printer on September 10, 1954; in galleys on February 3, 1955.)
41. Colonel O. Zakrezhevskii, "The Influence of the Development of the Means of Warfare upon the Military Art," in *Marksizm-Leninizm o voine, armii i voennoi nauke, Sbornik statei,* Moscow, 1955, p. 195.
42. Unsigned editorial, "The Great Strength of the Leninist Idea of the Defense of the Socialist Government," *Vestnik vozdushnogo flota,* No. 4, April, 1955, p. 8.
43. G. Starko, "The Atom Bomb and Its Military Employment," in *Atomnoe oruzhie,* Moscow, 1955, p. 203.
44. "The Speech of Comrade G. K. Zhukov," *XXth Congress Report,* pp. 481-483.
45. M. Kozin, "The Organization and Tasks of MPVO [The Ministry of Antiair Defense] in Residences," *Voennye znaniia (Military Knowledge),* No. 3, March, 1956, p. 18.
46. Guards Major General of Tanks V. Voronchenko, "On the Influence of the Development of Military Equipment on the Manner of the Conduct of War and Military Operations," *Red Star,* July 26, 1956.
47. Marshal of the Soviet Union G. K. Zhukov, "A Speech at the All-Army Meeting of Crack Troops, March 16, 1957," Moscow, 1957, pp. 12-13.
48. Lieutenant Colonel of Engineers B. Surikov, "The Development of Antiair Defense," *Red Star,* March 23, 1957.
49. Lieutenant Colonel of Engineers, Candidate in the Technical Sciences, M. Pavlov, "The Anti-atomic Defense of Airfields," *Sovetskaia aviatsiia,* June 5, 1957.
50. Deputy of the Supreme Soviet of the U.S.S.R., Thrice Hero of the Soviet Union, Major General of Aviation I. Kozhedub, "Always on Guard," *Sovetskaia aviatsiia,* February 17, 1957; Colonel Iu. Pshenianik, Docent, Candidate in the Military Sciences, "On the Role of Aviation in Modern War," *Sovetskaia aviatsiia,* March 17, 1957.
51. *Knizhnaia letopis' (Catalogue of Books),* the weekly organ of the publishing industry, lists all the editions. An early standard version, *Pamiatka naseleniiu po zashchite ot atomnogo oruzhiia (Popular Handbook for Defense against Atomic Weapons),* 1954, 32 pages, has not been available for this study.
52. *Pamiatka naeleniiu po zashchite ot atomnogo, khimicheskogo i bakteriologicheskogo oruzhiia (Popular Handbook for Defense against Atomic, Chemical and Bacteriological Weapons),* Moscow, 1957, 61 pages.

53. V. I. Skopin, *Militarizm (Militarism)*, Moscow, 1956, pp. 67, 68. The second edition, Moscow, 1957, contains substantially the same text on pp. 75, 76.
54. M. M. Gvozdev and V. A. Iakovkin, *Atomnoe oruzhie i protivoatomnaia zashchita (Atomic Weapons and Antiatomic Defense)*, Moscow, 1956, p. 6.
55. "Interview with Henry Shapiro, Correspondent of the American United Press Agency, November 14, 1957," *Pravda*, November 19, 1957.
56. *Ibid.*
57. *Sovetskii patriot* for February 11, 12, and 13, 1958, contains the texts of speeches at the Moscow conference where these facts were announced.
58. The material on Soviet naval views is derived from the following Soviet sources: Captain of the Second Rank (Commander) A. Kvitnitskii, "The Arming of the American Navy with Guided Jet Missiles," *Red Star*, September 4, 1956; Admiral V. Platonov, "Modern Views on the Conduct of Military Operations at Sea," *Red Star*, December 16, 1956; Captain of the Second Rank (Commander) K. Romanov, "Landing Operations in the Plans of the American Admirals," *Sovetskii flot*, January 5, 1957; Admiral L. Vladmirskii, "Modern Naval Construction," *Red Star*, February 15, 1957; Professor, Rear Admiral N. Pavlovich, "The Naval Art and the Development of the Military Equipment of the Fleet," *Sovetskii flot*, March 6, 1957; Rear Admiral A. Kruchenykh, "On the Character of Modern Military Action at Sea," *Sovetskii flot*, March 23, 1957; Rear Admiral V. Andreev, "Sea and Ocean Communications in Modern War," *Red Star*, April 25, 1957; Captain N. Nikolaev, "The Navy in the System of the Armed Forces of the U.S.S.R.," *Sovetskii flot*, May 29, 1957; Captain N. Gordeev, "The Defense of Naval Bases in Modern Conditions," *Red Star*, May 27, 1957; Captain P. Zhelezniak, "Aerial Means of Search for Submarines," *Sovetskii flot*, June 8, 1957; Candidate in Naval Sciences, Vice Admiral A. Kruchenykh, "On the Influence of Rocket Weapons on Fleet Tactics," *Sovetskii flot*, November 15, 1957; Lieutenant Colonel of Engineers B. Surikov, "Anti-missile Defense of Ships," *Sovetskii flot*, January 7, 1958; Doctor of Technical Sciences and Captain of Engineers [Naval] G. Migirenko, "Explosions and the Defense of Ships," *Sovetskii flot*, February 15, 1958; Captain of Engineers [Naval] A. Kilesso, " 'The Achilles' Heel' of the Aircraft Carrier Fleet," *Sovetskii flot*, March 20, 1958.
59. Captain of the Second Rank (Commander) K. Romanov, "Landing Operations in the Plans of the American Admirals," *Sovetskii flot*, January 5, 1957.
60. *Ibid.*
61. Captain D. Shavtsov, "Command of the Sea," *Voennaia mysl'*, No. 7, July, 1955, p. 14.
62. Major General, Doctor of Technical Sciences, G. I. Pokrovskii, *Rol' nauki i tekhniki v sovremennoi voine (The Role of Science and Technology in Modern War)*, pamphlet, Moscow, 1957, p. 24.
63. "The Speech of the U.S.S.R. Minister of Defense, Marshal of the Soviet Union G. K. Zhukov," *Red Star*, March 20, 1957.

64. Colonel I. S. Baz', "Soviet Military Science on the Character of Modern War," *Voennyi vestnik (Military Herald)*, No. 6, June, 1958, pp. 19-29.

65. Hero of the Soviet Union, Major General of Tank Troops O. Losik, "The Important Condition for the High Mobility of Troops," *Red Star*, March 30, 1957.

INDEX

Acheson, Dean G., 109-110
"active defense":
  Soviet in 1941, 195-197, 199, 201
aggression:
  Soviet; *see* wars, aggressive Soviet
airborne forces, 254-255
aircraft, pilotless, 231
air defense systems:
  Soviet, 175-176, 216, 238-239
Air Force:
  Soviet, 41, 175, 216, 226, 229-232,
    234-235, 238
  U.S., 175, 179
Armed Forces:
  political role of Soviet, 134

bacteriological weapons, 216
Baibakov, N. K., 153
balance of power:
  changes in, 1-2, 228
Balashov, Major, 48
Bandung Conference, 147
Beria, L. P., 119, 132-133, 138
Bernal, John D., 140
Boltin, E., 237-238
Braiko, P., 191
budget, military, 99-105, 112-113,
  119-120
Bulganin, Nikolai, 15, 73, 78, 82,
  87, 104-105, 119-120, 147, 155,
  160, 170
Bullitt, William C., 118

Carney, Robert B., 118, 183
Catledge, Turner, 84

Chalik, E., 55, 60
chemical warfare; *see* warfare, chem-
  ical
Chou En-lai, 228
Churchill, Winston, 115, 124
  Churchill-Molotov   Correspond-
    ence, 116-117
civil defense:
  Soviet, 243-246
Cobham, Sir Alan, 230
Communist Party, Soviet Union:
  role of, after Stalin's death, 134-
    135
  December, 1956, Plenum of Cen-
    tral Committee of, 154, 158
  February, 1957, Plenum of Cen-
    tral Committee of, 153-154

deterrence, 12, 14-16, 18-24, 70, 72
  ff., 240, 250-251
doctrine:
  Soviet military, 5, 8, 32-34, 40,
    168-171, 174, 176
  see also "active defense": Air
    Force, Soviet; ground forces,
    Soviet; missiles, ballistic; Navy,
    Soviet; pre-emptive attack; Rot-
    mistrov; surprise attack; Talen-
    skii; war
Dulles, John Foster, 17, 105-110,
  113, 118, 147

Eisenhower, Dwight D., 17, 69, 82,
  96-98, 107

263

OTHER VOLUMES OF RAND RESEARCH

Air War and Emotional Stress: Psychological Studies of Bombing and Civilian Defense, by Irving L. Janis. New York, N. Y.: McGraw-Hill Book Company, Inc., 1951.

Approximations for Digital Computers, by Cecil Hastings, Jr. Princeton, N. J.: Princeton University Press, 1955.

Behind the Sputniks: A Survey of Soviet Space Science, by F. J. Krieger. Washington, D.C.: Public Affairs Press, 1958.

The Berlin Blockade: A Study in Cold War Politics, by W. Phillips Davison. Princeton, N. J.: Princeton University Press, 1958.

The Compleat Strategyst: Being a Primer on the Theory of Games of Strategy, by J. D. Williams. New York, N. Y.: McGraw-Hill Book Company, Inc., 1954.

Dynamic Programming, by Richard Bellman. Princeton, N. J.: Princeton University Press, 1957.

Efficiency in Government through Systems Analysis: with Emphasis on Water Resource Development, by Roland N. McKean. New York, N. Y.: John Wiley & Sons, Inc., 1958.

The French Economy and the State, by Warren C. Baum. Princeton, N. J.: Princeton University Press, 1958.

German Rearmament and Atomic War: The Views of German Military and Political Leaders, by Hans Speier. Evanston, Ill.: Row, Peterson & Company, 1957.

The House without Windows: France Selects a President, by Constantin Melnik and Nathan Leites. Evanston, Ill.: Row, Peterson & Company, 1958.

International Communication and Political Opinion: A Guide to the Literature, by Bruce Lannes Smith and Chitra M. Smith. Princeton, N. J.: Princeton University Press, 1956.

Introduction to the Theory of Games, by J. C. C. McKinsey. New York, N. Y.: McGraw-Hill Book Company, Inc., 1952.

Labor Productivity in Soviet and American Industry, by Walter Galenson. New York, N. Y.: Columbia University Press, 1955.

Linear Programming and Economic Analysis, by Robert Dorfman, Paul A. Samuelson, and Robert M. Solow. New York, N. Y.: McGraw-Hill Book Company, Inc., 1958.

A Million Random Digits with 100,000 Normal Deviates, by The RAND Corporation. Glencoe, Ill.: The Free Press, 1955.

Mobilizing Resources for War: The Economic Alternatives, by Tibor Scitovsky, Edward Shaw, and Lorie Tarshis. New York, N. Y.: McGraw-Hill Book Company, Inc., 1951.

The Operational Code of the Politburo, by Nathan Leites. New York, N. Y.: McGraw-Hill Book Company, Inc., 1951.

The Organizational Weapon: A Study of Bolshevik Strategy and Tactics, by Philip Selznick. New York, N. Y.: McGraw-Hill Book Company, Inc., 1952.

Propaganda Analysis: A Study of Inferences Made from Nazi Propaganda in World War II, by Alexander L. George. Evanston, Ill.: Row, Peterson & Company, 1959.

Psychosis and Civilization, by Herbert Goldhamer and Andrew W. Marshall. Glencoe, Ill.: The Free Press, 1949.

The Rise of Khrushchev, by Myron Rush. Washington, D.C.: Public Affairs Press, 1958.

Ritual of Liquidation: The Case of the Moscow Trials, by Nathan Leites and Elsa Bernaut. Glencoe, Ill.: The Free Press, 1954.

Smolensk under Soviet Rule, by Merle Fainsod. Cambridge, Mass.: Harvard University Press, 1958.

Soviet Attitudes Toward Authority: An Interdisciplinary Approach to Problems of Soviet Character, by Margaret Mead. New York, N. Y.: McGraw-Hill Book Company, Inc., 1951.

Soviet Military Doctrine, by Raymond L. Garthoff. Glencoe, Ill.: The Free Press, 1953.

Soviet National Income and Product in 1928, by Oleg Hoeffding. New York, N. Y.: Columbia University Press, 1954.

Soviet National Income and Product, 1940-1948, by Abram Bergson and Hans Heymann, Jr. New York, N. Y.: Columbia University Press, 1954.

Strategic Surrender: The Politics of Victory and Defeat, by Paul Kecskemeti. Stanford, Calif.: Stanford University Press, 1958.

A Study of Bolshevism, by Nathan Leites. Glencoe, Ill.: The Free Press, 1953.

Two Studies in Soviet Controls: Communism and the Russian Peasant, and Moscow in Crisis, by Herbert S. Dinerstein and Leon Gouré. Glencoe, Ill.: The Free Press, 1955.

Weight-Strength Analysis of Aircraft Structures, by F. R. Shanley. New York, N. Y.: McGraw-Hill Book Company, Inc., 1952.

West German Leadership and Foreign Policy, edited by Hans Speier and W. Phillips Davison. Evanston, Ill.: Row, Peterson & Company, 1957.